Schentz

Barbara Heitger/Alexander Doujak

Managing CUTS and New GROWTH

Barbara Heitger / Alexander Doujak

Managing CUTS and New GROWTH

an innovative approach to change management

2nd Edition

All rights reserved. No part of this book shall be reproduced, stored in a retrieval system, or transmitted by any means, electronic, mechanical, photocopying, recording, or otherwise, without written permission from the publisher. No patent liability is assumed with respect to the use or the information contained herein. Although every precaution has been taken in the preparation of this book, the publisher and authors assume no responsibility for errors or omissions. Neither is any liability assumed with respect to the use of the information contained herein. The authors and publisher specifically disclaim any responsibility for any liabilities, loss or risk, personal or otherwise, which is incurred as a consequence, directly or indirectly, of the use and application of any of the contents of this book.

If you would like to contact us for any information or requests concerning this book- please contact us per email: office@goldegg-verlag.at.

ISBN: 978-3-902903-00-6

© Dr. Barbara Heitger
Schwarzspanierstrasse 15/1/5
A-1090 Vienna
Telephone: +43.1.40 93 646
E-Mail: office@heitgerconsulting.com

Dr. Alexander Doujak
Lainzer Strasse 80
A-1130 Vienna
Telephone: +43.1.306 33 66
E-Mail: office@doujak.eu

1st Edition: 2008
2nd Edition: 2013
Goldegg Verlag GmbH, Wien
Telephone: +43.1.505 43 76-0
E-Mail: office@goldegg-verlag.at
www.goldegg-verlag.at

COMMENTS ON THE FIRST EDITION OF "MANAGING CUTS AND NEW GROWTH"

Robert Fritz (Consultant, U.S., author of "The Path of Least Resistance for Managers"/Co-author of "The Managerial Moment of Truth")
"Managing Cuts and New Growth is a breathtaking contribution to the management literature by virtue of its scope, depth, practical wisdom, and originality. Here is a book of timely significance. Here is a book that addresses how organizations can truly move from the traps of contradictory objectives that limit growth, to restructuring the fundamental elements in which complexity and internal conflicts are able to be transformed and aligned. Barbara Heitger and Alexander Doujak are masters of change management, and Managing Cuts and New Growth is a must read for anyone who is involved in the field."

Jan A. Poczynek (Business Consultant, Vienna)
"Contemporary timelessness. Translated internationality. A re-updated change management in times of crisis. This book addresses consultants and managers likewise. It offers a thorough overview on the subject of transformation of organizations and sufficient links to enable a transfer to practice. Overall it is a strong mix of models, methods, practical relevance, case studies and interventions. The levers for successful change management become very clear, especially by dedicating individual chapters to the emotional turmoil in change processes and to business factors, confirming their high priority in changes."

Daniel Riedl (Member of the Executive Board, Immofinanz AG)
"Barbara Heitger and Alexander Doujak illustrate the benefits of systemic consulting as a self-help tool. I would highly recommend this book to everyone who deals with change (and who doesn't as a manager?). They address the challenges posed by ongoing changes and show how to navigate new situations even without solutions pointing towards the way forward. This book is also for those who, rather than seeing change as a cost-cutting exercise, embrace it together with the social dimensions which are the hallmarks of true and successful transformations."

TWO EPISODES

(1) "Flirting in February, engaged in March, married in April – and top results in December"

A regional branch of an international software corporation is undergoing fundamental change – from software supplier to "solution provider". Instead of relying on the traditionally successful software sales, its new business process model banks on holistic solutions for customers.

This new marketing approach makes comprehensive know-how a prerequisite for the units with direct customer contact. Moreover, a new management level is taking over domestic business control, and the "old" management team has been given responsibility for an entire region.

A diversely staffed change team is commissioned to implement the new organizational structure and anchor the new processes. A further, clever condition set by corporate management adds even more suspense: The business results of the ongoing year must not fall short of the plan.

One thing is clear: Renewal of this kind calls for immense innovative power and, at the same time, hard cuts – abandoning the previous self-image and the strategy and routines of everyday business. Inciting radical renewal in times of success while venturing into unknown territory: This is a real management challenge.

(2) The old masters become production managers

A small subsidiary of an international production group specializes in the development and production of custom orders in an economically shaky product line that has been operating in the red over several years. A major turn-around project in the production line is anticipated with deep anxiety by the "old masters".

Radical repositioning is called for: The new strategy – converting from piece production and custom craftsmanship to small series of specialized products, means organizational restructuring: Less development resources, new business or production processes, coupled with a change in self-image of those involved. "The old masters and experts" who control the product from A to Z are to become part-specific serial workers. Anxiety concerning job loss increases tension, as there is no definite guarantee that the new product will be a success. The results requirements, in contrast, are clear and demanding. Hope for a secure future and concentration on results improvement alternates with doubts and feelings of helplessness and loss regarding previous successes and the "industrial artisan identity". Hard cuts need to be made as an economizing measure, and positioning for new growth needs to be developed.

Two episodes that reflect the change circumstances in many enterprises: Both management situations are highly demanding – not only in terms of growth and renewal objectives, but also hard cuts – accompanied by emotional turbulence.

TABLE OF CONTENTS

Comments on the first edition of "Managing Cuts and New Growth" 5
Two episodes 7

CHAPTER 1: Same old Tune or new Composition? 15
1. What change & line managers think about 15
2. Three images of change management 20
3. Negative statements predominate 21
4. Trends in change management 21
5. Change management as daily business – our experiences as consultants 22
6. What follows from all of this? 25
7. Same old tune or new composition in change management? 26

CHAPTER 2: In the Jungle of Change Concepts 31
1. A map provides orientation 31
2. What change directions are there? 33
3. Concepts of change – an overview 36

CHAPTER 3: Un:balanced Transformation 51
1. Transformation as radical and comprehensive change 52
2. Un:balance 60
3. An initial balance sheet – old and new images of transformations 66
4. Hard cuts 69
5. New growth 80
6. Management agenda for the development of radical innovations: What to do? 85
7. Ten ground rules for a climate that promotes innovation 88
8. Hard cuts and new growth as simultaneous and parallel objectives 91
9. Un:balanced Transformation 93
10. The overall control of hard cuts and new growth requires an integrated set of architectures, interventions and leadership skills 95

11. Strategies for the architecture and management of hard cuts and new growth ... 96
12. Overview of change architecture and organization ... 100

CHAPTER 4: The Power of Figures ... 105

1. When are companies successful? – some models ... 106
2. What counts? The correlation between change and value creation: Studies ... 109
3. Success or failure – what counts in change management? ... 111
4. Better not – what speaks in favor of not measuring change processes? ... 114
5. Then why measure and evaluate? ... 114
6. Agenda for good controlling concepts in transformations ... 115
7. Agenda for effective evaluation ... 116

CHAPTER 5: The Logic of Feelings ... 121

1. Feelings in the change arena ... 121
2. The four basic categories of feelings – a look backstage ... 125
3. Interventions: What are the main points to consider? ... 129

CHAPTER 6: New Change Challenges ... 133

1. Article I: Cheating the Coincidence ... 133
2. Article II: Let It Be … ... 146

CHAPTER 7: Case Studies ... 159

Case I: my.change, my.chance ... 159
Case II: A 130-year-old company becomes Internet leader ... 175
Case III: Live and let die ... 184
Case IV: An unlikely couple? ... 196
Case V: Growth and Renewal through Business Model Innovation ... 211
Case VI: On a Treasure Hunt for Innovation ... 222

CHAPTER 8: The Phases of Change — 233
Phase 1: Interrupt the routine – we need to change! — 238
Phase 2: Imagine the future – develop architecture, chart the route! — 243
Phase 3: Make brave decisions – jump into the deep end! — 248
Phase 4: Implement change consistently — 252
Phase 5: Master the high-altitude challenge – consolidate success — 257
Phase model overview — 262

CHAPTER 9: Interventions, Designs, Architectures — 265
Phase 1 interventions — 266
Phase 2 interventions — 289
Phase 3 interventions — 305
Phase 4 interventions — 320
Phase 5 interventions — 333

Appendix — 357
How this second edition came about – acknowledgements — 357
Brief glossary — 359
Bibliography — 363
The Authors — 371

CHAPTER 1

SAME OLD TUNE OR NEW COMPOSITION?

"Change projects aren't what they used to be – gone are the days of clearly defined projects focusing on a single topic, on strategies, downsizing, organizational development or IT matters."

This statement was made by a top manager in a freshly merged enterprise to whom we spoke during post-merger integration. Is he right? Have the topics, requirements and dynamics of change evolved and does change management, if it is to be successful, need to come up with a new composition instead of playing the same old tune? If – and only if – this is true, does it make sense to rethink the self-image, concepts and toolbox for managing change – and in particular "transformation", its more radical and all-encompassing variant?

We will begin by elucidating this central question – "Do we need a 'new composition' for successful change projects?" – from two perspectives: Firstly as seen by top executives and change managers, and secondly from the point of view of our own experience as change process consultants.

1. What change & line managers think about

The following quotations represent a distillation of the most important results we gathered from interviews conducted with top managers during and after change projects.

"On the one hand we have the hard-core restructuring specialists with their radical clear-cutting methods and their figures – and on the other we have the gentle organizational developers, heading into the void with their humanitarian touch!"

This quotation clearly demonstrates the divide between hard-core downsizing and change projects that focus on evolutionary development. The marked derision that is often felt by the proponents of the one approach for the other stands in the way of the integration or the temporary interlocking of the two that is necessary in certain phases. Whatever is not part of one's own approach is rejected in that of the other.

> *"It's best to just shut your eyes and take the bull by the horns – get it over with quick – it's just part of my job."*

This quotation from a manager given the responsibility of making radical cuts is symptomatic for a behavior pattern that can be described as "blind charging". In critical, emotionally unnerving phases of a change process, this leads to negative experiences in personal relations that undermine the future of new growth instead of promoting it. The pressure on individuals becomes so immense that, at first glance, burying one's head in the sand seems the most rewarding of options. Conflicts become acute, "cooperative capital" is "destroyed", and employees' commitment to the company suffers a hard blow. Particularly when proper communication of hard cuts is neglected, the psychological contract between employee and company becomes brittle.

> *"Anxieties and opposition were blocking everything. To be honest, I didn't know any more what we could do."*

Understanding, coping with and working with the emotional intensity of the radical change processes managers experience in their environment – and in themselves – is definitely one of the greatest challenges of change management. As a manager, how do I deal with critical and highly emotional change situations, given that management is traditionally expected to reach rationally defined objectives, provide security, know the best way forward and communicate all this with assertiveness and consistency? Dealing with collective uncertainty is anything but trivial – especially if one is directly involved. A strong sense of self and knowing one's own patterns in dealing with change are absolute necessities. That is the one, very personal side of the matter, which concerns one's own resources and also one's own limitations in dealing with changes. The other side is about acquiring new knowledge about managing changes: Managers need an "inner map" that shows them which dynamics to expect when making hard cuts and which to anticipate in the case of new growth. Understanding the logic of feelings in such processes is extremely beneficial – it enables managers to proceed constructively and accelerate the change process.

> *"There is a huge contradiction here. On the one hand we're always hearing 'people are our most important capital', and three sentences later comes the statement 'the only thing that really counts is shareholder value' – and that means downsizing, dismissing employees."*

This quotation is one among many which demonstrates how polarities need to be brought together in change projects, as they keep getting more extreme. Both statements are true: Human resources are indeed enterprises' most important capital and, in the end, effective change is always expressed in employee behavior. At the same time, market success is measured in performance figures or share prices. Everything that increases employee productivity – and in the short term this includes staff reduction – registers positively on the stock exchange. We do not believe that these polarities can be stabilized and balanced. Like surfing, it is more a matter of utilizing the waves that generate imbalance to get ahead and to find a balance in the midst of motion.

The trick lies in working with these contradictions in their polarity and with all their pros and cons, and deciding one way or the other as the process moves ahead. For managers, this is easier said than done: The "good old" hierarchy calls for directness, clarity and objectives free of contradiction. The more turbulent and fast-moving the corporate environment is, the less feasible this becomes. Managing more contradictions requires more open change processes – making space for "changing change".

> *"It's all well worded and glossed over, but nobody believes it."* (And a few sentences later): *"Internationalization is our only chance."*

> *"There are constantly new change projects underway here – I can't even count them all. Then, at some point, they quietly fade out."*

How can companies succeed in making clear why and in what direction changes need to be made? Clear orientation in terms of "why" and "where to" is a must for generating change energy. When change projects are carried out at increasingly shorter intervals and under ever-changing banners, it becomes very difficult to activate staff. Mistrust increases, and an attitude of: "Look, another new cow is being herded through the village, but this change, too, will pass" sets in. The inflation of change initiatives creates "change resistance" – neither managers nor employees take announcements as seriously as before. Stability is anchored in the informal networks of long-standing collaboration: So we get a lot of waves on the surface, but calm and stability in the deep. Why does this happen?

We believe that the initiators of change programs overestimate organizations' capacity for and capability of change, and that "creating a sense of urgency" (Kotter) should not be overused as an initial impetus if it is to remain convincing.

> "Then, all of a sudden, the machines came to a standstill – the warhorses and the old masters were gone, and nobody knew what to do next."

This quote is typical for projects with simultaneous hard cuts and new growth, and shows how rapidly "organizational memory" and important tacit knowledge can be lost in the endeavor to achieve short-term economizing objectives at full force. This is a frequent side effect of the "grab the bull by the horns" attitude that endangers projects' long-term success.

> "Our situation was totally different – incomparable with change projects in other firms. We just jumped right into the deep end."

Here one's own change management is described as being absolutely unique. Exchanging experiences and best practices with other companies is not on the management agenda. This is an attitude we have often encountered, particularly in projects involving hard cuts. Clearly, a great deal of apprehension exists about learning from the experiences of other firms that have been in similar situations. We have identified three reasons for this. Firstly, the pressure for change is so high that companies do not allow themselves much time for planning. Secondly, there is a prevailing belief among companies that systems are rapidly changeable – comparable with mechanical adjustments, where the engineer turns a screw and the change is effectively managed. Thirdly, hard cuts generate negative emotions such as fear, embarrassment, guilt or failure – the desire to exchange experiences such as these is limited.

> *"We were completely trapped in our internal struggles. What was happening on the market, the goals we wanted to reach with customers – this all faded into the backdrop."*

This comment substantiates how strong the pull of internal dynamics is when there are contradictions to be managed and the hot phases of change projects are underway. A strong orientation on internal processes is, of course, repeatedly necessary and does not pose a problem when it is consciously set as a priority. But if the market and the original goals of the change project move out of focus for a longer period of time, this becomes hazardous.

> *"The external experts brought in clever concepts and developed new ideas – which they couldn't have come up with without our input – and then they left. Since then, it's all been just gathering dust."*

This statement demonstrates how demanding it is to effectively link truly innovative – or even radical – external input with the company's internal knowledge capital. Quite frequently, external experts are called in for a pilot project, and implementation is initiated separately – often much later as a "re-launch" – and in some cases never. Many other interviews also showed that decision-makers frequently delegate hard cuts and innovations in their own business or new organizational concepts to external consultants. Confidence in the innovative competencies of one's own corporation is low. Skills for strengthening the innovativeness of organizations and teams have yet to become standard management know-how. Still, most managers we talked with declared themselves in favor of joint control of hard cuts and new growth.

> *"It was change per decree – like a Potemkin village. Nobody believed in it and nothing happened!"* or: *"There were two worlds: My day-to-day business, where I was sorely missed while the workshops were going on, and the change workshops, which were like being on a cruise ship, totally surreal and detached."*

These statements represent two different approaches to change process management. The first reflects a directive approach "producing" words but no action – perhaps due to the initiators' lack of readiness for change, or to their lack of knowledge on how to implement complex changes. The second quotation portrays an understanding of change that sets aside both time and place for making changes, but fails to make a productive connection to daily business and is not really supported by commitment. Both approaches fail to grasp the entire complexity of hard cuts and new growth, so that lasting implementation is doomed to fail.

2. Three images of change management

On the whole, we encountered three prevailing images of change management in the interviews:

Change management as announcing and calling for change. This understanding of change emanates from the idea that the initiator acts like an engineer applying a lever to the organizational machine. The organization is altered externally by employing the right procedure (confidence in the expert – everything depends on having the right lever in the right place). The chances of this type of change project failing rise with its complexity, because the focus on traditional hierarchy and bureaucracy as steering principles poses a further risk factor. Typically the concept for change is finalized and announced – and then nothing happens.

Change management as a "series of workshops" is based on the assumption that the company changes when its people are involved in working on the change. Here, the attention of change management is focused on the "sum of people who need to change". The connection to the company as a "system" is neglected. The main emphasis is placed on relying on individuals and the security of relations to make the change succeed. In this approach, implementation and transfer of the change to the entire system and daily business are in danger of failing – particularly when dealing with radical changes.

The third view, which we feel does the complexity of current changes the most justice, sees **change management as a self-relational process** within the company – a process that requires a stable architecture. Self-relational means that every intervention generates reactions that, in turn, influence the change process itself. When one changes the shape of something, one is also being shaped by that action. A stable architecture makes it possible to mould the course of the change – which is subject to contradictory turbulences – into stable and reliable process elements ("process security" instead of mere expert security –

i.e., stability in the social architecture and the process, not in the absolute validity of concepts decided once and for all).

3. Negative statements predominate

If we look at the overall picture that emerged from the data and analysis of our manager interviews, one aspect becomes particularly clear. In the course of the frank discussions, we asked about the ups and downs of change processes, images and effects, "lessons learned" and personal outcomes. Critical and negative statements about change were significantly predominant. We presume four reasons for this:

1. Firstly, an understandable counter-reaction to the general public euphoria regarding change. Seen in this context, the discussions also had a "venting" function – which is important in change processes.
2. Secondly, changes of this intensity are new territory for everyone – both consultants and managers. Knowledge, experience and fine-tuned models are still being developed. Change management competence is a new field of general management.
3. Thirdly, managers in change processes are doubly affected. As both drivers and participants, they are also involved in all of the cognitive and emotional turbulences triggered by such processes. At the same time, by virtue of their function, they are called upon to provide orientation and to effectively organize changes.
4. Fourthly, we believe one needs to ask whether many of the positive changes that take place in companies are even perceived as such or labeled as "change". Reports from innovative companies (3M, Microsoft and St. Luke's) or startups show how much positive change simply happens – without being identified as such.

4. Trends in change management

Based on our continuous work in change projects, we phrased the following theses about what we see is happening in organizations regarding change.

1. **Change sucks!** "Change" became a synonym for cost-efficiency programs, downsizing, and continuouously condensing processes. Everything not optimizing value creation is dispensable.

2. **Change is global.** Organizations are searching for markets, technology and innovation worldwide. Not everybody is on board yet, but natural disasters as in Fukushima make us aware of worldwide interdependencies. Cultural topics increasingly become an agenda item for big corporations.
3. **You can't kiss organizations, but design them.** Since you cannot touch organizations, the possibilities to actively design them are still underestimated. There is not enough awareness of the consequences of organizational design for leadership and governance.
4. **Next. Next. Next. – Hyperinflation of projects.** In many organizations several change projects are going on but lacking a common logic. A lack of energy for and attention to the projects are the price they pay. The integration into a multi-change-project-management becomes necessary.
5. **Competence built up.** You can see a real professionalization regarding change management inside organizations. Many internal consultants are able to professionally support change. Changes are also taking place "on the go", e.g., that every manager now owns a Blackberry.
6. **It's actually about leadership …** Where managers show courage in living up to new expectations and new modes of working, change happens. It needs both an attractive vision and authenticity of direct leadership.
7. **… and about resilience.** Organizations that geared up to manage unforeseen turbulences are "fit for change". They are able to think in scenarios and became quickly adaptable.

5. Change management as daily business – our experiences as consultants

What developments have we as change project consultants observed in our clients' companies in the past years?

The **number and variety** of change management projects requiring simultaneous control is on the rise – and their interdependency is also increasing as a result.

Contrariety in change processes is a growing trend. An increasing number of projects pursue streamlining goals and repositioning, innovation or growth at the same time. More and more projects aim not only for evolutionary change ("We will become better"), but also radical change: A quantum leap ("We will become different").

The pressure to implement – i.e. to quickly and effectively consolidate change in the company – is growing. The efficiency of change management is a success factor rewarded on the stock market. Only few enterprises also measure the outcome and the success of change projects. *What have we actually achieved with the change?* This question is demanding. It is rarely asked.

Open-endedness and "moving targets" are increasingly characteristic for change processes. Unforeseeable external interventions, market developments or decisions affecting the project need to be integrated into the ongoing change process. "The changing of change" is a permanent issue. Hardly anyone believes in the simple feasibility of changes nowadays. That is the fundamental aspect of this development. In practical terms, it is a matter of building up process security in order to steer projects through the turbulence – to make sound decisions about when to bank on stability and when to bank on "changing change".

The reaction of both management and employees is more and more frequently *"Oh no, not again"* or *"This is an* absolute jungle of change concepts *we're moving in"*. This is an indicator for change fatigue in organizations, and also shows that change management resources – not only time and know-how, but first and foremost emotional change energy, the desire for something new – are limited, not inexhaustible.

Controlling the contradiction between internal and external orientation in change projects is demanding: Externally, it is often a matter of complying with the (short-term) logic of figures and maintaining focus on customer benefit – often this alone harbors ample potential for conflict. Internally, commitment and movement need to be generated. Internal dynamics – especially emotional escalation and blockages – consume a great deal of energy without bringing the process forward. As a result, all attention is focused inward, and the original objectives are lost from view.

With the pressure for change and the necessity to achieve objectives, the development of change management competence within a company tends to fall by the wayside. Change management competence can be assessed by answering the question: *"What are the strengths and weaknesses of the way we initiate, conceptualize, launch, implement and anchor change concepts?"* On the personal level, this is a matter of the social and cognitive change management competence of the key players. On the organizational level, change management competence is determined by resources and the patterns of the organization's behavior as a system in the process of change.

"Change is good." Those in support of preservation and stability are readily labeled anti-change and conservative. Those rooting for change are progressives, the winners. The quote from Tom Peters, *"Nothing is more constant than change"* has become a firmly anchored ideology in many enterprises. This statement also betrays a belief in the rapid changeability of systems. The equally important need for anchoring and stabilizing is easily lost sight of. The consequences are change projects that generate lots of waves on the surface and are "sloughed through" without changing the enterprise's in-depth structure, its entrenched action and decision-making routines. Core identity, typical patterns, positioning, the market, customers and partners are perceived and dealt with the same way as before. This may be a successful – even if unconscious – compromise (changing on the surface, but not in the core) if one wants to do the "change ideal" justice *and* fulfill one's own need for continuity. But such a compromise hardly brings results. Many projects aiming for hard cuts and new growth separate conceptual work from implementation. They begin with analyses, data comparison, strategies and organization concepts developed by external experts and submitted to top management for decision. Managerial personnel and employees tend to take in this model with ambivalence – as perhaps innovative and well-thought-out content-wise, but poorly suited to the company's deep-rooted identity and specific daily business, a judgment which of course also portrays the need to hold on to the status quo. The result is a lack of energy to implement changes and an absence of commitment. In the second act – often with a new cast – an implementation project is started, either internally by management or externally with new consultants. In the meantime, valuable time has passed and the chances for dealing with new concepts in a productive way have disappeared.

Another separation we have frequently observed is the "split" into two types of change projects: Those with "hard" goals, streamlining projects very much oriented on immediate economic success on the one hand, and on the other hand growth-oriented projects that concentrate either on a change in company culture or renewal and innovation. Each of these contrasting project types produces a management concept and criteria for success that cancel out those of the other. Streamlining projects focus on the reduction of "deficits" (lower costs, staff reduction, etc.). Growth and potentials are not an issue (*"you can't shrink to suc-*

cess"). Growth-oriented projects tend to have difficulty focusing on measurable success and resource limitation. More often than not, "hard cuts" win over new growth, because they are more radical and tend to make it difficult to maintain the delicate prerequisites and incentives for renewal. New growth as transformation – i.e., as "becoming different" and not merely "getting better" – also means, for all concerned, questioning and eventually giving up ingrained routines and stable patterns of co-operation and perception. In the first place, this must be really worthwhile and, in the second, it needs to be steered very skillfully.

6. What follows from all of this?

On the basis of our experiences, interviews and compiled survey results, we can draw the following conclusions:

In addition to result-oriented performance indexes, qualitative factors such as consistent strategy implementation, management quality and innovative strength are becoming increasingly important criteria for companies' success. Change management generates more visible value creation than before.

The readiness and ability to conceive and realize complex change projects effectively and quickly are success factors for managers, and represent a competitive advantage for companies. This particularly applies to projects that make hard cuts and at the same time aim for innovation or new growth. Contradictory dynamics are typical for these change projects.

Change management requires professionalization; in the past, this area of competence was not a standard item on managers' and consultants' "agendas". The need for orientation and repertoire in this area is growing.

As managers and consultants, we need to develop an understanding of how organizations can change in a way that does justice to the complexity of turbulent transformations (neither change by decree nor change as a series of workshops). Once we have mapped this out, we can develop structures, designs and interventions that do justice to hard cuts on the one hand and innovation and the typical dynamics of the different phases of change on the other (Chapter 2).

How we picture change determines how we act, how we as consultants and managers "navigate" and control change. Naturally, this also determines our perception of success – our self-image is a vital factor as well. A realistically positive image of ourselves, our company and its potential is a considerable source of energy.

We need a better understanding of what constitutes hard cuts and what characterizes new growth. Only then can we decide where within the change process they can be linked, and where it is advisable to let them run on their own, in parallel or one after the other (Chapter 3).

Change is a highly emotional issue. Changes spark off turmoil in organizations – and in individuals. Understanding the pattern and "identity" of their own organization is important for managers and consultants, as is understanding themselves as individuals in the change process. Perceiving the logic of feelings in others and ourselves, and utilizing this understanding with "empathetic distance" as a motor and a resource is highly productive – and often makes the difference between success and failure (Chapter 4).

7. Same old tune or new composition in change management?

We believe that managers and consultants wishing to make changes that aim for hard cuts and new growth will depart from long-standing ideas about how change can succeed. We have experienced this in a variety of situations, and this has prompted us to develop our own concepts for systemic management and systemic consultation further, to prepare and test specific instruments for change projects that aim for simultaneous hard cuts and new growth, and to write this book.

Thoughts of people affected by change

(1) change manager

… My assignment is so vague … I'm going to be confronted with horrible emotions … this is going to be a real downer … corporate management has no idea what's really going on down here … how am I supposed to keep track of the big picture? … of course, the assignment is challenging, and I do enjoy taking on new tasks … there's a lot of potential for me personally, if I do manage to bring the organization up to par … but my standing will really suffer if I don't … What can I actually achieve on my own? … I need a good team to support me … how can I involve customers … but it's way too early for that, anyways … water cooler gossip is reaching storm force, there's talk of entire departments being shut down … even if I do have an opinion of my own, I can't say anything about it officially … the first pilot projects are touching down … there's a few good results already … customer feedback is encouraging … no idea how I'm going to manage my private life in the next 6 weeks … I've got to call my wife … How can I get some quiet and stability? … but this is an appealing task, after all … it's not my first project, I've accomplished a lot in the past … but this one is extremely complex and challenging … what will things look like in 5 years? … everything will be entirely different … I'll probably be working on another project by then … what criteria do managers use to measure performance, anyways? Who evaluates this? … staff, management …? … How do I bridge the gap between staff and management? … this is a real sandwich position I'm in … who were my role models before? … which role model fits this situation? … How do I organize this process so that I don't have to do an 80-hour week? … I'm looking forward to the next team meeting … the subprojects in downsizing need a lot of emotional support … how do I treat the losers? … how do I curb the euphoria, or is it a bad idea to dampen enthusiasm when we're aiming for growth? … What were the real crises in my life, how did I overcome them, what coping strategies did I have? … I've accomplished so much already … the next large-scale event – just thinking about it gives me heartburn … I'm used to speaking in public … but it's all so emotional … I hope they'll be able to keep it under control … on the other hand, it's always a thrilling experience to surf through those big events … it's exciting to be at the center of attention … I think my presentation will go really well … I've always been good at the informal networking part afterwards … so many questions … what really keeps me going is this basic feeling of strength …

CHAPTER 2

IN THE JUNGLE OF CHANGE CONCEPTS

> *If we take findings indicating that the growing diversity and importance of change management requires a new formula seriously, we need a "roadmap" on which we can position different types of change.*

With different situations and different needs, the goals of change vary. They generate different dynamics in companies, and each case requires specific structuring and direction.

One of the difficulties managers face lies in finding the approach that is most appropriate for their particular situation; a sense of orientation is called for.

1. A map provides orientation

The following map positions different types of change projects according to two dimensions.

The first reflects how high the company's **need for change** is in relation to its market. In systemic terms, this is a matter of assessing the need in relation to the external environment. The pivotal question is: *Do we need evolutionary, gradual change in our company, or do we need a radical change (transformation)?*

The second dimension describes the company's **capability for change.** In systemic terms, this is about assessing the ability of the system for self-organization and self-development. This involves three aspects. First of all, competence in diagnosing the external environment – the market, competitors, value-adding partners, customers – and internal aspects such as strategy, structures, social aspects, processes, human resources, core competencies, innovative potential and change patterns. Secondly, the ability to decide where maintaining stability is in order and where to bank on evolutionary development and transformation. The third essential ability is change management competence in a more specific sense: The personal, contextual and social competence to shape change processes and develop an appropriate control repertoire for the company. The organization's openness for change is also a factor here.

If the capacity for change is low, then strong, more directive top-down control is required in the change process. In contrast, a high capacity for change calls for more indirect control, by establishing a framework (structure and processes) and incentives for self-initiative and self-development (bottom-up and crosswise networking).

The following image shows the positioning of typical change objectives and concepts in the combination of both dimensions: Necessity for change and capacity for change.

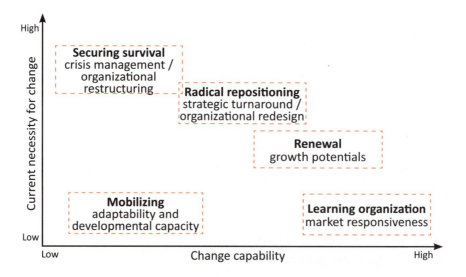

How can this map help initiators and those responsible for change?
- It provides clarity about different assessments of planned projects at a very early stage, thus leading to necessary discussions about diagnosis and objectives and their consequences for architecture and control. This makes sure the initiators of change are all heading in the same direction.
- It facilitates the concrete decision about which change management concept (architecture, roles and process) is best. It also averts the precipitate transfer of concepts and methods successfully applied in the past to newly

emerging, possibly differently positioned problems, because it indicates the fundamental strategies appropriate for each type of change.
- As a "portfolio map" it serves to position ongoing change projects in a company in relation to one another, and thus to provide a picture of the intensity and the directions of change the company is undergoing. This is important for the overall control of changes in progress. If a project's positioning shifts during its course, the map can indicate the necessity for "changing change" (moving target).

2. What change directions are there?

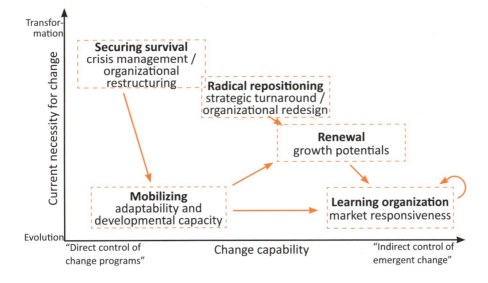

Survival
Reorganization projects are about survival, recovery and retreating to navigable water. Mastering acute crises is vital: The current pressure for change must be lifted, business must be stabilized.

Mobilizing
If the objective is **mobilization**, the change initiators want to increase the capacity for change of individuals and systems in success phases. By promoting timely learning, they aim to prevent crises from emerging. However, the perceived necessity for change may also increase in the process.

Radical repositioning

The aim of **radical repositioning** is to return to calmer waters through a combination of proactive turnaround (anticipating a potential crisis) and strategic redesign, and thereby to increase the organization's capacity for change.

Renewal

Renewing oneself as an enterprise – with no crisis looming on the horizon – means finding, testing and integrating innovative potentials for growth and development: Renewing one's identity.

Learning organization

In a **learning organization**, change happens as an element of day-to-day business (emergent change). Market, incentive & control systems, as well as corporate culture, encourage development and innovation.

> **Examples:**
>
> **1.** Several planned major projects have not been completed in an international telecommunication company – this means a 2nd quarter in the red. Corporate management announces a crisis.
>
> **2.** The personnel division of a recently merged international production company has fallen into complete internal disarray – despite competent experts. Its performance is generally assessed negatively, in part without justification. The various products and business processes have broken free; they are only sparsely linked to each other, and have come unlatched from the overall development of the company. The plan is to give new focus to the value creation of the Human Resources division, allowing it to reposition itself as a division with a new strategy and a self-understanding that corresponds to the changed situation of the entire company (internationalization, pressure to innovate and financial pressure), and to drastically reduce costs. A new manager takes over the direction of the department.

> **Examples:**
>
> **3.** The new board of an organically evolved and diversified corporate commercial trade group, with a long-standing tradition under family ownership, decides to initiate a change project that targets strategic repositioning and simultaneous corporate restructuring. The company is successful, but growth rates have clearly declined; the old way of doing business is no longer practicable. The top priority is to strengthen innovative power (E-Commerce and value chain with suppliers and customers), get the company back into the swing and build growth potential for the future.
>
> **4.** The established, thoroughly structured "customer services/maintenance" department of a systems company is offering an increasing number of more and more complex business services and generating the major share of the company's profits. The management team decides to establish a TQM (Total Quality Management) process to consolidate success in this qualitative and quantitative growth phase.
>
> **5.** The accounting teams of an IT provider that offers complex service projects are rated using individual and team-oriented indexes that measure profit contribution, customer satisfaction and power of innovation. In the informal setting of internal marketplaces, they exchange knowledge and experience. The best performers in a given area are entrusted with tasks for all (competence center). A "Customer Parliament" (open discussion forum) is held annually.

Five examples – five very different change situations, each with a different goal and generating different company dynamics – and each requiring a specific type of control and architecture. If we start with the outlined examples, the positioning for each could look roughly like this:

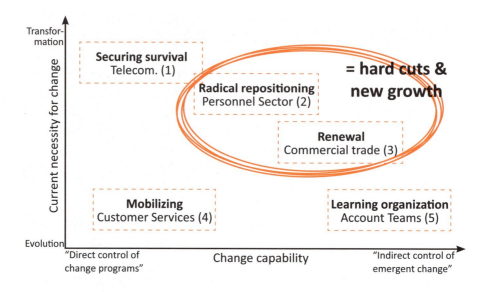

In this book we concentrate on change projects involving hard cuts and new growth. By that we mean projects aiming for renewal and radical repositioning (examples 2 and 3 above). Both involve a radical change of the previous corporate identity (transformation!) despite the absence of acute existential crisis. In fact, the opposite is the case: Sufficient individual and organizational resources and competence for change exists. This is the combination which, in comparison with the other change concepts, generates the most intensive contradictions. In short: This is about becoming somebody different, despite already being good. In the case of self-renewal, this inevitably also means experiencing separation from the "old identity" as a hard cut. In the case of radical repositioning, it means making hard cuts as a streamlining measure and simultaneously generating innovative energy. Before we focus on the specific features of these two change types in relation to the concept of "Un:balanced Transformation", let's take a look at the individual concepts positioned on the map.

3. Concepts of change – an overview

In the following, we will briefly introduce the individual concepts of change. First, we name the typical triggers and objectives. This is followed by an indication of priority measures. We then explain where special attention is required for steering the change process, and what specific challenges the respective concepts present.

	"Securing Survival" Example: Managing Reorganization
Change drivers	Losses over a long period, market slumps or crashes lead to a liquidity crisis and diminishing trust of stakeholders (customers, value-adding partners, employees, shareholders, banks, general public, etc.) – i.e., short-term or medium-term existential crisis.
Objectives	Survival – Increase liquidity, re-establish positive performance figures and regain stakeholder trust – Regain leeway for shaping the future and stabilizing day-to-day business
Priorities	Hard cuts all around – reduction and concentration on a few main points: Capital/liquidity – employees – preventing losses – Re-assess business portfolio and assets – Re-engineer core processes (suppliers, production, distribution) – Downsizing and retention of good employees – Cash & liquidity management – Stabilize day-to-day business – Negotiations with banks, suppliers, customers (or proprietors)
Steering	Essential aspects of the change process design: – Stringent and results-orientated top-down control ("push principle") – Set up change architecture parallel to day-to-day business as a special crisis organization, i.e., strong crisis committee, own communication center and crisis teams (comprehensive, innovative and well-staffed, operative experts) who work out reorganization concepts and hold the line during implementation – Consistent, intense and target-group-specific crisis communication concerning the situation, consequences and objectives or milestones of the management of the reorganization, both internally (managers, employees, staff representatives) and externally (media, banks, suppliers, customers) – Partial replacement of the management staff (new arrivals are unblinded by everyday routine and relational complexities) – Development and intense communication of positive images concerning the short-term future – Control of results across the line

"Securing Survival" (cont.)	
Example: Managing Reorganization	
Challenge	– Take time for diagnosis and win commitment for the crisis; i.e. communicate and act "firmly but sincerely" (see the chapters "The Logic of Feelings" and "The Power of Figures"). – Manage the "survivor syndrome". – Establish new managerial personnel as a team (anticipate a future attitude of co-operation during crisis management).

"Mobilizing"	
Example: TQM, Kaizen	
Change drivers	Market stability or continuous successes have securely anchored routines in day-to-day business. Management is convinced that their branch is becoming increasingly dynamic; the team is (all too) accustomed to security.
Objectives	Strengthening the company's change capacity and readiness for the future and boost entrepreneurial action, i.e., customer and result orientation – More dynamic power: Promote creativity and innovation – Ability to invest in more profitable growth and future potentials
Priorities	Activities for evolutionary (quantitative and qualitative) growth: – Communicate business strategy, business plans and business ratios, establish a link between top-down and bottom-up activities – Increase transparency about what each individual contributes to corporate success – Establishing incentive and qualification systems for entrepreneurial innovation and for quality increase – i.e., comprehensive development of potential and know-how for managerial personnel and employees – Heavy investment in training and further development of management systems (to make them more entrepreneurial) – Provide continual impetus by means of customer/employee feedback – Control and communicate optimization measures of the day-to-day operations

	"Mobilizing" (cont.) Example: TQM, Kaizen (cont.)
Steering	Essential aspects of the change process design: – The commitment of senior management and stringent, result-oriented middle-down and bottom-up control are integrated into a firmly directed – and, if necessary, very formally controlled – overall process. – Training, training, training. – The change architecture secures integrated corporate development and the long-term buildup of potential, e.g., by means of an interdisciplinary control team with the intense involvement of middle management. Teams on the working level are issue-specific and staffed according to business processes or daily business; equipped with change know-how, they bring substantial innovations forward. Group events are marketplaces for the exchange of results and promote motivation, co-operation and competition, as do performance systems and criteria. Intensified project work breaks up divisional structures and brings first experiences of successful change. – "Dream teams" (e.g., "mavericks") provide a protected domain for innovative thinkers and their ideas. – Successes need to be displayed, communicated and experienced.
Challenge	– The transition to a high-performance organization (that generates continuous innovation) means switching from "push" control to "pull" (learning organization). – Broad organizational change, necessitating a high level of commitment and consistency in management – substantive ("becoming better") as well as temporal ("becoming faster") evolutionary progress.

	"Radical Repositioning" Example: Business process re-engineering; post-merger integration
Change drivers	Early warning signals showing future business success in danger, the negative development of important business ratios or pronounced market changes and new business potentials make a radical redesign of business, strategy and core processes necessary.

Concepts of change – an overview

"Radical Repositioning" (cont.)	
Example: Business process re-engineering; post-merger integration (cont.)	
Objectives	Streamlining, growth or innovation: – Stop the decline of value and loss of potential by means of a proactive turnaround (anticipate potential crisis or address latent crisis) – Develop and implement strategic reorientation (new business understanding, vision, strategy, redesign structure, processes, leadership) – Realign company culture alongside the proactive strategic turnaround
Priorities	Hard cuts and new growth (quantitative and qualitative): – Developing rationalization measures and (possibly) downsizing measures (hard cuts), new vision and new business understanding – Benchmarking, best practice comparisons and gap analyses – Redesign of strategy (growth and potential objectives; innovative growth) – Redesign of structural organization, core processes and systems (leadership, performance, Human Resources and IT systems) – Evaluating, reinforcing and promoting core competencies – Investment in leadership competence and the development of the competence of staff for the "new business"
Steering	Essential aspects of the change process design: – A transformation that makes use of inherent capacity for change requires "push and pull" steering – Stringent, continuous management of the anticipated crisis or hard cuts, consistently controlled all down the line; if necessary, crisis teams/committee (hard cuts – "push"); management of the transition phase – A clear top-down start for strategic reorientation; senior management controls substantial orientation, new business understanding and fundamental decisions (particularly on personnel issues) ("push") – As early as possible, however, establishment of "breakthrough teams" and strategic change teams (innovators and strategists) in order to utilize the company's self-organization, potentials and resources. Development of innovations, which are piloted in the company at an early stage. ("Pull": Authorized change teams and managers with challenging objectives and incentives for successful change) – After well-chosen pilot projects, rapid formation of operative business units (not thousands of small projects)

"Radical Repositioning" (cont.) Example: Business process re-engineering; post-merger integration (cont.)	
	– Set-up of integrated transformation architecture aligned towards co-operation and competition for both "hard cuts" ("push") and "new growth" ("push and pull") not only with elements that can promote hard cuts or new growth separately, but also with an overall control team that integrates both elements in its interventions ("push-to-pull" control) – Market links (change from outside to inside; customer and market impulses or pilots) and incentive systems that boost cultural change – Support measures: On the one hand for the productive implementation of hard cuts, on the other for training and coaching in change management and leadership. This means new expertise and target-group-specific coaching, e.g., for those leaving the company/affected by hard cuts, for change managers working in the midst of contradictions, for central key performers and for middle managers, who are the vital interpreters and multipliers. – Consistent control and evaluation of change processes to enable flexible management – Utilization of quick wins as motors – The change process anticipates the future business culture and is a rehearsal stage for the future identity
Challenge	The necessity of hard cuts and new growth generates extremely contradictory dynamics, both in the "logic of figures" (the achievement of short-term successes and at the same time the buildup of long-term potentials) and in the "logic of feelings" (disappointment, aggression and elation). It holds out the promise of a bright future and prospects of success, but also means parting from the old, taking on risks and tolerating uncertainties. The management principles are "push" (obligatory, clear and binding decisions that provide orientation) on the one hand, and "pull" (interventions that open things up and encourage experiments, self-control and innovation) on the other. Deciding when to use which calls for meticulous diagnosis and considerable leeway and acceptance in both vertical and peer-to-peer co-operation.

Concepts of change – an overview

"Renewal" Example: E-business integration, developing and introducing a new strategy and organizing business areas accordingly	
Change drivers	Future scenarios or benchmarking/gap analyses indicate serious crisis potential and/or future opportunities. This calls for the development of a challenging new "mission" or business idea.
Objectives	Buildup and consolidation of growth and future potential; expansion of the basis for profitable growth: – Develop and anchor a new vision and strategy as a "future magnet" for more innovative business action – Conceptualize and implement innovations – Strengthen capacity and eagerness for innovation – If necessary, adapt structures, processes and systems (leadership, performance, HR, IT …) – Link strategy work with work on processes and corporate culture
Priorities	Both new growth and hard cuts as a departure from central corporate identity elements and practiced routines – despite success (!): – Combine innovation initiatives and future work scenarios with benchmarking and learning journeys – Develop/evaluate visions and variations on business models and business designs; invent challenging images of the future – Design and evaluate strategy variations – Start widespread innovation initiatives; rely on "pull" and self-starting/internal market; promote numerous ideas – Qualification in the areas of change, innovation and leadership – Business plans and pilots/simulations for testing – Link strategy work with redesign of organization and leadership – Implementation by future units and their managers – Continuous controlling – focus: Market and customer relations and the implementation of innovations
Steering	Essential aspects of the change process design: – Senior management provides overall orientation and incentives/framework for innovation-driven activities (more "pull" than "push") and makes central, fundamental decisions – The architecture of change is characterized by high-performance teams, learn-by-doing pilot projects and simulations linked according to market relevance (wherever possible, focus on decentralized self-control, create and promote "small revolutions", reinforce and protect innovation cells)

"Renewal" (cont.)		
Example: E-business integration, developing and introducing a new strategy and organizing business areas accordingly (cont.)		
		– Hard cuts should only be made where new growth entails a considerable change of previous identity (e.g., redesign of organization, leadership etc.) – this calls for clear directives and supportive change management. – Competencies in the fields of change management, leadership and knowledge management are vital. – Incentives through customer/market impulses and integration of value-adding partners. – Plan (!) and communicate quick wins as a motor.
Challenge		Transformation through innovation is often hard to realize without acute success pressure inciting readiness to undergo radical change (*"Why do we want to change when we are already successful?"*). Perception barriers and "reluctance" to apply seemingly unnecessary hard cuts further diminish the will to change. In addition, innovative transformation necessitates the readiness to relinquish or to destroy the existing state ("creative destruction").

"Learning Organization"	
Example: Companies such as GE, Hewlett Packard, Sony, 3M, Microsoft	
Change drivers	– Change drivers arise from day-to-day business, i.e. there is no specific trigger, but an abundance of widely scattered self-started change initiatives. – Vision, control systems and the culture of these enterprises provide a setting and incentives conducive to self-development and emergence of change, i.e., no independent, specific change architecture.
Objectives	Promote high performance and innovation in alignment with the company's vision; the corporate culture in such enterprises is strong, and characterized by statements such as: "Stay number one"; "We are the elite"; "We're successful, and we have fun"; "We believe in ourselves". – The attitude is: "We shape the future"; or, even more pointedly: "We 'invent' our future".
Priorities	– In these companies, continuous improvements and innovations are integrated in day-to-day business more than in others. – These companies can be characterized as learning organizations and innovative enterprises.

Concepts of change – an overview

	"Learning Organization" (cont.) Example: Companies such as GE, Hewlett Packard, Sony, 3M, Microsoft (cont.)
Steering	– Concentration on smaller business units (internal market, rapid implementation) and on individuals (incentives for self-development and personal mastership). – External connections and internal networking promote the necessary business-oriented combination of co-operation and competition in learning organizations. – Polycentric changes require careful control. This particularly concerns systems and structures that enable employee development (personnel development, leadership system, innovation systems, incentive and goal systems). – Departure rituals are an effective means for coping with constant change and transformation of identity; they provide space for the "other side" of change.
Challenge	The implementation and maintenance of the "learning organization" as a long-term corporate philosophy calls for constant reflection of the current status and perpetual – even if small and carefully-dosed – interventions to stir things up. "Panta rhei – everything is in flow" also applies to the learning organization. Continuous development is vital to maintain this state.

(1) Peter Senge's concept of the five disciplines can be mentioned here as an example for the "learning organization". You will find our "learning organization questionnaire" and the "corporate test – learning and innovative organization" in the chapter "Interventions, Designs, Architectures".
(2) Patrick Lagadec's crisis management model is an example of the "Survival" change concept.
(3) Examples of the "Mobilizing" concept are the TQM model of Philip B. Crosby, W. Edward Deming, Kaoru Ishikawa and Joseph M. Juran.
(4) The business re-engineering model of Michael Hammer and James Champy is an example of "Radical Repositioning".
(5) Typical advocates of the "Renewal" concept are Gary Hamel and C.K. Prahalad, with their model for the development of "groundbreaking strategies".

Now back to our initial question: What actually sets radical repositioning and renewal as "Un:balanced Transformation" apart from other change concepts?

What these two concepts have in common are qualitative innovation objectives and – simultaneously – quantitative growth objectives in a transformative sense – the objective of being different, not merely faster or better. There is also a common "absence" of existential crisis, which once perceived as such, concentrates all energies on coping. These shared characteristics are what sets these two concepts apart from the others. Where they differ from each other is in the intensity of hard cuts. In self-renewal, this intensity is associated with the relinquishing of one's previous identity during the implementation of transformative innovation. In the case of radical repositioning, on the other hand, hard cuts need to be made at an earlier stage as a streamlining measure (downsizing, reduction).

> **Thoughts of people affected by change**
>
> **(2) Top executive**
> … but it's absolutely clear where we need to head … we need to turn this company upside down … there's no way things can continue as they have up to now … growth fantasies … we need to access new markets, new clients … and never forget that we need to improve efficiency significantly … I think this will have positive effects on the stock exchange, too … in the last years there's been 30% rationalization in the traditional departments … we need to keep up with that … how do I get my people moving … some of them are putting in a good effort … but the overall company is a sluggish mass … we could have been way ahead by now … how do I convince my works council … should I take an aggressive stance? … or is involvement a better idea? … the most important thing is to strengthen the people who are ready to move … but that handful probably won't be enough … I need strong groups … my contract runs for another 3 years, I can achieve a lot by then … but the results need to be visible next year, too … I guess that's the squaring of the circle … how do I manage this combination … analysts don't see the big picture … how do I bridge the gap to the outside … we need to rid ourselves of the old structures and processes … if only we had consensus on the board … but I need to assert myself there … how do I wake these people up, I think we need a huge campaign … individual talks won't get me any further … … our entire communication needs to be readjusted … what motivates my people to move with me? … what the customers are saying is actually really impressive … we really need to speed things up, be faster, get new projects up and running … the quarter results don't actually look bad at all – now, while we have enough leeway, is a good time to make the cuts and take the blow … I need a clear numerical statement from accounting, and a scenario calculation

Concepts of change – an overview

Thoughts of people affected by change (cont.)

… nobody here has any idea how much I have to buffer off … I'm so proud of the innovation team … we need to strengthen them even more … nobody's really getting the entire picture, I need to communicate more … we're going to be number one, I am totally convinced … where are the best levers … where will they have the most effect … I've reached the limits of the usual management meetings … their potential is exhausted, I need a new way of doing this … how do I manage the balance between winners and losers without losing my staff in the small-scale areas … I need to keep the key players at all costs … but I also need to promote new people … I need to replace John … he's not going to make it much longer … even if he has been with the company for a long time … but maybe that's why … I need a good solution for this … why am I doing all this anyway? … I need to share the workload … things shouldn't depend wholly on me … what if I have an accident? … Pete is under a lot of stress … makes you ask yourself what the meaning of all this is … I'm responsible for my people …

(3) Employee
… we're doing just fine, why sink costs yet again … corporate is driven by the stock exchange … every year, another change project … another cow being herded through the village … always a new endeavor, before we've managed to stabilize our processes after the last one … if I only knew what the new project will mean for me … corporate has again forgotten to consider the consequences … just breeze in with a decision and milestones without backing it up with a real plan … every year the same old palaver about how serious the situation is … they're just afraid for their bonuses and stock option … the truth is that they have no idea what our core business is about and how sensitive our processes are … how well we work together … and now, again, downsizing … it destroys so much … if we just stick with our old concept and do it even better, profits will go up … the upheaval in the team … we've just managed to settle down and now here comes another blow … my colleague says that they want to get rid of us entirely … I can't find my position in the new organization chart, I think they only tell us half the truth … but I'm not letting them take me for an idiot … maybe I should take a look outside, see what my job perspectives are … should I join in on one of the projects? … what are the chances of this whole thing succeeding, what's the real reason behind it? … or are they just playing the reorganization game to stay on track without risking too much … what are the rules of the game this time? … it would actually be nicer to be part of the growth activities …

Thoughts of people affected by change (cont.)

innovation … securing the future … words without much substance … but the project team is really stepping on the gas … I think I'll join them … so I'll have to talk to the project leader … right, this is my chance to get myself noticed, and I'll have direct access to information … Joanne's handed in her resignation … no way she's taking this, she says … that's also a way of dealing with it … I just need to keep my options open, whether I stay on the lookout here or outside the company … I've heard there's a good agency … on the other hand, I've really gotten used to the colleagues, to the team, and we've achieved so much in the last year … it would be crazy to give this all up and not to stick with it … that things can't go on this way is absolutely clear … and so what if the others won't join in … if management does the right thing … they have, in the past, so …

CHAPTER 3

UN:BALANCED TRANSFORMATION

Change initiatives that set both cuts and growth as their goal are on the rise. In a survey by Capgemini[1], 37% of the managers questioned identified organizational growth as the main goal of a transformation process, and 44% the reduction of costs.

Boston Consulting's Innovation Survey 2010[2] revealed that innvoation is a top-three agenda item for 71% of respondents. However, 86% of Ernst & Young's survey[3] participants stated that they had cost-reduction initiatives and 38% named severe downsizing as parts of the changes caused by the world economic crisis.

Projects and situations where these goals are pursued simultaneously are particularly challenging, since they are about absolutely contradictory goals. On the one hand, they are streamlining projects; on the other hand, their concern is to stimulate growth. And often – even today – the desire to change is not driven by looming existential crisis. On the contrary, the idea is to embark on large-scale changes despite operation in the black. The challenge consists in maintaining the ability for self-reflection in the midst of recognition and applause. Nobel Prize winner Elias Canetti formulated this challenge very clearly: *"Success listens only to applause. To all else it is deaf"*. This is the one side of the matter. As for the other: Hard cuts alone are not enough. *"You can't shrink to success"* or *"You can't shrink your way to greatness"*, as Arthur Martinez, CEO of Sears, is often quoted as saying.[4] But quantitative growth alone (e.g., mergers)

---

[1] Capgemini Study: *Change Management Study 2010: Business Transformation*, Capgemini, 2010.
[2] BCG Study: *Innovation 2010 – A Return to Prominence – and the Emergence of a New World Order*
[3] Ernst & Young Survey: *New Chances in Difficult Times*, 2009
[4] *Business Week*, January 8, 1996.

measured in terms of profitability ratios and stock market acceptance has not proved sufficient, either. Quantitative *and* qualitative growth – through innovation – are required. The most productive innovations are not evolutionary, but radical ones. Continuous improvements and best practice efforts in companies have their limits. Within existing sectors they often lead to strategic convergence. Business enterprises are becoming increasingly similar, a development that is intensifying competitive pressure and diminishing return on innovation. This can always be observed when innovations are imitated: When business models like that of Dell are emulated throughout the computer industry, or when VW, BMW and DaimlerChrysler offer all classes in their product range. Benchmarking and evolutionary innovation have reached their limit when they become hindrances for radical innovations. This is why strategic turnarounds and self-renewal as change objectives call for more than mere evolutionary innovation – they call for transformation.

1. Transformation as radical and comprehensive change

"Transform: To change in composition or structure, to change the outward form or appearance of, to change in character or condition." (Merriam-Webster Dictionary)

A transformation is radical because it changes the identity of essential elements. It is comprehensive because it involves the entire system. It changes the substantive orientation (vision, strategy and objectives) of an enterprise – its structures, processes and systems. But it also changes the "psychological" contract between the company and employees, and the relations to customers and value-adding partners. This means a radical change in corporate culture, even if the latter does not let itself be influenced directly. Hence, transformation means essential changes for the company as a social system.

A practical example
A business information service company that is over 130 years old finds itself looking at completely new prospects. Technological innovations and the success of the Internet have opened up opportunities to generate new products. New target groups can be addressed via new distribution channels. However, this also means a rise in competition and transparency. What was once a local, sheltered market is becoming a global marketplace.

A further source of change pressure is the imminent retirement of the company's CEO after 30 years – during which his person played a highly representative role in the company's public image.

In this case, transformation specifically means:
- How do we build up an internet-based area of business that will increase the internet turnover share from zero to 70% in two years – with consistent profitability throughout the company?
- How do we change our management structures from an autocratic family business to a team-oriented, young organization?
- What kind of international co-operation do we need to enter into in the next year to secure chances in the global market?
- How do we secure our local market? Which markets should we retreat from?

A brief theoretical interlude

As systemic-oriented consultants, we are faced with the question of the controllability of transformations of this kind. The term "systemic" refers to a specific theoretical background[5] – systems theory.

The most important premises of systems theory are:

Companies are thought of as open social systems. Social systems control themselves (autopoiesis, self-reproduction). Living systems operate within their own boundaries. Maintaining these boundaries is a life-preserving mechanism and the objective of self-reproduction, which – for enterprises acting in the economic system – occurs in the constant renewal of solvency.

Social systems are operatively self-contained, and function according to specific patterns, with more or less permeable outer boundaries (structural linkage with other systems) which open and close selectively: Much of what takes place in the environment is not perceived, or does not show up on the observation screen. Social systems can never "entirely" observe themselves and their surroundings. Perceived reality depends on the selected perspective (principle of reality construction in highly complex social systems). Social systems are self-referential. Whoever enters into a relationship with self-referential social sys-

---

[5] See Königswieser, Exner, 1998, pp 25; Rudolf Wimmer, *Organisationsberatung* 1992, p. 59.

tems is not merely active as an observer and agent, but is also being "shaped", i.e., affected via interaction. The dynamics, the system's patterns, have a feedback effect. Systems theory does not view employees and managers as elements of the system, but rather as making up the system's "environment" with their feelings, resources and experiences. Their actions and communication, however, are part of the system, which depends on these and their effects (successful customer accounts, reliable controlling, etc.).

How are social systems determined?

For one thing, by how they regulate the relationship between their parts and the whole (differentiation versus integration). The tension of this relation is managed via control and organization. Free play or interaction between parts and the whole can be controlled via strategies and objectives, as well as negotiation processes (internal markets), common values or a strong culture ("we belong together"), structures (hierarchy) or individuals (leaders). On the other hand, systems determine themselves by shaping their relationship with the environment. How does a system set its boundaries, who belongs and who does not? Who is perceived as belonging to the relevant environment and who is not (stakeholders, e.g., proprietors, customers, partners, competitors, employees, politics, etc.)? How permeable should the boundaries be? If they are too open, the system is subject to turbulence, and gradually loses its identity. If they are too closed, the enterprise overlooks essential market trends. The system-environment relationship determines how the market and environment reproduce themselves in the system (strategy, marketing). The third determining factor is the meaningfulness of the system and its capacity for development. The question "Why do we exist?" addresses the system's core identity and determines answers concerning the direction of further development.

With its view of the corporation as a social system, systems theory differs substantially from other, conventional conceptions. If the enterprise or organization is thought of as a "machine" (Taylorism, bureaucracy), then "to manage" means to act like an engineer who "pushes the right button" from the outside and, mechanistically, achieves the desired effect. His actions, being those of a practiced technician, are calculable – and he remains unchanged in the process.

This model only functions for stable and clear situations. Another frequently encountered model conceives of a corporation as the sum total of its employees. Hence "logical" interventions aim to motivate and to change the workforce, forming teams and relying primarily on participation.[6] This conception is suitable for projects aiming for evolutionary change, but even under these conditions it entails the risk of a strongly inward orientation.

If we take the premises of systems theory seriously, interesting working hypotheses for the management of transformations follow:

- Although transformations begin and end with "the conducting of business" – meaning that they begin and end with people and their actions – they are not directly, linearly controllable ("if-then" mechanism).
- They trigger considerable confusion and turbulence in the system. As intervening parties, change managers and consultants are part of the process, and are at the same time themselves affected by the resonance and tension fields they have helped to create.
- In order to counteract this high degree of openness and unpredictability with adequate security and stability, transformation processes require stable intervention and steering architectures – i.e. "vessels" in which diagnostic and decisional work can be carried out on a continual basis (e.g., steering teams, Sounding Boards).
- The more perspectives "reality constructions" integrate (production, sales, services, customers, consultants, etc.), the more profitable they are.
- A willingness to make mistakes and to try things out in experiments that provide rapid feedback is a sine qua non. The effects of change interventions and experiments are not foreseeable at the outset.
- Tension between clear measurable objectives and transformation as an open process with an uncertain outcome is a constant. Objectives and success criteria must be reexamined time and again and often need to be redefined when the current diagnosis indicates that new priorities are in order. Every intervention in ambivalent, complex situations requires a solid diagnosis. In this respect, it is helpful to know one's own "observation categories" or patterns as well as one's own perceptive sensorium. The aim of the diagnosis is to get a picture of the system's relationship with its environment (stakeholders, protagonists), of its patterns and specific logic (control) and of its identity (historic self-image and future), and to arrive at as good an understanding as possible of how the system reacts – in terms of cooperativeness or conflict. The diagnosis helps in the determi-

---

[6] See Glossary for the definition of the term "intervention".

nations of effective interventions for the transformation, whether on the level of objectives and tasks (substantive dimension), the level of architecture (the organization of the transformation, including the social dimension: *"Who will the change involve?"*) or on the level of the process (*"milestones"* as a temporal dimension: *"When should which steps be taken?"*). The question of resources (time capacities, budgets, technology) also calls for determining the status quo. The systemic management of transformations is a paradox.

What are the impacts of transformations?
Transformations are radical and comprehensive. The following model provides an illustration of the dimensions in which they take effect.

What is the impact of transformations?
Transformations are radical and comprehensive. This model illustrates in which dimensions.

Transformations affect all elements of this "management map". They require interventions that integrate all of these elements in line with the transformation. The most effective area to begin with (lever and maelstrom effect) is determined by diagnosis.

Experience has shown that structures and processes are often the focal point of transformation efforts, as is the redefinition of strategies (business model, stakeholder values, targeted future, strategic objectives, success factors and potentials, core competencies and control systems and instruments for strategy implementation). At the same time, the (often neglected) factor of corporate identity work – *"Who do we want to be?"*, *"What makes our enterprise meaningful and thus creates commitment?"* – often entails a renewal of the "material-psychological" contract with employees – building commitment for change. For instance, at a large group event with top managers of an international pharmaceutical company with external growth objectives and efficiency programs on the agenda, a patient spoke about how significantly the firm's products had improved his life. This made the importance of identity work apparent, and gave a strong impetus for work in this area.

Transformation and culture – often neglected?

For corporate culture, transformation means a change in the mental models and patterns that have constituted past and present success. They are often taken for granted, having an invisible effect on day-to-day business, and the protagonists are often less aware of them than external observers. Mental models are important resources; they provide orientation and establish community and identity. They draw boundaries, standardize and assist in everyday routines. They comprise the pivotal dogmas and values of corporations. As "reality constructions come true", they contain internal images of oneself – images of one's own resources and abilities but also of one's deficiencies and problems – , of personal history and options for the future, of the market, customers, employees and other stakeholders. In the everyday language of management, this is called "corporate culture".

These mental models explain how the enterprise conducts itself, what is important and which cause-and-effect chains "exist". They facilitate the interpretation of events as they occur, and steer decisions. Their drawback for transformation processes is that they also always generate perception barriers. The exclusion of other assumptions and other possible reality constructions blocks access to their potential for innovation and change. It is not without reason that branch-revolutionizing ideas typically come from "greenhorns" or career changers – and not from the "established stars" of the industry.

Transformation and the individual – changes begin and end with the employees

For the people involved, transformation means drafting a new image of the future, and deciding whether or how the corporate change corresponds to their

> *own identity and prospects for development. It is necessary to understand the "why" and "where to" of transformation to be able to concretize one's contribution, to understand the personal meaning, to sound out the individual consequences of change and to decide for or against it. This commitment (meaning, conviction and energy) emerges from communication, from reflecting, experiencing and deciding – never from mere information. Transformation means renewing the material-psychological contract between the employees and the enterprise, and reviewing and rebalancing the various reciprocal currencies (money, fun, challenge, security, etc.).*

In terms of content, this is a matter of learning new things, practicing new behavior and knowledge – and changing. Success in this process of adopting the new – brought into motion by means of commitment, learning and doing – comes with experience, experimentation, practice, evaluation, adaptation and repetition. To integrate new elements of identity means to let go, relinquish and "overwrite" previous security-providing aspects such as specific roles or habits. Only by doing and experiencing can the new be integrated into the old. This is the only way of determining whether something can work in one way or another – for instance in the case of a sales representative, previously an expert in direct customer contact and now taking on responsibility for the design of customer relations as key account manager. These learning processes require enthusiastic experimenting and the tolerance to make mistakes and the willingness to get lessons learned out of them. The change in identity can be supported by providing orientation from the beginning via simulation or in pilot projects – with quick and direct feedback loops – and via incentive systems that rely on the market and cooperative competition: ("*Which pilot project was the most successful with customers?*" etc.). This development takes time to process, both substantively and emotionally.

For individuals, it is not merely about reinventing one's "relationship with oneself" in terms of self-concept and self-image (e.g., changing from artisan to assembly line worker, but having a secure job in return; changing from product salesperson to key account manager etc.). Most often, personal working relationships are also in transition. Colleagues leave the company or are made redundant, others change departments. New rules of the game alter opportunities and risks for relationships in the work process, the quality of which is vital – both personally and for the company. Self-management is required – and allowing oneself time for the transition phase. Transition is a process of letting go of a situation one has outlived and managing a fundamental reorientation.[7]

This transition phase takes different forms, depending on the individual combination of hard cuts and new growth. It always takes time – as we all know from experience, even if it is sometimes difficult to allow ourselves and others to take this time. Nevertheless, corporate employees often spend more than two-thirds of their waking hours in the company; this fact alone makes the importance of the personal dimension of transformation plain enough.

The first phase of transition is that of letting go, which involves a withdrawal of dedication to the "outlived" context and the process of identifying elements that no longer match one's own identity. This also causes disillusionment, feelings of meaninglessness and disorientation. The second phase is like a neutral zone between the old and new world. This is the time to retreat, process the loss and integrate the change into one's own biography: *What is coming to an end? What significance does this have for me? What do I want now? How could I make use of the future? How do I decide?* The third step involves concretely making the new beginning (new and old have been integrated for the new phase) and re-investing one's energy and motion back into the flow of life. The emotional aspects of this process are described in the chapter "The Logic of Feelings".

Transformation and external stakeholders – often pushed aside to the day-to-day routine

External relations with customers, value-adding partners, shareholders and other stakeholders are an essential – often insufficiently highlighted – dimension of change. The transformation can only begin to have an effect when the relationship to the relevant environments has changed. Transformation cannot be experienced "internally" until one's outward appearance has changed and one receives different feedback etc. from the outside. The inward-oriented dynamics of some conventional change processes do not allow this opening until late in the transition, or ignore its necessity completely. Deliberately observing and dealing with environments can be a source of valuable resources for the transformation.

---

[7] Compare Johanna Krizanits, *Selbstmanagement in Transition*, Hernsteiner 1/2002, pp. 16 ff; and "Phases of Change", Chapter 7 below.

Integrating customers and partners in the process (e.g., through "Customer Parliaments", open forums with partners, or empathetic customer observation) strengthens customer and partner relationships, and frequently brings unexpected potential for innovation to light. Transformations often also necessitate altered behavior and change from external stakeholders, making it all the more important to involve them early on and win them over for change.

We have established that the effect of transformations is both radical and comprehensive. But why "Un:balanced Transformation"?

2. Un:balance

> **Examples**
>
> Employees are brooding over an unusual staffing decision: Why has an absolute newcomer – from a completely different area of business – who has no knowledge of the products and no relationship with regular customers – been chosen as our new marketing director?
>
> The corporation's head has proclaimed the following goal for the coming year: Each national unit must triple results.
>
> Despite a 25% turnover increase this year, senior management has announced a hiring freeze. The rationale: "The economic recession in America will reach Europe; we need to begin cutting overhead now."

Transformations need a powerful "unbalance" as an impetus to compensate the absence of existential crisis. Imbalance can arise from the anticipation of future crises, for instance, or setting unrealistic, demanding goals for qualitative and quantitative growth.

These must clearly signalize that "business as usual" or mere optimization is no longer sufficient; only when a clear imbalance is perceived will the system start moving towards transformation. Imbalance only emerges when it is made visible, is communicated and clearly perceived. There are companies with divisions operating in the red for years on end without change ever having been deemed necessary.

Possible initiators for unbalance that render it more or less legitimate and addressable within the organization are: "Objective" external factors (economic weakness, technology developments, competitive trends, etc.) and/or internal factors (absence of a strong vision, fossilized organizational structures, repetitive errors in business procedures, etc.) or inspiring visions (business pioneers in founding phases, new managers, etc.).

The necessary communication of imbalance always triggers irritation and anxiety – or the sense of a new age dawning and commitment. Concern arises, but at the same time relief, as in "finally – a clear, decisive course and initiative". Launching a transformation is not possible without this upheaval – maintaining balance as a management method freezes development. Again, the described change situations mean abandoning traditional concepts of organizational development that aim for normative harmonization of corporate and staff objectives and rely on open, consensus-oriented development processes. Managers know this from experience, but drawing the consequences is highly challenging in emotional terms, particularly for longstanding senior staff. Reinforcing imbalances means taking risks, braving accusations of polarization and injustice and questioning deep-rooted corporate relationships. Considered in systemic terms, managers are often made symptom bearers in phases of imbalance. They are assigned attributions that do not apply to them as individuals, but to their function and their role. Many employees feel insecure and project their fears and worries onto those who trigger these emotions. Things are seen in terms of "good and evil" and intense personalization results. Despite the consequential discomfort for others (and oneself) of taking on responsibility for the organization's future, managers must give developmental ideas priority.

In the course of the ensuing change process, it is important to provide "containment" – a structure that is both strengthening and protective for employees and managers. In the midst of change, it is vital to establish stability and security zones in order to effectively implement change and regain balance.

On the whole, what is needed is an accomplished interplay between creating and promoting imbalance on the one hand ("unbalancing"), and providing balance and stability ("rebalancing") on the other. This is why we speak of "Un:balanced Transformation".

Un:balanced Transformation encompasses the deliberate control of both imbalance and balance, and thus achieves a kind of "balance of a higher order". Putting it visually: The change leader generates waves on which he must then surf ahead.

The manager's change repertoire
What type of management intervention is necessary, and when? The following intervention typology (based on systems theory) provides orientation:

Manager interventions have a **closing effect** when they generate obligation – e.g., directives, target agreements, personnel decisions or a new organizational structure. They have an **opening effect** when they create leeway and incentives for empowerment or experiments. The alternating mix of opening and closing decisions is another element of the meta-management of an Un:balanced Transformation.

In terms of content, it is a matter of harnessing the following elements for the Un:balanced Transformation:
- Identity and vision
- Contents (strategy, objectives, day-to-day business)
- Structure, processes and steering systems
- Individuals and their relationships
- Relationships with other stakeholders

This means devoting time, money and other resources (knowledge etc.) to the management of these dimensions.

Intervention Dimensions	Intervention Effect/Examples	
	More closing, obligating	**More opening, experimental**
Behavior	Rituals Habits Consistency in everyday routine	Surprises Humor Playful experiments
First-order decisions steer day-to-day business	Decisions in day-to-day business Direct instructions Operative guidelines/objectives	"Do what you think is right …" Operative leeway
Self-observation/diagnosis and communication thereof create orientation for future decisions	**Controlling** Customer surveys Reviews Staff surveys Staff discussions Analysis	Benchmarking Best practice comparisons Learning journeys Evaluation Scenario work
Second-order decisions change the framework	**Introduce new strategies,** structures and processes, incentives and payment systems, management and control systems	**Pilot project competitions** "Green meadow" projects Create incubators Innovation markets

Manager change repertoire (Heitger/Jarmai)

Day-to-day operations and continual improvement and innovation call primarily for "closing" interventions via behavior, first-order decisions and meta-communication – these stabilize and anchor. They also generate concentration and focus energy on the existing. Any behavior always constitutes an intervention that goes beyond its immediately intended objectives and results. It is observed, interpreted and referred to in the behavioral decisions of others. Studies show that employees orient themselves by the behavior of senior management to the same degree as on their words. However, their most important reference is the behavior of their immediate supervisor. Rituals, symbols and day-to-day behavior have a considerable impact.

First-order decisions mainly refer to day-to-day business – such as deciding how to respond to a customer complaint. These interventions do not change "meta-decisions", framework, substantial direction, organization, or resource development and distribution.

Self-observation and communication thereof – i.e., acting not as a protagonist, but rather as an observer – means pausing to determine and diagnose the status quo. These are closing interventions: Controlling, statistics and evaluations, appraisals (e.g., staff appraisals), reviews, audits, but also feasibility studies. **Second-order decisions** change the basis for day-to-day business. They affect orientation (meaning, strategies and objectives), framework or control (structure, processes and systems), individuals and relations, i.e., the allocation of money and resources.

"Closing" means that the change is definitive, provides new orientation and generates commitment. The intensity of change can be evolutionary (e.g., Kaizen results are implemented, processes optimized, personnel decisions made) or, as in the case of transformation, a quantum leap. Implementing hard cuts (dismissing employees, closing a department, giving up a business segment, etc.) is part of this process, as is implementing radically new strategic positioning involving the redesign of organization, processes and systems. When working on transformations that aim to achieve both hard cuts and new growth, "systemic innovation" is necessary: To cultivate new growth on fertile ground, more opening interventions are necessary. Opening interventions enable testing and experimentation. They also generate insecurity and irritation which – when "dosed" as the system requires, spur the venture on into new territory.

Without focus, or the "big picture", and without directed challenge, opening interventions cause arbitrariness and noncommittal behavior and can lead to destructive chaos. The predominance of closing interventions generates constriction, incapacitation and immobilization.

Traditional leadership concentrates primarily on closing interventions, while leadership in transformation processes advocates opening interventions as well.

Every intervention is "relatively" opening and closing – the respective degree is determined by the addressees and their perception. Examining your own interventions in these terms is a good trial run for the intended impact and your personal management repertoire. In our practice, we have repeatedly experienced that interventions promoting innovation in transformation processes receive much less explicit attention than they deserve – with the exception of best practice examples such as 3M, Microsoft, etc. in which they are an integral part of corporate culture.[8]

Leadership and transformation

Dealing with hard cuts and new growth in changes poses an immense challenge for change managers in terms of role diversity. The roles of doer, manager and controller are familiar to managers from their daily business and traditional management practice. Less familiar are the roles that demand the "opening" decisions that are necessary for promoting new growth: The roles of pioneer, coach, change architect, strategist and innovation leader.

Innovative interventions destabilize and cause "creative destruction". They create new challenges that cannot be overcome with conventional approaches. They generate energy, incentives and a productive setting for the development of new, creative solutions. Un:balanced Transformation also means new demands for managers: This can mean the termination of historically successful functions to release energy and make way for the new, which requires foresight, lateral thinking, confidence in productive destruction and persuasiveness – coupled with determination. Both substantially and emotionally, this is no easy matter, as it means exploiting the room for free play that arises from insecurity, risk and openness for the future.

	Closing	Opening
Behavior	"Doer"	Pioneer
1st order • day-to-day business	Operative manager	Coach
Self-observation	Analyst/ "consistent controller"	Creative observer/ "good nose"
2nd order • change of setting	Change architect Strategist	

(Manager: vertical axis; Innovation leader: vertical axis; horizontal arrow across Change architect / Strategist row)

---

[8] Incidentally, literature on topics such as innovation, knowledge development and "revolutionary leadership" also shows that the demand for systemic interventions in this field is increasing.

3. An initial balance sheet – old and new images of transformations

During radical transformation processes, managers and consultants should abandon these old "convictions":	These approaches are more productive in transformations:
"Maintaining a balance between fields of tension and contradictions accelerates change." – Balancing stabilizes – but also preserves the present.	Change management as management of unbalance and balance: – Only clear unbalance yields energy for change.
"Cooperation is more important than competition." – Cooperation harmonizes, but also waters down differences.	Competition and co-operation interplay: – More competition, especially between teams, stimulates changes.
"Conflicts must be de-escalated." – Defusing conflicts stabilizes, but at a high price (repression, new things cannot emerge).	Transformation needs conflict: – De-escalate primarily emotional conflicts and induce cognitive conflicts – these may be on the same issue –, but in a productive setting. This creates a clear understanding of pro and contra, promotes a proactive mindset, creates innovation and prevents errors.
"Feelings are a side-effect in transformation processes; we have to accept them." – This attitude facilitates concentration on figures, data and facts. But the consequences are implementation blockers.	Feelings are the motor for all phases of change: – Utilize feelings as important resources for the departure from the past and the integration of changes into the new identity.
"Transformation decisions require a broad consensus." – Consensus secures acceptance, but reduces the radicality of change (dilution).	The combination of top-down decisions and bottom-up involvement is crucial: – Meta-decisions per decree are a necessary risk; they create clarity on the future value of hard cuts and new growth, and what the road to the future will look like.

"Transformation is change planned top-down; management accounting and controls are a success factor ("planned change")." – Change managers as engineers who turn the right screws. – Change architectures of this design fail because they are not "chaos- and error-friendly".	Transformations are a squaring of the circle – "planned quantum leap" (planned change) and at the same time self-generated change "emergent change". – Change managers as protagonists and observers, as both designers and the designed, who also undergo change in the process – This necessitates flexible control as "work in progress", and stable change architectures that live up to the specifics and dynamics of hard cuts and new growth (self-organization).
"A good concept makes up 90% of success." – Good concepts provide important ideas, but often overlook the process of docking to the system and integrating the new. – Separating conceptualization and implementation does not work.	From step one, concept development must be interlinked with implementation work. – "What would happen if …" scenarios provide important impulses for implementation, familiarize the idea of transformation and create transparency. – The dynamic of overall change can be experienced in small, straightforward implementations.
"Now the others need to change. After all, we initiated it." – The "changers" become the "preservationists" of the planned transformation. Opposition escalates; the process comes to a standstill.	For all those involved, transformation also means (more or less extensive) personal change. – The willingness of the initiators to change has a multiplier effect.
"It is important to always involve everyone." – Involvement creates commitment, but also means that deceleration, weariness and "reaction inflation" set in, which are difficult or impossible to deal with.	Clear-cut and step-by-step integration according to phases and stakeholders. – Commitment and the ability to implement change are strengthened.
"Before we can step outside, we need to have solved everything on the inside." – The "solutions" merely anticipate stakeholder interests, the learning effect is negligible.	Integration of relevant environments from the very beginning. – Generates energy for change, provides valuable feedback information and increases speed of implementation.

"We focus just on the process. The way is the goal." – Objectives and results are lost from sight. or "These objectives and results must be achieved. This creates commitment." – Turbulences and unforeseeable circumstances cause set objectives to lose value (false priority).	Managing the tension between clear objectives and result criteria on the one hand, and transformation management as an open "work in progress" on the other hand, calls for repeated adjustments. This means constant re-determination of whether objectives and success criteria should be kept stable or developed according to progress (flexible objectives through continuous "objective – environment" checks).

4. Hard cuts

"Un:balanced Transformation" involves hard cuts and new growth: What exactly is meant by "hard cuts"?

Here are a few examples:

1. The management of a technology corporation (that has seen only growth in its history) decides upon its first downsizing program due to "red figures" over several quarters and not enough customer projects in the pipeline. Everyone feels that this will be a turning point in the company's history, even if there is no concrete threat to corporate existence (yet). A strategic turnaround is necessary to reduce costs.

2. *In the wake of a merger process, restructuring is planned for the IT section of an industrial corporation. Certain functions will be outsourced to an external service provider, who will take over part of the staff; others will be dismissed. Several departments in the sector will be consolidated. The integration process is linked with streamlining objectives and new strategic positioning.*

3. *A production company in a multi-corporate enterprise is switching from individual or custom production per order to serial production. Redundancies are pending if the company fails to generate more proceeds from larger series. The team's pride lay in their ability to oversee the entire technically complex product as masters of their trade. This identity will now be lost. The switch from unique master artisan workshop to serial producer is felt as a hard cut throughout the company.*

4. *A successful, thriving corporate group in family possession initiates "strategic renewal". Similar businesses will be consolidated into profit centers in new strategic business areas in order to strengthen synergies, innovation and competitive advantages. For some in the company, this means a loss of autonomy and the necessity to redefine their identity in the corporate group.*

These examples show a broad spectrum of "hard cuts" to be dealt with. In the first two examples, it is a matter of radical corporate repositioning. The initial challenge consists in streamlining, achieving a marked boost in efficiency and reducing costs.[9]

In the third and fourth example – classic renewal projects –, growth and future potentials as "change drivers" are the focus of attention. Designing a new identity that secures future growth and success potentials is vital. At first glance, the current situation is not "existence-threatening", as in extensive downsizing programs; the "hard cuts" are of a different nature. They consist in a departure from the "old identity", signifying a separation from deeply anchored self-images – and particularly from sources of pride and success – in the implementation of renewal. And this in a phase of current success!

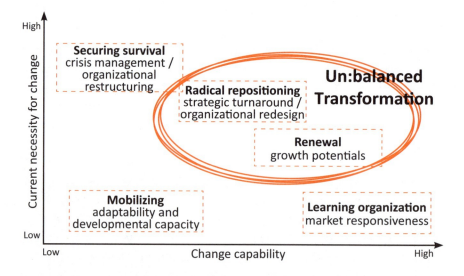

When we talk about "hard cuts", we mean all interventions in the change process that are perceived as a loss of previous core identity.

The two variations are:
- **Hard cuts as downsizing,** which in their strongest manifestation consist in the active separation of employees from the business enterprise or in

---

[9] Clearly, development initiatives need to be launched at the same time. We address this issue in the next chapter.

extreme cases the closure of a plant or organizational units; hard cuts can also consist in cost reduction.

- **Hard cuts as "separation from central elements of previous identity"**[10] in the course of developing a new, entirely different identity (the weakest manifestation).

In our work, we have noticed that attention tends to be focused more on the development of theory and practice for "hard cuts as downsizing" – particularly in the U.S., where more downsizing projects were observed at the end of the 80's and 90's than in the German-speaking region. However, the second variation of "hard cuts, as separation from central elements of identity" is not a familiar topic in management literature. We believe that both variations present similar dynamics, even if in different intensity. Nonetheless, when we speak of hard cuts in the following, we are referring to their stronger manifestation – the necessity for staff reduction.

Corporate downsizing is hardly anything new. In recent years it has often been management's tool of choice for improving competitiveness. Ironically, new research by HBS Professor Teresa Amabile suggests that creativity, a vital weapon in the competitive arsenal of most organizations, may be seriously handicapped by the very action intended to increase a company's competitive position.[11]

Studies show that fewer than 30 percent of downsizing efforts have achieved the anticipated profitability. This statistic suggests the real downsizing losers are organizations and stockholders. Similarly, the low unemployment figures reflect that downsized workers are no longer helpless victims. Many organizations are downsizing in one area while ramping up hiring in others. This decrease and expansion procedure has been coined as employee churning, and this practice contributes to financial losses. The good news is every market imbalance finds ways to correct itself, and modifying strategies during downsizing can increase the statistics of profitability and organizational success. [12]

---

[10] We understand the dimensions of identity to include the system's meaning, its specific form of self-organization and steering, the relevant environments and the relationship with them and the system's reality constructions concerning past, present and future.

[11] Jacobs, Peter K. *Minding the Muse: The impact of downsizing on corporate creativity*, 23 May 2000, http://hbswk.hbs.edu/item/1518.html

[12] Turner, Freda, "Downsizing: Who is the real loser?", WebPronews 2003

The "Wall Street effect" contributes significantly to managers' sense of urgency. In contrast to former times, downsizing is rewarded with a rise in share prices, at least on a short-term basis. The pressure for (short-term) shareholder value from managers of larger (pension) funds[13] is increasing. Managers profit directly from trends as a result of stock option programs ("Dunlap syndrome"). On the other hand, best practice comparisons generate pressure to emulate practices that are more efficient in comparison. Managers who implement the same measures as many others are not as harshly criticized when these misfire as those who run aground with an unusual measure ("sharing the blame").[14]

Hard cuts, e.g., staff reductions are usually accompanied by the argument that pressure has arisen "from outside" (*"We must – we have no choice."*). Rapid polarization of (presumed) losers and winners (or those spared) is the result, and the focus is on short-term reductions that can be verified in figures and other, similar cost-cutting measures. The prevalent mindset is deficit-oriented ("eliminate weaknesses" instead of "build up strengths"). Successfully mastering hard cuts becomes an increasingly crucial ability with the rising turbulence in market and industrial sector development. However, downsizing is an increasing management trend – no longer merely a means of countering crises, but also an agenda item in companies with outstanding results.

Is traditional staff reduction successful?

The Wall Street Journal reports the following downsizing results, showing the "Percentage of Firms That Achieved Desired Results"[15]:

- Reduced expenses 46%
- Increased profits 32%
- Improved cash flow 24%
- Increased productivity 22%

---

[13] "The chief executives from 52 U.S. firms, having dismissed more than 1,000 employees between January and August, can lean back in satisfaction: Their salaries, including bonus, increased by 20 percent last year. A much stronger increase than seen by their 'more humane' colleagues." Spiegel online [magazine], 30 August 2000, quoted in: Kieser, Alfred: "Downsizing – eine vernünftige Strategie?" in: *Harvard Business Manager*, 2/2002, p. 32.

[14] Kieser, Alfred "Downsizing – eine vernünftige Strategie?" in: *Harvard Business Manager*, 2/2002, p. 32.

[15] Hunter, Scott "The negative effects of downsizing", www.associatedcontent.com, 2007.

- Increased ROI 21%
- Increased competitive advantage 19%
- Reduced bureaucracy 17%
- Improved decision-making 14%
- Increased customer satisfaction 14%
- Increased sales 13%
- Increased market share 12%
- Improved product quality 9%
- Technological advances 9%
- Increased innovation 7%
- Avoidance of a takeover 6%

Franco Gandolfi has compared several studies on the results of downsizing from 1990 to 2004 (Gandolfi 2008), and in all of them, the downsizing companies were outperformed by those with stable employment in the long run. Some surveys indicated short-term financial improvements for about one third of downsizing companies, but the overall picture shows clear indications that downsizing does not live up to its promise.

The special nature of hard cuts
How can this marginal success rate in downsizing projects be explained? What dynamics do cutbacks trigger?

Key capacities and problem-solving potentials are lost
This does not merely concern the professional competencies of those who leave, and is not merely a matter of their tacit knowledge, but also their social competence in working relationships and their "relationship capital" with customers, colleagues or value-adding partners.

The "material-psychological contract" between employee and company is put off balance
Naturally, this applies foremost to those who leave or those for whom the company reduces or worsens the terms of the contract considerably (loss of competencies, interesting work areas or salary cuts). This emotionalizes, disappoints and creates an intense need for communication between employees and decision-makers.

The search for scapegoats or distrust and accusations, particularly regarding managerial personnel, are the consequences. Employees ask themselves whether and under which conditions they will stay with the company. Good, sought-after professionals are more inclined to change jobs. The danger of losing pivotal know-how sources is considerable. Others withdraw into "inner resignation" and withhold their personal involvement. Energy levels and commitment decline.

Management focus on operative contents
With hard cuts, there are so many substantial decisions to make that managers are inclined to disregard emotional reactions, primarily because these are often unpleasant. This strengthens the dynamics of distrust and feelings of neglect.

Cost of upheaval
Who is now responsible for what? How will business procedures continue when our team is dissolved? Who's taking on the responsibilities of those who are leaving? Disorientation destabilizes day-to-day business.

Uncertainty and lack of information
The need for information is high. Information flows quickly, but it is often random or of inconsistent quality – depending on managerial personnel. It becomes tinged with rumors and takes on a life of its own. Everyone is in search of official, secure information.

Work pressure increases – the same number of tasks, or even more, need to be accomplished with fewer resources (overwork and stress).

The "survivor syndrome"[16]
The experience of those who remain in the business enterprise has a special dynamic that American researchers have coined the "survivor syndrome". The initial feeling of relief among those remaining changes abruptly in the course of the process. In the event of massive changes, nobody in the organization remains unaffected. As mentioned above, hard cuts elicit strong emotions. The question preoccupying everyone is: *"Can it affect me (if not now, perhaps in the future)?"* Those remaining also feel the consequences; they cannot retreat from

---

[16] C.f. Noer, p. 33.

what is happening, and observe at close range how the company deals with the painful process of hard cuts.

Among the symptoms of the survivor syndrome are reactions such as personal fear for one's own future, depressive states and persistent distrust – particularly towards superiors. The employees feel guilt (often subconsciously) towards dismissed employees, like traitors who have abandoned or taken advantage of their colleagues. As a result of the loss of trust in management, the willingness to change jobs increases – especially in key performers with good chances on the job market. Trust and empowerment diminish, jeopardizing important innovative resources. Hard cuts are a fundamental intervention in the employee-company relationship. The "material-psychological contract" – and the various material and immaterial currencies between business enterprises and employees – is disrupted. This "living" contract goes far beyond a formal legal agreement (money and benefits in return for performance or time), and undeniably determines work behavior, attachment to the company and commitment. Polarization (*"Is this necessary?"*; *"Whose fault is this?"*) and all-too-personal appointment of blame result from this underlying situation. If all of these issues can be worked on with the "survivors", the numerous negative effects of downsizing can be minimized.

Decision-makers are also affected
Managerial personnel are not spared, either. For them, hard cuts lead to emotional reactions such as guilt, withdrawal, cynicism and alienation. However, these "negative" feelings are often projected onto the employees. Due to a misconception of "strength", it is particularly difficult for managerial personnel to be aware of their own feelings, to accept them and use them as a resource.

Disrupted networks and teams
As a result of downsizing, working groups are altered – frequently in their structure, but always in their relationships with other groups or individuals. The interaction of roles is redefined and the loss of team members disturbs the power balance within the group. This leads to necessary reorientation phases[17] and the situation is often intensified by long, drawn-out decision-making processes concerning personnel. The groups' performance declines, in some cases

---

[17] C.f. Tuckman's model of ideal phases of group formation: "Forming – Storming – Norming – Performing – Adjourning", 1965.

significantly. The absence of team support means that the organization is providing fewer emotional safety handles and stability for personal identity.

Avoiding mistakes at all costs and loss of innovative potential
On the level of the enterprise as a whole, downsizing destroys cooperative capital and tacit knowledge. The reduction of staff interferes with deep-rooted informal networks, which are important for innovative corporate action ("entrepreneurial networking").[18] "Defensive routines" (risk nothing; be circumspectly diplomatic) and bureaucracy increase as employees try to keep everything under control in order to avoid making mistakes.

Consequence: "Sorcerer's apprentice effect"
In the wake of hard cuts, opposition towards change increases and lobbies multiply. The collective organizational culture becomes brittle; its sense of community is disrupted. The sense of being overburdened increases – dedication and commitment to the task and creativity diminish; a great deal of innovative energy is lost. Focusing on short-term successes increases the danger of losing long-term potential. Communication becomes restrictive ("only the good news") while conflicts multiply ("the cake slices get thinner and thinner").

This is why hard cuts often – if they are considered and introduced singularly – fall victim to a type of "sorcerer's apprentice effect"; downsizing conjures up exactly that which it was intended to reduce: Productivity costs!

Unsettled customers and value-adding partners
Will my contact person remain the same? How will the hard cuts affect our future relationship? What future potential does the company have now? Does its strategy match my development visions? Will the "hard cuts" also affect me? Should I invest any further in this relationship or not?

Customers, suppliers and partners are not at ease, and have a great need for orientation and communication.

---

[18] Dougherty, D./Bowman, E.H., "The Effects of Organizational Downsizing on Product Innovation" in: California Management Review Vol. 37, 1995, pp 28–44.

Economic crises

The sociopolitical consequences of hard cuts and downsizing sometimes mean economic crises for individuals, customers and value-adding partners – in extreme cases, for entire regions, which means that enterprises are faced with the question of how they will position themselves socially. This has a further repercussive effect on the enterprise's image in the region, on the market, and as an employer.

> *Due to all of these factors, hard cuts in the process of restructuring may succeed in the short term (if one neglects the often considerable restructuring costs). There are few well-established models for carrying out restructuring – the existing ones are imported from the U.S. Due to the already critical pressure for action in such management situations, the negative dynamics of hard cuts multiply. Short-term successes are often dearly paid for with long-term costs – productivity declines, success potential is lost, and commitment to the company is weakened. This particularly applies to radical hard cuts.*

"Downsizing as a continuous process" is part of everyday business for "top performers". It means a consistent and comprehensive consideration of costs as the responsibility of every employee. This conception of downsizing is evolutionary, creates a maelstrom for innovation and does not entail the negative spirals described above, since it avoids the uncertainties of radical hard cuts.

Yet what is to be done when the hard cuts of radical downsizing are up for discussion?

The management agenda for hard cuts: What to do?

Innovative streamlining measures are no longer a rarity, e.g., "lending" employees to customers and suppliers, or flexitime models. Hiring freezes, salary cuts or unpaid leave are further common solutions. Only if these alternatives do not suffice should staff reduction be considered.

Make a realistic prognosis of the concrete results to be expected from the hard cuts – beyond short-term cost reduction. *Where will they create competitive advantages? For which long-term future plans are they an important step?* Link downsizing and strategy!

Plan hard cuts comprehensively and base them on a stakeholder diagnosis
What will mobilize the various involved parties, and how can they contribute to success? This question concerns the perspectives of customers and value-adding partners, possibly also those of the press or the region. But above all, it concerns those leaving, those remaining, their superiors, senior management, the works council, HR, finance and legal experts and corporate communications, to name just a few. A comprehensive core team is a sensible measure for the professional development of a diagnosis and plan, plus experts who are called in when the need arises. This planning phase makes up about 50% of the activity related to hard cuts! The team concretizes the content, ground rules and scope of the downsizing package. The more transparent, fair and comprehensible, the better; the more possibilities of choice the addressees have, the better. The more intensely immediate superiors are involved and prepared to fulfill their functions fairly and clearly, but sincerely and with respect, the better. Management training is part of the planning process: *How do I deliver bad news as a superior, how do I retain important top performers, how do I lead those remaining?* For managers, intense communication is a must – communication of the business situation, the next steps in the transition phase, of very specific (even if provisional) interim solutions, customer communication etc. This is what managers need to prepare themselves for, on both functional and emotional levels. Particularly in the beginning, this planning process requires confidentiality and direct communication among managers, or workshops beyond the realm of day-to-day business. The broad involvement and intense training of managers takes place shortly before the announcement of the cuts.

Communication: As clear and precise as possible – open – interactive – with messages that convey both contents and emotion
The reasons, objectives, ground rules, steps and dates of hard cuts are at the center of interest, and help define the answer to the most important question: *What does all this mean for me?* The initial communication is a key factor for success. Linking the logic of figures with the logic of the task (strategy, customers, etc.) – and foremost, with the logic of feelings – is crucial at this stage. For managerial personnel, this includes making their own personal perspective clear: *What does this program mean for them personally, for their history, their relationship with the enterprise and with colleagues? How does the manager want to go about leading staff in this phase?* Esteem, clarity, presence, listening and ongoing discussion – these are the ingredients for success. A communication plan (*who, why, with whom, when*) that provides the opportunity for group dis-

cussion or Q&A is a further essential part of the announcement of cuts. Diverse, consistent and regular communication, as well as the physical, substantive and emotional accessibility of senior management is particularly crucial – there is no such thing as too much communication in this phase!

Implementation as announced and offers of support

The implementation concerns all stakeholder groups. Those who stay experience that those who leave are treated fairly, clearly and respectfully, that they receive support, and that adequate allowance is made for the process of parting as appropriate to the business culture of the company. This creates trust. Face-to-face communication is most effective at this point. This phase is all about working with the remaining personnel, if necessary, on personal questions (workload, commitment, etc.), but above all, collectively planning the transition phase as it affects day-to-day business (business plans, organization). This includes ideas for structuring one's own work newly or differently, or for optimizing internal processes. Offering training sessions and communication platforms (large group events, "Communities of Practice" meetings) signalizes the beginning of a new phase and strengthens commitment and trust for the future. Coming to terms emotionally with this process can take time (see the chapter "The Logic of Feelings"). Leadership and management are in demand on all levels, and – as tension and pressure are considerable – managers need relief and support in the form of coaching, counseling, short intense training sessions or info packages regarding the matter at hand. Human resources departments are "high performers" in this phase. They develop strategies and packages for those leaving, for those remaining, for high performers (retention programs) and above all for managerial personnel, on whom things depend the most in the situation of hard cuts: Employees take their cues first and foremost from the behavior of their immediate superiors.

Continuous monitoring and evaluation of results

Results of hard cuts can only be measured and monitored insofar as clear, quantitative goals were set from the very onset, ideally on the basis of the stakeholder analysis and in terms of the hard cuts' contribution to strategy. Defining which criteria define success for each target group keeps the downsizing process in motion and ensures a clear conclusion.

Two tips for criteria definition:
1. Since hard cuts reinforce a deficit-oriented attitude, it is important for each target group to ask:
   – What do we want to achieve (e.g., in relation to high performers)?
   – What do we want to avoid by all means?
   – What do we want to preserve?
2. Also include externally orientated criteria that encourage innovation – e.g., customer satisfaction in the downsizing phase.

A core team continues to deal with steering and monitoring the process; the responsibility for the substantive implementation lies above all with executive management. Their interventions are primarily of a clarifying, stabilizing nature, i.e., balancing uncertainties and turbulence, and generating trust and commitment for new growth. This requires new managerial skills in understanding the logic of feelings in changes. Our observations of how managers react personally in these situations have clearly shown us: The way we deal with the feelings of others usually mirrors how we relate to our own emotions.

5. New growth

The world market leader in truck cranes has consistently expanded its product range in recent years with new lifting aids for industrial use. Now, a new idea is revolutionizing the entire company. In future, business will no longer focus on developing individual new products, but on acting as a service provider and systems supplier for the entire logistics chain: "E-logistics" is born. A new business area is being established, internet startups are being bought up and integrated and new distribution channels are being created.

"New growth" describes the side of transformation that is about "reinventing" oneself. Ideas, courage and an eagerness to experiment are what is needed. At the center of attention here is the entire corporation's innovative force. But here we are not – as is usual – considering this innovative strength directly in relation to product innovation, but rather in relation to the readiness and the ability of the organization and the people involved to develop and test innovations and promote them during implementation.

Not only new products, but also new business models or core processes can be objects of innovation. In other words, it's all about the innovative capacity or innovativeness of the company. Innovation experts (e.g., Tushman), strategy and corporate development experts (Leifer, Schrage or Hamel) and knowledge management experts (Nonaka, Takeuchi, von Krogh, Ichijo – see the bibliography for more details) deal with innovation in this sense.

In order to differentiate the intensity of innovations, we find the following distinction important: Evolutionary innovations have the goal of becoming faster, better, larger, more efficient or more comprehensive. It is a matter of optimizing the existing ("exploitation"), regardless of whether one is dealing with products, services, business processes or management systems.

> *Radical innovations, by contrast, effectuate new breakthroughs (e.g., by "exploration"). They presuppose a perception of things and standards that are different from what is customary. This is the variant of new growth that we are interested in here.*
> *As the following diagram shows[19] radical innovations call for a steering mechanism quite different from that for continuous improvement (evolutionary innovations) or hard cuts. The innovation side of a transformation process follows a logic that is completely different from that of day-to-day operations and also different from that of hard cuts, both in terms of figures (focusing on future potential rather than on short-term cost minimization and profit) and feelings (a spirit of optimism, animated curiosity and a readiness to take risks rather than the worries, anxiety and also aggression associated with hard cuts).*

---

[19] According to Tushman; c.f. Hambrick, p. 331.

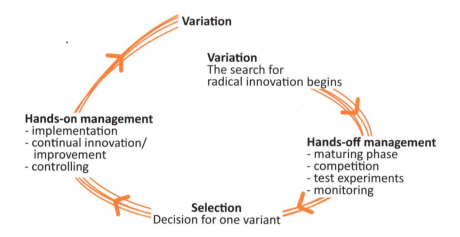

What is special about new growth: Facts and figures

In Fortune Magazine's annual rating of the "most admired companies", innovative power is the foremost ranking criterion. Financial analysts also rank innovation at fourth place in immaterial criteria for investment decisions.[20]

Success factor: Radical innovation

> "Sometime over the next decade your company will be challenged to change in an unprecedented way." [21]

Of the nearly 1,600 executives BCG surveyed worldwide in the innovation study 2010, only 55% said they were satisfied with returns on innovation spending. More than two-thirds (71%) said they considered innovation a top-three priority, versus 64% in 2009, but only 61% said they plan to increase innovation spending. For jumping on the wagon of economic recovery, 84% of respondents name innovation as an important or extremely important lever.[22]

Radical innovations account for high results in revenue and profit growth, whereas evolutionary innovations bring an average profit and growth only.

---

[20] Becker, Huselid, p. 9.

[21] Gary Hamel, *The Future of Management*, Harvard Business School Press, 2007.

[22] BCG Study *Innovation 2010 – A Return to Prominence – and the Emergence of a New World Order.*

Among 108 companies, 86% of business expansion emanated from extending existing business lines. This type of expansion produced 62% of total revenues, but only 39% of total profits. Blue ocean businesses (businesses that had a radical innovation at its core) almost reverse the figures: Their expansions accounted for 38% of total revenues and 61% of total profits. [23]

Radical innovations particularly emerge in enterprises with: High functional orientation and high flexibility (unbureaucratic), with clear and compelling strategies or visions, highly diverse and creative staff, stronger focus on service experiences rather than technology, and a high level of enthusiasm for change.

Radical innovation as the invention of new business concepts

Who has been most able to exploit the changes in your sector in the past 10 years? The most frequent answer to this question is: Newcomers, by "changing the rules of the game" (discontinuous, radical innovation). There are definite limits to one's own power of imagination. Most members of one sector share a common blind spot, focusing on or disregarding the same areas. This marks the other side of radical innovation: The difficulty of breaking free of the daily routine, of day-to-day operations and perceiving things in a radically new way, thinking and making decisions "out of the box". Pushing forward radical innovations is one of the greatest challenges in management. Interestingly, those "newcomers" that recreate whole industries are often made up of people coming from big corporations. They just did not find the space, time, resources or encouragement to make their ideas reality in the more rigid structures of a corporation.

Best practice – top performers' strategies for more innovation

Promoting – or even better, provoking – new growth of this nature is no trivial matter. On the one hand, it means abandoning unquestioned elements of day-to-day business (reality constructions, implicit images and assumptions about oneself, customers, competitors, the market, managers, employees, as well as action and decision-making models that may have proven successful in the past). On the other hand, it also means promoting openness and incentives as well as allowing mistakes, so that something "totally different" can emerge and mature. So what type of management intervention is required?

---

[23] Kim, Chan and Mauborgne, Renée, "Blue Ocean Strategy: How to Create Uncontested Market Space and Make the Competition Irrelevant".

The following features are what makes the top performers among the most innovative companies stand out from the rest.

Innovation is a fundamental capacity in these organizations and not merely a matter of launching new products.

If we make a distinction between managed innovation (systematically planned, focusing on many evolutionary innovations) on the one hand, and open-ended innovation on the other (flexible, less structured, interactive, networked and open for all types of renewal (even radical), where the development of new things has a value of its own and innovation is a core competence), we see that this open-ended innovation dominates among the top performers in innovation.

Openness and protection for new ideas: New ideas – no matter where they come from – are gathered, concretized and tested in a protected environment. Top performers assess new ideas much later than others (protecting them in the vulnerable phase). Incentives and reward systems promote innovation and attract risk capital, serving to promote the development of ideas without the usual restrictions.

The company culture and working climate in the top performer companies is characterized by the following:
Employee involvement in setting challenging goals motivates and generates energy.

Generous leeway in the organization of work and communication, and good networking (information, knowledge exchange) are important motors for motivation and innovation (trust and openness as maxims). These companies have defined standard time and resources for the investigation and discovery of ideas and potentials (in contrast to less innovative companies, where high operative time pressure is common).

Support for ideas and productive debates: Top performers avoid premature appraisal and criticism; instead, they utilize specially developed creativity tools and team processes that promote the flow of ideas, diversity and contributions from all sides (intense utilization of IT in the idea management process, IT as a marketplace), the overall idea being to challenge each other productively with critical questions. The criteria by which performance is measured also permit taking risks and experimenting. Leadership in the top performers is not "top-down", but rather situational, facilitating and encouraging, creating an innovative climate. The development and selection of managerial personnel plays a vital role.

Employees who prove to be "innovation champions" are profiled as role models in the most innovative companies. Customers and value-adding partners are involved in the innovation process.

6. Management agenda for the development of radical innovations: What to do?

This section focuses on the developmental phase of radical innovations. These cannot be forced or directly managed. They call for opening interventions that cultivate fertile ground on which innovations can grow and flourish.

- **Challenging images and visions for the future:** These make it necessary to develop new perspectives and to think differently from before. They work like magnets, bundling and aligning energy and attention.
- **Autonomy** provides time and resources for dealing with what is new. Tolerance for errors and freedom of movement enhance motivation to familiarize oneself with and work on new topics. The organization facilitates access to knowledge and networking opportunities.
- **Redundancy** (through common language and experiences) raises a team's potential for finding new solutions. This is often endangered by downsizing processes, particularly when companies centralize or decide that certain competencies need only be fostered and developed by a single person.
- **Internal diversity** reflects the complexity and dynamics of the external market in the company. Differences are openly acknowledged and freely accessible (open communication, informal, strong communication culture; "Communities of Practice").
- **Creative chaos, flexible alliances and internal fluctuation** prevent one-dimensional departmental thinking and functional barriers to the perception of innovation (career paths with overlapping functions, opportunities for exchange in informal, self-steering networks).

- **Strong ties to the outside of the organization** especially with customers and suppliers bring in new needs and ideas. They also make newer concepts like "Open Innovation" much more successful.

Barriers to innovation

Innovations can also make hard cuts necessary. This happens when their implementation requires the abandonment of familiar, historically successful core elements of identity.[24] Karl Weick investigated this phenomenon in his study *"Drop your tools or you will die"*. [25]

Karl Weick specifically investigated the reasons for the reluctance to abandon accustomed tools when in danger. Basis for the investigation were examples in which experts (e.g., firemen, pilots and seamen) did not drop their profession-specific "tools" in crisis situations, and thus put themselves in great danger, or even died. A frequent example were firefighters who were unable to escape forest fires in time, because – despite repeated exhortations – they refused to leave their heavy equipment behind. After all, it had served them well in the past. *"Drop your tools or you will die"* is therefore synonymous with flexibility and the ability to let go of the "learned and accustomed". Learning to understand the urge to hold on allows one to create more leeway for innovation. The lessons learned from these accident studies can easily be transferred to organizations. So why are customary tools not abandoned? In-depth interviews revealed the following barriers:

- The message "drop your tools and run" is not heard.
- The rationale and urgency to do so were not communicated.
- If the unaccustomed instruction "drop your tools" comes from strangers or individuals who are not trusted, it remains without consequence.
- The tools give their owners the feeling of acting effectively, of being able to influence their environment; they provide emotional security, especially in dangerous situations.
- There is often not enough practice in letting go of one's own tools quickly and effectively – someone unused to improvising feels paralyzed and helpless.

---

[24] This is probably also one of the main reasons why newcomers to a sector (62%) are usually the ones to fundamentally change its ground rules. (Gallup poll; c.f. Hamel, p. 23).

[25] Weick, 1996 (see bibliography).

- The action that is to be taken without the tools is unfamiliar and frightening because it was never tested. The new, which is supposed to take the place of the tools, is unknown. Abandoning the tools would mean admitting a mistake, having failed as an expert.
- Social dynamics take effect – if others stick with their tools, the conviction *"it's not that bad, we don't need to do anything different"* takes hold.
- The conviction that dropping the tools would not make a big difference is prevalent.
- Tools are the expression and symbol of professional identity. What are managers or experts without the tools, systems and instruments they use?

The BCG Innovation 2010 report lists the four biggest obstacles to successful innovation:
- A risk-averse corporate culture
- Lengthy development times
- Difficulty in selecting the right products to commercialize
- Inability to adequately measure performance[26]

But what can be done to make "letting go" easier and to overcome innovation barriers?

1. Increase attention and send out very clear messages, particularly in upheaval. Check whether they have "arrived". Messages must come from C-level.
2. Make a strong case for action.
3. Strengthen trust in stable networks.
4. Steering and the ability to maintain control are based on knowledge: *"If bad comes to worse, we'll switch to "autopilot" and revert to the old pattern ("panic button"); it's hard for us to accept the vacuum between old and new."* Address this phenomenon and provide encouragement with personal examples.
5. Learn and practice releasing the burden of knowledge and tools; being able to let go – as a management exercise, repeatedly create new contexts for practicing letting go.

---

[26] BCG Study *Innovation 2010 – A Return to Prominence – and the Emergence of a New World Order*

6. Increase the ability to improvise and to employ substitute actions. Practice error-friendliness (particularly difficult for experts).
7. Scrutinize social dynamics, in particular those of groups; highlight the risk of "majority ignorance"; make dogmas visible.
8. Practice for emergencies (*"what do we do if …"*); achieve a new identity by taking creative alternative action.

Interventions that promote innovation also destabilize and initiate "productive clear-out". They create new challenges for which "conventional approaches" are unfit. And they generate energy, incentives and a productive setting for the development of inventive, new answers. This also means that managers face new challenges. "Un:balanced Transformation" can mean questioning or abrogating "historically successful functions" to create space and energy for new ways of doing things. This requires foresight, thinking outside the box, courage for productive "destruction" and the power of persuasion, coupled with determination. In terms of function and emotion, this is an immense task, as it means utilizing the gap between insecurity, risk and openness for the future. Radical innovations always go hand in hand with positive turbulences.

7. Ten ground rules for a climate that promotes innovation

Incentives and interventions for innovative organizations and corporate cultures – innovation rules

1. **Create challenges by setting dreams and (seemingly) impossible demands as goals:** They make it clear that "more, better, faster" do not suffice, that new thinking is in order and that intensity (speed, energy and resources) is necessary for innovation.
2. **Expand and stretch the limits of your own field of business:** What is at the forefront and drives us on are missions and meaning, not the existing business. These are what gives us the courage to venture out and to write off previously acquired social and intellectual capital (e.g., Virgin Atlantic: *"Our business is about creating memorable moments for our customers"*; Schwab: *"We are the custodians of our customers' financial dreams"*).
   Radical innovations arise from "new" and creative ways of defining problems and asking questions. New mental images and widened horizons re-

veal new landscapes for innovation, different from the usual ones which allow only gradual improvements (at best).

3. **Exploit differences as a productive force:** Challenge and question contrasts – this is one of the most important motors for innovation. In order to achieve this, differences must first become visible. Bringing together multi-perspective ways of looking at things in interactive settings makes differences transparent and creates fertile ground for new ideas ("Customer Parliaments", empathetic customer observation (video) and evaluation by interdisciplinary teams, scenarios with the most innovative customers and partners). Teams and large group events are particularly suitable for reaping ideas and improvement from the productive force of differences.

4. **Let new, revolutionary voices have a say:** Whoever "thinks young", has recently joined the company, is a specialist in another field or is inexperienced in the area at hand can effectively question and identify the "old boys'" perception barriers and – what is more – bluntly bring the most impossible ideas into the game. Inverted mentoring – when senior managers select young, high-potential employees and learn from their views on trends and the future – is an intervention in this direction, as is the "shadow cabinet", where teams of "young lions" work out the priorities they would set as a management team. This is often discomforting. "Difficult adapters" and headstrong lateral thinkers often make an unwieldy first impression and are rarely perceived as productive in the classic sense. But innovation calls for people other than CIP experts. Other voices also get a say when companies tune their aerials to the periphery – actively bringing in experts or new employees from the outside (especially from other sectors) and utilizing their resources. This also includes consulting and involving employees who are not part of the established center of the enterprise, but rather act "on the fringes".

5. **Create open markets for ideas, capital and talents:**
   - **Ideas:** Interactive large group events such as open houses or internal innovation trade fairs – perhaps also with customers, where supplies and demands are negotiated – are examples for open markets.
   - **Capital:** "Business Angels" can also be established as risk capital providers within the company; innovation budgets with competition-oriented ground rules create market-like situations and incentives.

- **Talents:** Facilitate personnel changes (e.g., link titles to individuals, not to positions; issue phantom shares for founding teams in new areas, etc.); attract resources (pull effect) instead of distributing them.

6. **Promote a large number of quick, low-risk and small-scale experiments:** This "Lightweight Innovation" poses two challenges: the protection of ideas (do not submit them to stringent ROI accounts when they are still delicate seedlings) and tolerance for error (experiments that strand are not failures). This developmental phase of radical innovations is concluded by a selection process.

   An initial idea, judged favorably in terms of value creation, becomes an experiment. The experiment proves feasible and customer feedback is positive. It now becomes a "venture", where revenue, sustainability and developmental capacity need to be verified (piloted in a genuine operation, e.g., a new business procedure or business model). Positioning the project in a development process such as this one provides orientation when it comes to making decisions in its regard.

7. **Differentiate and divide:** Concentration on small market shares or niches – everybody is an "entrepreneur". Cell divisions make room for new business models. "Communities of Practice" ensure that knowledge and experience are shared.

8. **Organize excursions into foreign worlds:** These can be for example *learning journeys* (see case study "On a Treasure Hunt for Innovation") that explore innovative topics in other enterprises (innovations need the cycle of "experience-observe-evaluate"/"develop-test-evaluate"/"allow to mature-decide") or *empathetic observation* of customers (video and interdisciplinary evaluation teams; observation of customers in their use of products) in order to identify latent, unconscious customer needs. An *innovative alliance* can be formed with leading customers or partners (i.e., those who challenge the enterprise because they are innovative and demanding themselves) in order to develop future scenarios in workshops, exchange employees (e.g., "high potential", lateral thinkers) and exploit their experiences for innovations. *Sabbaticals* and *living in new, foreign worlds* should be supported, starting with *attending specialist conferences* from other disciplines and gaining inspiration and implementing ideas (e.g., Japanese car designers living with an American middle-class family for several months in order to understand what automotive needs are central for the U.S. middle-class market). Setting up *Open Innovation* platforms proved to be beneficiary by building on the knowledge of crowds.

Different spaces for innovative work other than those of day-to-day business also work as a symbol, helping to accelerate the transition from one working mode to another within teams.

9. **Develop and examine innovative strategies by means of indexes:** *What percentage of our products is younger than three years? How much turnover do we generate? How many of the clients we advise are leading innovators in their industrial sector?* These are examples of questions that accelerate innovative endeavors in the focus of management.

10. **Strengthen independence and autonomy in individuals and teams:** In an atmosphere of openness, challenge and intense communication: e.g., innovation trade fairs with leading customers and selected partners, competitions with productive debates that utilize conflicts as a motor. Innovations address the "whole person"; pursuing ideas requires being able to try things out, having time for experiments – constant operative pressure hinders the emergence of the new. At the start, ideas need protection from the managers of day-to-day business and from customers. Like seedlings, they require an incubation period. They do not grow faster if they are tugged on. Performance pressure is productive for innovations, whereas operative time pressure is not. Innovations need to mature; they require discipline, commitment, challenge and a great deal of freedom. They flourish in a culture of self-assurance and performance, in which there is latitude for alternating between tension (intense work) and relaxation (letting go – doing something completely different). For many companies, this is something new and unusual. Unlike the tasks of day-to-day operations, innovations cannot be accomplished like agenda items. For them to succeed, organizations need to have considerable openness and be able to accept what is new and different. This is what developing an innovation-friendly atmosphere is all about.

8. Hard cuts and new growth as simultaneous and parallel objectives

We have established how "hard cuts" and "new growth" can fail. What consequences can we draw from this for the planning of change? Does it make sense to carry these two types of change out in succession? First, restructure and downsize, then work on new growth, innovation and cultural change? This approach has a significant disadvantage: The whole process takes a long time (e.g., nearly 20 years for GE). Still, the fact that it does eventually lead to a positive future makes this succession more promising than the reverse order. Initiating new growth and innovation and then making hard cuts destroys trust in leadership and commitment to the enterprise. It creates an overall feeling of having been "betrayed and misled" with false fair-weather forecasts.

Both variations "spare" the system from having to actually live and work through the field of tension between the two objectives. Precisely this, however, – if successful – has an immense reinforcing effect on both system identity and organizational learning about transformations, while increasing the organization's maturity and future capacity.

"Un:balanced Transformation" **means the simultaneity of hard cuts and new growth.** On the one hand, the necessity for this comes from the outside. Pressure to make "quick changes" is on the rise. Market development is becoming more and more dynamic. The stock exchange listing of leading companies induces short-term capital market logic. But there are also "internal" reasons that speak in favor of simultaneity. Numerous studies substantiate that hard cuts alone do not bring significant yields (*"you can't shrink to success"*) and that successful re-dimensioning without corporate foresight is impossible. On the other hand, the results of growth strategies without hard cuts are frequently lower than expected. Ultimately, the most successful companies in terms of profitability, shareholder value, product quality and productivity are those that simultaneously initiate growth and implement hard cuts.[27]

The change map once again recapitulates our basic hypothesis: An integrated change process needs to combine the positions "radical repositioning" and "renewal", linking the objectives of hard cuts and new growth in a way that ensures coordination where necessary (close linkage), but also provides structures and processes in which the contradictory logic and dynamics of each of these objectives can develop productively. This means creating a provisional "two-handed" or "dual" change architecture for certain time periods[28], which provides control for hard cuts on the one hand, but at the same time lends protec-

---

[27] amanet.org study, 2001.
[28] Tushman (1997, p. 187) similarly suggests dual organizations to accelerate evolutionary innovations (traditional steering) on the one hand, and radical innovations (open, incentive-oriented substantive steering).

tion to innovations (as "subsidiary systems") and gives them room to grow. The following comparison illustrates the consequences for the change architecture.

9. Un:balanced Transformation

Anchoring hard cuts and new growth simultaneously

Hard cuts	New growth
– Direct, operative steering – Short-term and results-oriented action/stabilize – Optimize processes, costs and resources – Top-down approach, clear instructions and decisions, transparent ground rules ("push")	– Steering from the context (setting, incentives, framework) – Risk- and experiment-friendly action/unsettle, open things up, challenge – Let things mature, improvise, experiment; learn by doing; work intensively; break rules – Generate momentum that creates dedication and commitment to self-managed future-oriented pilot projects ("pull"): visions/dreams as magnets, encourage autonomy, create redundancy, strengthen and utilize differences, enable fluctuation and chaos – Develop and provoke other reality constructions (scenarios, goals) – promote creative conflict – managers as architects, promoters, leaders for innovation – Hands-off and open leadership

So what is special about the parallelism and simultaneity of hard cuts and new growth? One essential aspect lies in dealing skillfully with the inherent structural contradictions of both transformation objectives. This is not a case of "lazy compromises" or a "desperate attempt at integration", but rather the exploiting of contradictions.

	Hard cuts	New growth
Goals	Focus on short-term performance indexes, efficiency and economic capital	Focus on long-term success potentials for the future – investment and intellectual capital
Steering	Top-down – close, clear, directive, linear, by program – „planned change"	Involvement: Incentives for bottom-up and cross-section self-control and networking, open. Encourage emergent change
Contents	Lower resources/costs – focus on processes, structure, systems, possible downsizing	Involvement, innovative culture
HR	To be regarded as a cost factor	To be regarded as capital, a resource, „entrepreneurs"
Logic of feelings	Requires longer coping processes (worries, distrust, aggression, disappointment, leave-taking – gradual new commitment)	Requires concentration, community (teams are important) and a basic feeling of joy, challenge and confidence
Reality construction	Feelings of loss and defeat influence perception	Buoyant optimism, a combination of discipline and spirit of adventure influence perception (pioneers, winners of the future)
Architecture	Core team steers the process of hard cuts – intense involvement of HR and line managers in implementation	Support autonomous initiatives and structures and short-term experiments – conducted on the sidelines of day-to-day operation ("incubation" until matured)
Orientation	Pull towards the past and to the inside – a need for stabilization and renewal of the employee-company contract	Pull towards the future and to the outside – desire to "ignore" or overcome existing conditions
Executives	Producers, ambassadors and bringers of "bad news" – the situation calls for their presence in the roles of "implementers", coaches, communicators and crisis/transition experts (security, orientation)	Architects, enablers and promoters of innovation – the situation calls for letting go and strengthening autonomy, encouraging "revolutionaries" (pioneer spirit, new territory)
Motor/ motivator for people	Security and risk minimization, finding one's own position, maintaining stability	Involvement, challenge and free play, commitment. Performance in new, demanding areas

This polarity requires that change is steered on the basis of a deep understanding of the systemic dynamics of both objectives, on the part of senior management as well as the control team, on the part of those responsible for change management and finally also on the part of line managers who, after all, have to communicate these contradictions and ultimately anchor them effectively "in the field".

10. The overall control of hard cuts and new growth requires an integrated set of architectures, interventions and leadership skills

Transformation requires an integrated set of interventions to successfully enable integrated, consistent implementation and the development of a balanced, "transformed" system.

> *"Off-the-rack" solutions are not practicable for this type of change – transformation is always both a clearly managed, planned change program and also "emergent change" – emerging from the system's self-organization and self-steering. The process requires both aspects: on the one hand, stringent control; on the other, openness or redundancy. Moreover, it requires experimental fields and error-friendliness. The change has a feedback effect on itself. This complexity is what makes the process so unpredictable for controlled, linear management.*

Transformations require observer input, external ideas and sound work settings that differ clearly from day-to-day business with its pressure for operative results and routines. These conditions provide people with the freedom to switch roles and perspectives, particularly between the role of "protagonist" (deciding, acting and implementing) and that of "creative observer" (developing new interpretations and a new understanding of the system from an empathetic distance, playful experimentation with future images and ideas).

Transformations of this nature require strong "change leadership" that can perceive both sides – hard cuts and new growth – emotionally, and differentiate between them cognitively; overall control of such processes involves doing both sides justice. This means determining where within the change architecture independent elements and processes are necessary and where they should work in tandem – in alignment with the respective goals of hard cuts and new growth.

In our model, this can also mean dual change management architecture, particularly in the first three phases.

> *Every successfully accomplished transformation is more than a "turnaround", more than a mere recovery in figures. It generates new images of the future and translates these into strategies, structures and further development of human resources and culture. In the process, transformation not only changes the identity, business understanding, strategy, organization, culture, expertise and knowledge of employees. In transformations, the enterprise renews and strengthens its change management competence, its behavioral patterns in managing hard and clear cuts; it practices patterns of closure, of letting go of historically successful work and relations. And it rehearses living through phases of uncertainty, "the space between the old and customary and the new unknown" with the readiness to take risks, with experiments, and all the ups and downs that are a part of such phases. This means that the enterprise trains and improves its own change capacity – successful transformations bring about more than successful implementations in mere terms of content. Equally important is the company's gain in self-confidence, the assurance that it will also be able to shape future change processes profitably, because the experience of having successfully managed demanding changes builds strength. This is why changes in the system and in individuals that are perceived as having been successful are always investments in the future capacity and readiness of the system and its stakeholders for change. They provide confidence in the ability to also master future turbulences successfully.*

11. Strategies for the architecture and management of hard cuts and new growth

Just as architects plan spaces and create settings in which different things can take place, managers and consultants design the architecture for changes by deciding on the placement of social, temporal, spatial and substantive elements. "The architecture determines *that* something takes place and *what* takes place."[29] Architectural and strategic know-how is crucial for the success of a transformation. Just as there are schools of architecture with clear principles

---

[29] Compare: Königswieser/Exner, Systemische Intervention, Klett-Cotta, 198, pp. 47.

defining what constitutes "good" architecture, one can list guidelines or design options for shaping the architecture of change.

1. **Diagnosis**

   The change project should begin with thorough diagnosis of the system. Based on the diagnosis, plans are made for the principal architectural "foundation" of the change:
   - How broad/limited will the transformation be (how many and which stakeholders will be included)?
   - How superficially/thoroughly will objectives be planned (surface/depth structure)?
   - How extensively or openly/pointedly will the objectives be selected (what is the range of topics we want to address)?
   - Project- or line-determined control of the change initiative (anchoring in the line or interaction between line and project)?

2. **Architecture**

   The transformation as a "flexible, temporary enterprise" with the aim of implementing itself must be given its own, stable architecture. This requires elements that fulfill the following functions:
   - **Steering and decision-making**
     Aim: To establish a stable overall control of hard cuts and new growth, the interaction between the two, and consistent change leadership.
     Architectural elements: E.g., continuous dialogue with change initiator/board (continuous re-contracting), establishment of a steering team (comprehensive composition according to involved functions, levels and stakeholders) and controlling systems
   - **Working with content**
     Aim: Effective work with clear relevance to the strategic, organizational topics or to the business. Architectural elements: E.g., work teams, expert pools (e.g., on HR topics in hard cuts, IT teams, sales groups), core projects and subprojects
   - **Testing/simulating**
     Aim: To test the impact on the entire system on a small scale, as well as to learn and gather experience for implementation
     Architectural elements: E.g., pilot teams, pilot projects and simulation workshops with users and customers

- **Communicating**
  Aim: To ensure dialogue with all relevant stakeholders, i.e., their necessary commitment ("*There is no such thing as too much communication*") Architectural elements: E.g., major events, snowball systems, IT platforms and "open space" events, large group interventions
- **Giving and receiving feedback and impulses**
  Aim: "*You get what you measure*". This means procuring clear feedback and ideas regarding the content and the "how" of the change. Architectural elements: E.g., Customer Parliament, focus groups and Sounding Board
- **Develop and support resources**
  Aim: To develop the necessary skills and provide sufficient resources Architectural elements: E.g., group and individual coaching sessions, training and advanced vocational training, as well as change management competencies for important key individuals or professional back office support for the initiative

3. **Communication of contradictions**
Explicitly communicate hard cuts and new growth as contradictory objectives – link them ("*why both?*") from a future perspective.

4. **Dual management style**
For hard cuts: Top-down and hands-on; for new growth: Bottom-up and hands-off. This also includes dealing with the respectively different logics of figures (cost efficiency for hard cuts; investment in intellectual capital for new growth) and logics of feelings ("mourning the old" in the midst of dynamic change; mistrust and confusion regarding hard cuts; enthusiasm and optimism regarding new growth).

5. **Separation and combination of hard cuts and new growth**
Particularly in the beginning, it is important to create specific architectural elements for hard cuts and for new growth. In the first three phases, their respective dynamics are too contradictory to be integrated. The consistent integration of both elements in the architecture first becomes necessary in the phase of broad implementation.

6. **Determining the dramaturgy**
The behavioral sciences provide the following indications for change dramaturgy:
- As far as possible, tackle unpleasant experiences and difficult issues early on – this particularly applies to bad news and matters of dispute.

- As far as possible, bundle bad news and failures (no "salami slice strategy") and process them intensely.
- It is advisable to utilize architectural elements that end with a highlight and visible success, making the experience of the final situation a memorable one.
- Savor positive experiences/successes, and divide these into several sequences to optimally utilize them as resources (this particularly applies to the planning of "quick wins" and their communication in the company).
- Commitment can be strengthened – even in the case of hard cuts – by means of choice and decision options (e.g., compensation or outplacement consultation).
- Rituals and symbols – establishing them as "traditions" supports feelings of continuity and belonging in phases of great uncertainty.

7. **Business is business!**

Every change starts and finishes with the "business" (the purpose) of the enterprise. Therefore the fundamental principle is: To change from the outside in – not to initiate projects that merely address corporate culture, but to concentrate implementation in areas that are directly relevant to the business. Flexible control and the direction of the implementation must be evident from the very beginning, and the change process itself should be designed so that the targeted objectives and business culture can practically be experienced, anticipated in advance.

8. **Proceed according to "script", but remain open to dynamics, options, turbulences**

Following this precept represents one of the greatest challenges for top managers and steering groups. The ingredients for success are: A clear system of change monitoring and effective evaluation (see the chapter "The Power of Figures") as well as an open steering team that is capable of conflict and balances the contradicting demands of flexible target development and maintaining consistency at the same time.

9. **Consultants**

Consultants can support by taking over different functions:

(1) Consultants as experts who strengthen the enterprise, its management and the employees. Make use of consultants within limits. They contribute knowledge and skills that enterprises often lack, particularly in the beginning of organizational change processes.

(2) Consultants as "initial igniters" – they support management in their roles as change leaders, and do not personally lead the change process!

After the initial phase, management increasingly takes over responsibilities (no dependency and/or convenience!).

(3) Consultants as change management experts, architects, moderators and sparring partners in the change process ease the burden of those involved and facilitate higher concentration on the contents of change.

10. **Transformation always means changing one's own identity – changing oneself**

This requires a strong sense of self. Key players in the change process need to reflect on how they have experienced and dealt with upheaval in their own lives – in terms of content and emotion – and within their own relational network. Only what we have lived through ourselves – in reality or in our imagination – and have grasped emotionally, can we understand in others, whose reactions and feelings we are confronted with when working on clear cuts and new growth. This is about maintaining empathetic distance and being able to identify temporarily with diverse perspectives as a basis for successful communication (using oneself and one's own feelings as a "rehearsal stage and Sounding Board" for what takes place in the company).

The case studies in the last part of the book illustrate these strategies for shaping change in practice.

12. Overview of change architecture and organization

Those who wish to extend their knowledge can find more on **innovation** in the following books:
- Tushman/O'Reilly, *Winning through Innovation*
- Berkun, *The Myths of Innovation*
- Sutton, *Weird Ideas That Work*
- Duarte/Tennant-Snyder, *Strategic Innovation*
- Dyer/Gregersen/Christensen, *The Innovator's DNA*

On the topic of **knowledge management** and particularly knowledge development:
- Nonaka/Takeuchi, *The Knowledge-Creating Company*
- Krogh/Ichijo/Nonaka, *Enabling Knowledge Creation*

On the topic of **revolutionary leadership:**
- Hamel, *Leading the Revolution*
- Johansen, *Leaders Make the Future*
- Weick, *Making Sense of the Organization*

For details, see Bibliography.

> **Thoughts of people affected by change**
>
> **(4) Middle manager**
> … so, at least the personnel decisions are out now … and I'll be kept on, at least for the next year … but how do I tell my people … again, downsizing by 25% … this is the fourth wave of cutbacks … it'll be easy to break it to the new people, but the others won't understand … every year the same argument, now, the next upheaval … customer demands, market collapse, results, the elements are interchangeable … pressure is rising … and here I am again, sandwiched right in the middle … well, how much we can actually believe isn't clear … it makes me think about the other departments – we've cut back so much already, they should take a look at their own area … if corporate got the same instructions we do, they'd lose it … what gives me hope is the growth we're seeing in the X department … the ideas we've come up with there … and optimization is finally a sensible goal, we've always been ambitious … always a step ahead, even of other departments … I think we can do it … with a certain level of competitiveness … we'll reach our target, no question … but what will the price be this time … I'm growing skin thicker than an elephant … not sure if that's good … how can I motivate myself more … how will I manage this? … staying number one is so abstract … and what do I get in return? … it's the sportsmanship in competing with my colleagues that's more significant … and of course it's more pleasant than downsizing … maybe this balance is something that would go over well with my people … I think each of them will go for different things … I need people I can count on, and I need to focus on the right ones … I think I'll start some projects in my department … it should work with a handful of strong people … now that everything is in uproar anyways … now they've appointed another change manager … I'm curious to find out what his job description is … there's going to be a lot of commotion again … I'll need to protect my position … all the same, I'm looking forward to the new …

Thoughts of people affected by change (cont.)

(5) Customers

… they just need to get it into their heads that things need to move faster … they have no idea of the pressure we – our customers – are under … all the same, product quality and stability mustn't change … demands on our company are also rising … the last thing I can afford are insecurities in daily business … there's so much we have to do and organize ourselves … the new products they're promising seem to have a lot of potential, but will they actually work the way they say they will? … service is becoming more and more vital … we need to simplify things … interfaces … will they make it through reorganization? … maybe I should check out the competition … it may give us better reasons to stay with them … on the other hand, if we do manage to work on a process like this together, a lot could come of it … but we mustn't depend too strongly on a single supplier … I need more transparency on what's going on there … and this feeling – will they make it or not … I think they want to do it quietly, so we won't notice … and think things are still the same as before … but we have employees with contacts in their company … it's pure mayhem … our key account manager is singing us a different song, of course … but I think we need to be alert … I really like their idea of comprehensive project teams … that way we'll get more insight into their processes … supply chain … are we on the same page, or just neighbors … I think it's time to make some ambitious demands on these guys … this will keep up their will to change … "hang it higher" … that's what they need to sell to us, too … I've heard they're venturing out into completely new fields … makes me wonder what will become the core business with us regular customers … we'll need to watch them closely … if they send out the best people to the new areas, I'll really start to worry about our products … on the other hand, my hands are so full with daily business, that I actually just want to see results … think I'll be frank about this in my next meeting with them …

CHAPTER 4

THE POWER OF FIGURES

"Only what is measured can be managed" – this also applies to change management. But how do figures influence the objectives and the steering of transformation processes? Can their objectives be measured? And if so, how – given that transformations are a combination of control and turbulence in perpetual rebalance? Or are the words of John Lennon more fitting: "Life is what happens to you while you are busy making other plans."

One thing is for certain: you cannot run a business without figures. Businesses only maintain their viability (according to systems theory) through the constant renewal of solvency. Those who can no longer pay must file for bankruptcy or settlement. It is figures that provide companies with direction and the power and magic of figures are considerable; those who can best substantiate their position with figures always have a head start. Figures serve to formulate future objectives.

Figures are involved whenever a system's performance is evaluated. This particularly applies to businesses. In order to understand what a figure means in concrete terms, we need in each case to know the answer to these questions:

- What is being measured, according to what criterion, and what does this criterion bring into focus (e.g., turnover or profit, ROI or RONA)?
- In relation to what, i.e., what is the comparison criterion? (Is it a comparison over time, are criteria being compared with one another or are these being compared with others?)
- Who is measuring and what are their interests (e.g., analysts or employees)?

Everybody is familiar with these questions in the context of organizational evaluation. The criteria selected for the evaluation of an organization's success are determined by management, with various consequences for day-to-day operations and thus also for corporate development. Figures steer behavior; their function is like that of magnets, bundling, aligning and concentrating energy and attention. The selection and the interrelating of success criteria, as the integrated "numerical structure" of an enterprise, are important elements in the design of effective controlling architectures, as is the rapid and interactive feeding of results back into the system. Furthermore, the answer to the question "what defines corporate success for this company?" determines which transformation objectives show up in the target sights.

1. When are companies successful? – some models

The answer to this question depends on the mental models that define what an enterprise is actually about and what will consequently be the driving force for change processes.

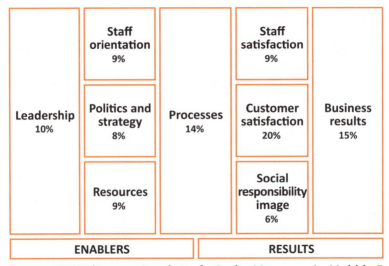

EFQM (European Foundation for Quality Management) – Model for Excellence

Many concepts have been developed for this purpose. Ratings and corporate evaluation concepts, such as shareholder value, focus on the capital value of an enterprise (viewing the enterprise as a commodity or share). The **EFQM** concept (see chart) differentiates between qualifiers and results, thereby focusing attention on results and development potentials (viewing companies as producers of products or services).

The **Balanced Scorecard** (BSC) – developed by Kaplan and Norton in their book with the same title – combines the customer perspective with that of internal business processes, and the dimension of finances with that of learning and development in a "steering map" for strategy implementation.

The Balanced Scorecard (Kaplan/Norton)

Kaplan and Norton illustrate the tension between the poles of external and internal orientation on the one side and short-term or long-term orientation on the other, as well as the necessity of deciding whether balance or imbalance is the most suitable priority.

Finally, another model – still in development – is the Intellectual Capital Navigator (see next page), in which Edvinsson (formerly responsible for knowledge management at Skandia) further develops the Balanced Scorecard to also reflect a company's intellectual capital. Models like this act as 'radar' for the future potential of intellectual capital – and say more about a company's innovative capacity than past-performance-based financial figures.[30]

Edvinsson suggests rating the market value of a company according to financial capital on the one hand and intellectual capital on the other. (It would be im-

---

[30] Edvinsson/Malone, *Intellectual Capital*, Piatkus London, 1997, pp. 69 ff.

portant to compare this model with other concepts, in particular those for corporate evaluation. Such a comparison is still outstanding.)

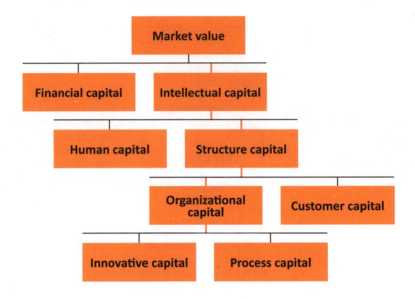

Intellectual Capital Navigator
As with the Balanced Scorecard, specific objectives and indexes have to be determined for each focus. For instance, the criteria for measuring "intellectual capital in customers" can relate to different customer types, duration of relationship, customer role and contribution, customer support measures and customer success.

All of these models provide specific observation patterns and thereby exclude others. This has consequences not only for the steering of daily operations, but also for decisions concerning transformations and their objectives. With EVA and shareholder models, transformation goals will tend to focus on financial objectives and therefore be more likely to take hard cuts into account, whereas with EFQM as a basic model, evolutionary goals are more likely. The Balanced Scorecard will highlight the dilemmas between hard cuts and new growth, whereas the Intellectual Capital Navigator rather draws attention to innovation objectives and knowledge as "invisible capital".

2. What counts? The correlation between change and value creation: Studies

In its annual "most admired" list, Fortune Magazine (March 2011) rates companies according to the following criteria:
- Quality of management
- Quality of products and services
- Innovation
- Long-term investment value
- Financial soundness
- People management: Ability to attract, develop and keep talented people
- Social responsibility
- Use of corporate assets
- Global competitiveness

According to a study by Ernst & Young[31], 35% of the information on which financial analysts and portfolio managers base their investment decisions is non-financial information. Criteria are ranked as follows:
1. Implementation of corporate strategy
2. Management credibility
3. Quality of corporate strategy
4. Innovation
5. Ability to win and retain employees with potential
6. Market share
7. Management expertise
8. Payment systems attuned to shareholder interests
9. Leadership in research
10. Quality of essential business processes

In another study by Ernst & Young[32] three quarters of the respondents (76%) agreed that financial reputation is important. Financial reputation is primarily about building trust with, and demonstrating competence to investors. When asked about the features of the companies they admired, investors frequently

---

[31] J. Low, T. Siesfield, Measures That Matter, Ernst & Young, Boston, 1998
[32] Ernst & Young, "The Drivers of Financial Reputation", 2007 EYGM Limited.

mentioned characteristics such as high degree of visibility, consistency, longevity, honesty and financial strength.

These studies show that successful change management can no longer be measured merely in terms of turnover and higher profits: More than in the past, it creates competitive advantage, strengthens innovative ability and brings the implementation of corporate strategy forward. Foster and Kaplan point out that in the American "Standard & Poor's Index", the 90 companies listed in 1920 had an average age of 65 years. In 1998, the average affiliation with the "Standard & Poor's 500 Index" was a mere 10 years. The ability to effectively and innovatively change or progress ahead of the market is of growing significance.

But why set new growth and hard cuts as simultaneous objectives? The American Management Association (www.amanet.org) annually evaluates management surveys and shows that on a long-term basis, companies that simultaneously cut and create new jobs show better results in productivity, quality, profitability and shareholder value.[33] In these companies, new growth and hard cuts are managed evolutionarily and can be considered part of daily operations.

A Capgemini survey[34] shows that transformations come in various shapes. Cost cutting, not surprisingly, is a consistent theme, with almost half of the respondents agreeing that it was a major goal. The main transformation goals are:
- Restructuring/reorganization (57%)
- Cost reduction/rightsizing (47%)
- Growth initiatives (37%)
- New corporate strategy (35%)
- Mergers/acquisitions/demergers (25%)
- Changed market strategy/approach to customers (23%)
- Other reasons (1–12%)

---

[33] Survey 2001, p. 3.
[34] Capgemini: Change Management Study 2010 – Business Transformation.

3. Success or failure – what counts in change management?

More and more studies – most of them American – are focusing on drivers and success factors for change processes.

Joyce and Kilman have identified the following as the most effective levers for the success of radical change:

1. The market as driver: The more competition there is on the market, the more successful the change project. Competition clearly wins out over other motives (e.g., changing corporate culture or other inward-oriented objectives).

2. Changes that have been consistently promoted for more than two years: Those are significantly more successful than those planned on a shorter-term basis. Anchoring and consistency of implementation as a central message for lasting change also means not concluding change projects prematurely and not "herding through" one change topic after the other.

3. The more employee participation, the more success: This generates commitment and facilitates the integration of tacit knowledge.

Change projects characterized by these three factors had significantly better results than others.

According to the McKinsey Global Survey[35] the most successful transformations of business performance occur when executives mobilize and sustain energy within their organizations and communicate their objectives clearly and creatively. Executives further improve their chances for success if they significantly raise employee expectations, actively change people's behavior, and engage the attention of individuals at all levels of the organization, from senior management to the front line.

IBM conducted a truly global study on what is "Making Change Work" in 2008. They asked over 1,500 people from Europe (34%), Asia-Pacific (37%) and the Americas (29%) about the challenges and success factors of change projects.

---

[35] McKinsey Global Survey: *Organizing for successful change management*, July 2006.

They found that in both categories, so called "soft factors" were – in general – much more influential than "hard" ones.

The main challenges in change projects were found to be:
- Changing mindsets and attitudes (58%)
- Corporate culture (49%)
- Complexity is underestimated (35%)
- Shortage of resources (33%)
- Lack of commitment of higher management (32%)
- Lack of change know-how (20%)
- Lack of transparency because of missing or wrong information (18%)
- Lack of motivation of involved employees (16%)
- Change of process (15%)
- Change of IT systems (12%)
- Technology barriers (8%)

The factors that make change successful are as follows:
- Top management sponsorship (92%)
- Employee involvement (72%)
- Honest and timely communication (70%)
- Corporate culture that motivates and promotes change (65%)
- Change agents (pioneers of change) (55%)
- Change supported by culture (48%)
- Efficient training programs (38%)
- Adjustment of performance measures (36%)
- Efficient organization structure (33%)
- Monetary and non-monetary incentives (19%)

A comparison of these challenges and success factors shows that a firmly anchored corporate identity and culture that promotes change, with top management support, transparent and rapid up-front communication are crucial for the success of change projects – findings that are well substantiated in the concepts of the learning organization.

Which factors impede change?[36]

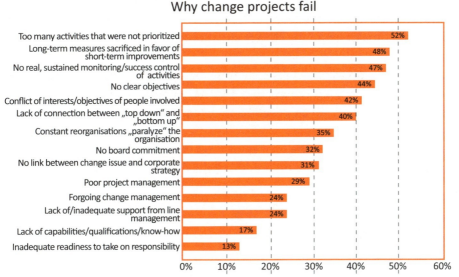

The pitfalls of change management
Why change projects fail

Factor	%
Too many activities that were not prioritized	52%
Long-term measures sacrificed in favor of short-term improvements	48%
No real, sustained monitoring/success control of activities	47%
No clear objectives	44%
Conflict of interests/objectives of people involved	42%
Lack of connection between „top down" and „bottom up"	40%
Constant reorganisations „paralyze" the organisation	35%
No board commitment	32%
No link between change issue and corporate strategy	31%
Poor project management	29%
Forgoing change management	24%
Lack of/inadequate support from line management	24%
Lack of capabilities/qualifications/know-how	17%
Inadequate readiness to take on responsibility	13%

It is evident that so-called "soft" factors such as organizational culture, tradition and resistance are actually the "tough" factors, as they are perceived as the greatest obstacles. It is challenging to give up what is familiar (culture, tradition), and to negotiate what to preserve and renew (taking resistance seriously as a signal and a message).

What is remarkable about these studies is that they fail to include the architecture and the master plans of change projects (see case studies below) among their objects of investigation. We consider both of these elements to be essential factors for the success of transformations, as they provide a stable framework for the paradox between control and turbulences.

Now that we have discussed how figures and the models behind them affect change objectives (the "what"), and which factors are presumed critical for the success or failure of change (the "how"), we can ask: What does change management look like in practice? Do companies actually measure the objectives and the process of transformations?

---

[36] Capgemini, Change Management Study, 2005.

4. Better not – what speaks in favor of not measuring change processes?

Controlling and evaluating transformation processes disrupts the flow of events. It is a source of irritation and brings even more complexity and pressure for decision-making into the change situation.

The results are occasionally disenchanting, and in emotionally charged situations (see section "Hard cuts") they lead to withdrawal or escalation and a search for scapegoats: To aggression and defensiveness. Measuring takes time.

Measuring also reduces the leeway of those involved. Injudiciously selected measuring criteria generate undesirable behavior.

5. Then why measure and evaluate?

Both measurement as the controlling of selected key figures according to transformation objectives and evaluation as a diagnosis of the transformation's overall impact on the company – with all intended and unintended consequences – are powerful interventions in the course of change events. It has to be made clear for what they are meant to be an engine and a multiplier, and what their primary effect is supposed to be. Change processes are always – if not officially, then on the "black market" – evaluated on the informal corporate stage.

For "Un:balanced Transformations", we consider the mix of **controlling**, i.e., the continuous measurement of objectives, content and processes on the one hand, and **evaluation**, i.e., a qualitative diagnosis of the system that gives an overall picture of all positive, critical, intended and unintended effects on the other, to be a necessity. This makes it easier to successfully create a bridge between goal orientation (controlling) and open steering of the process that can react to the unforeseen (evaluation).

Effective controlling ensures:
- Appraisal of change success
- Clarification of current goal achievement
- Prioritization and control
- Motivation and activation of those involved

Evaluation ensures:
- Diagnosis and learning (understanding of the system)
- Participation, motivation and communication
- A comprehensive perspective in setting the course
- Acceleration and efficiency: The right "levers" are pulled and measures taken in the interplay of planned change and self-steering

6. Agenda for good controlling concepts in transformations

Controlling starts with a diagnosis and the clear definition of prioritized goals for the transformation.

What should be measured when controlling changes? In Un:balanced Transformation projects, a Balanced Scorecard adapted for change projects has proven very useful (e.g., in kickoff workshops with steering teams).

On the basis of the vision and the strategy that has been decided upon for the transformation, the following steps should be taken:
- First, concretize the transformation objectives for each of the four Balanced Scorecard dimensions; compile indicators and success indexes in relation to the following two questions:
  - "What will we definitely achieve or change, e.g., in the customer perspective dimension?"
  - "What will we definitely preserve in the customer perspective dimension?"
- In a second step, clarify which guidelines and prerequisites need to be taken into account in the three other dimensions when tackling the customer perspective (i.e., in the finance, innovation and process dimensions). This procedure not only defines indicators and indexes for change objectives and stability, but also sets "early warning signals" in the other dimensions. In this same way, the control teams work through all four dimensions. This constitutes at the same time a joint effort to identify turbulences that can be expected in the course of the transformation.
- In the third step, the intensity of the objectives and their effects is estimated and their significance noted as increasing distance from the center ("*Un:balance*").

The four scorecards resulting from this process tend to be overly complex, making it necessary to reduce the overall picture to the most important key target figures and early warning indexes.

What does the controlling process look like – who measures when, who discusses the results and makes decisions?

- **Who:** Someone whose authority and neutrality are recognized
- **When:** Before important forks in the road, e.g., along the five change phases or agreed milestones
- **Process:** Controlling and steering belong together, hence the processing of results by decision-makers and important "co-authors" of the transformation (client, initiators, steering team and those responsible for implementation, depending on the architecture and the phase)
- **Communication** of the results and the related steering decisions generates commitment and trust

7. Agenda for effective evaluation

Unlike controlling, evaluation should not be allocated to the control team or decision-makers. It should be a separate element in the transformation's architecture. Evaluation requires an outside perspective and impartiality, since it is a matter of keenly perceiving intentional and unintentional effects and dynamics, understanding these and reflecting them back to the respective initiators in the form of a diagnosis. Impartiality in evaluation means (in contrast to controller neutrality) being able to temporarily identify oneself with the different perspectives of those involved in order to understand reactions, actions and responses, and develop hypotheses about their dynamics and effects on the overall system. Systemic evaluation requires know-how in the fields of inquiry and diagnostics, so that manifest and latent issues arising from the survey can be presented to the client in a productive way. In order to develop a differentiated overall picture of "effects and side-effects", distance and impartiality are required – which those at the epicenter of events lack. It is usually the control team, the project or change manager or top management who commission evaluation. In practice, several variations of evaluation have proven effective.

> **Examples are:**
>
> - Evaluation through **qualitative group interviews** with customers, employees and managers
>
> - Evaluation through **empathetic observation** of how customers use products in everyday life – according to conscious and subconscious needs – in order to evaluate innovative potential
>
> - A **workshop with feedback groups** representative of the different stakeholders, who do diagnostic work moderated by consultants at the beginning of a change project, thus contributing to the tailoring of target-definition and transformation architecture. In later phases, particularly after pilot projects, workshops of this nature can provide valuable ideas if the pilot projects are simulated, their results assessed and opportunities or risks evaluated.
>
> - **Open individual interviews** with stakeholder representatives: Particularly in the beginning, these lay a solid foundation by means of initial diagnosis for first, pivotal steering team decisions (objectives, architecture, team staffing, phases, milestones, master plan, communication strategies and appropriate controlling)
>
> - The combination of a brief **questionnaire** with five to eight quantitative questions (increases comparability) with open interviews of stable **evaluation teams** for each area makes a very efficient evaluation. External interviewers inquire about important milestones, and the anonymously evaluated results are discussed in the control team. In addition, each area manager receives the evaluation of his or her area.

Since such evaluations are sensitive interventions, it is essential to clarify meticulously the following questions and points with the client – regardless of whether one is acting as an internal or an external expert:
- What is the evaluation supposed to achieve?
- What is the subject of the evaluation?
- What form should the process take?

- Who will be interviewed? (As many multiple perspectives as possible is useful.)
- Who will control and organize the process?
- How will the participants be informed and involved in the process?
- Diagnosis transparency: With whom will the results be discussed, to whom will they be communicated?
- Confidentiality agreement (no person-specific evaluation)
- Evaluation result/diagnosis as an intervention: It is chiefly the evaluator's responsibility to present the diagnosis in a form that strengthens the system's self-control. This requires competence in inquiry and diagnostics.

The setting for reflection and processing of the diagnosis should be clarified in a detailed agreement with the client: This could take place as an item on the control team agenda, as feedback discussions in line management, by means of reflection in workshops or in large-scale events with subsequent working groups. Comprehensibility, professionalism in terms of methodology (interview manner and diagnosis) and communication (setting and design) are indispensable. Thus, evaluations become one of the most effective instruments for dealing productively with turbulences and inherent dynamics in transformations. Based on the current evaluation one can decide whether new goals and priorities should be set or not. Evaluation enables decision-makers to see the big picture. It provides – in systemic terms – productive reality constructions, and enables the "authors of the change process" to maintain distance, composure and collective commitment for the next steps.

CHAPTER 5

THE LOGIC OF FEELINGS

Feelings are the motor behind the implementation of changes. If we understand their function and dynamics, we can react appropriately and utilize them creatively for the system.

It is important to understand the fundamental difference between the "logic" of feelings and the logic of figures or the logic of the task at hand. Feelings are not directly controllable, or calculable in terms of duration and intensity. Every feeling – whether fear, anger, sorrow or joy – has an individual function and its own special value in the change process, as well as its own logic in relation to perceptions, time rhythms and action patterns. All these diverse, in part conflicting logics have their own meaningful and important role to play in the change process in an organization. Only those who observe and understand feelings can control them – by strengthening their productive aspects and exploiting their potential.

1. Feelings in the change arena

Up one minute – down the next: It is easy to understand that projects involving both hard cuts and new growth generate emotional polarities. At any given moment during a change, a great diversity of feelings are in play, some of which can be very strong and antagonistic (not all members of a company experience the same feelings at the same time). On the other hand, a change process also runs through a series of emotional phases that follow one another in sequence. Fear, anger and disappointment have a function that is not to be neglected and is no less important than that of joy, enthusiasm and courage.

Idealization of change: The ideology that "change per se is positive" leads to an idealization of change, which simultaneously results in blind spots in change processes: Insufficient acknowledgement of previous successes as a result of change idealization, perception of previous changes as wrong turns rather than as important steps to build on, diminished appreciation of continuity and stability as necessary and promising factors – both internally and on the market.

All of these result in resistance and inner withdrawal on the employees' part. This leads to the formation of a company with "two worlds", that is, "change enthusiasts" who say: *"Great, this is just what we want! This is our future. It has our full support!"*, and "change opponents" who go into resistance, reject the project and feel it is bad for the company. The effect on the overall system is a well-known phenomenon: A great deal happens, but nothing changes. The system remains stable, balanced between change advocates and preservationists. This is what makes it vital to consciously weigh up what aspects of corporate identity should be preserved, in order that people's need for stability and continuity not be swept under the carpet. As we all know, emotional matters that are pushed aside tend to re-emerge time and again.

It never turns out the way you expect: When dealing with hard cuts and new growth, those involved find themselves in the midst of considerable uncertainty. They feel the need for orientation, but are instead incessantly confronted with new stimuli. What works one day can look completely different the next. Unanticipated business options lead to collaborations or fusions; unexpected crises necessitate definite responses. What started out as change management quickly becomes 'the changing of change'. These projects are emotional roller coasters that also affect their initiators: The changers also need to change – they ride the roller coaster along with everyone else.

Feelings know no time: In our encounters, we connect with the predominant emotional context last experienced in the system or in the relationships. Think, for example, of a memorable encounter with someone in the past. This could have been an annoying or a pleasant experience. Although you have not seen this person for ages, the moment you meet him or her again, the feeling from the past is immediately present.

So how organizations react to feelings and how they deal with them plays a considerable role, particularly in times of upheaval.

The well-trodden paths of practiced routines: If certain reactions occur repeatedly, these feeling, thought and action patterns are incorporated into the organization and become part of what can be described as everyday culture or everyday dynamics: Typical everyday behavior. They form a well-trodden path which everyone takes without thinking and where the tiniest sequences can trigger the usual pattern.

Once this emotional pathway is set, change can only be achieved by stirring up – intense – feelings, as everyone tends otherwise to follow the well-trodden path. That is why, figuratively speaking, considerable effort is required to "build new roads". Once sentiments such as *"Anything that comes from the sales department is useless"* or *"Our meetings are for the most part frustrating"* establish themselves, they become entrenched patterns of collective feeling, which have a strong influence on an organization.

Stick to the facts, and please be positive!
So what is the principal attitude of organizations toward feelings? Organizations understand themselves to be task-oriented systems. This was particularly true of traditional bureaucracies. Positions with specific tasks, responsibilities and competencies were linked with each other in formal processes. The interchangeability of "position-holders" was intentional. By comparison, today's organizations are increasingly becoming systems that virtually demand emotion from their employees – particularly positive feelings of enthusiasm, self-initiative, courage and a certain degree of productive aggressiveness (*"We are battling for market leadership!"; "We will conquer the market at full tilt!"*). The individual comes before the job – the whole person is called on in terms of commitment, flexibility or innovation. At the same time, people need to tolerate much more fear and uncertainty than in former times. Key words are: Empowerment, entrepreneurship, restructuring. On the other hand, managers are seldom prepared for dealing with critical situations and unpleasant feelings in an understanding way. This is not a reproach, merely a statement of fact. In this connection, one can also observe that "negative" feelings in enterprises are generally experienced as disruptions and are more or less "prohibited", whereas "positive" feelings such as enthusiasm for the company are occasionally even prescribed.

The division into "hard reorganizers" on the one side and the "soft organizational developers" on the other is a further common phenomenon in companies. Both qualities are necessary for a constructive developmental process, but precisely not as opposing sides – this prevents genuine debate, which is vital to the further development of organizational identity.

Sticking to the facts does not work: Feelings are contagious and develop their own dynamics. Two brief anecdotes illustrate this:

A manager announces to the assembled workforce that costs must be cut, and then basically says: *"Ladies and Gentlemen, we're seeing bad figures, so we need to cut 10% of our costs and downsize staff by 10%. Do you have any questions about this?"* – very businesslike and not by any means unfriendly. What is the effect? Not surprisingly, feelings of fear and anger emerge, and thoughts such as: *"How cold-hearted!"*; *"Am I merely a cost factor?"*; *"How can the company treat us like this?"*.

The manager of a company that just lost a gigantic, crucial project says to the severely unsettled workforce: *"There is a sad and unpleasant reason for our gathering today. We've lost a project in which we had placed considerable hope. I find this very disappointing and upsetting because we have also lost possible turnover – but that's just the way it is. I want to think about how this happened, and what led to it. Then we can draw conclusions and take the necessary steps to get back out of this difficult situation."* What effect does this have? Quite different!

Both of these statements are, systemically spoken, interventions. The second statement integrates the prevailing emotions and creates social acceptance for negative feelings, making it possible to cope with both the content and the emotions associated with the loss of the customer's project. In this particular case, it led, in terms of social interaction, to more open debates and more "teambuilding" (disputes are bonding!), and in terms of content to pragmatic, new ground rules and support measures for the pre-sales phase and project acquisition. Without the power source of emotions, these results would have been unachievable.

The *"logic of feelings"-loop*

2. The four basic categories of feelings – a look backstage

Let us now have a look at the individual categories of feelings. It has proven useful to differentiate four basic categories (see the diagram "The 'logic of feelings'-loop"): Firstly fear, uncertainty and worry, secondly anger and aggression, thirdly sorrow and disappointment and, last but not least, optimism, joy and courage. What are the respective functions of these feelings? What are the dynamics and the logic of the way we deal with them? And what consequences do we need to draw from this? All of these feelings are necessary for successful change. Seen from the perspective of the logic of feelings, the first challenge is to disrupt everyday routines – which, with their emotional patterns, work like well-trodden paths – and awaken interest in the fact that things are now going to change, that something new is coming.

1. Fear, uncertainty, worry: Cut and run!

Function: The function of fear is to bundle energy and concentrate on a focal source of danger. Fear helps to recognize that "Something is changing here, and it could be threatening". The first reaction is typically an impulse to escape "I want nothing to do with this". But in organizations, there is often also an initial reaction along the lines of "Fantastic, now finally something is changing" – an inversion of the flight impulse. In radical change, this can be a way to initially keep fear at bay. It then expresses itself in informal ways, and rises to the surface later. Fear and escape are also a way of winning time to gather strength and realize the seriousness of the situation "I need time to come to terms with this and confront it."

Dynamics, logic: For one thing, fear generates denial, because at first, nobody wants to see what is happening. For management, the typical reaction is "But we communicated this already, what's the matter with these people? We've told them three times. Do we have to say it a fourth time?" However, cognitive understanding is not the problem here. Often, messages of this nature actually do need to be communicated three times or more, because only frequent, persistent communication ensures that they "touch down" emotionally. It would be a counterproductive intervention to ignore fear, along the lines of "We must keep fear at bay." Equally counterproductive would be the statement "Now we are going to figure out how to implement this", i.e., continuing only on the rational level. Because emotionally, people are not yet ready to work on that level. If one observes teams in situations such as these, it becomes obvious that they are simply unable to come up with ideas. This has nothing to do with their cognitive abilities. Fear needs a time and a place to express itself, and stabilizing management interventions so that energy blockades can dissolve again. It is not without good reason that one says fear makes you "dim", it narrows the field of vision. But fear also mobilizes, makes it clear that "this is serious" – and this is necessary for "Un:balanced Transformation".

What needs to be done?
The most effective approach for managers is to work on this topic personally; for instance by addressing the topic with the help of questions such as "Have there been situations in which I myself ever truly experienced hard cuts? How did I feel? What did I do? What helped me? What was difficult for me? How do I think the employees will react in this case?"

At the outset, it is difficult to even find a way to address the fear, since in many organizations this topic is never dealt with other than informally. This is why it is advisable to create settings with informal character, for instance with the proposal "Take a walk with your partner and discuss your thoughts on this – what it means for you, what irritates you, what appeals to you." Once one recalls how one has dealt with fear personally in the past, one quickly realizes what could help and motivate. Reactivating this knowledge is particularly important for management teams who are designing the change.

The most important thing that managers can do is send the message that fear is actually allowed. Fear is part of the process; it has the important function of creating attentiveness. It is important to describe the positive function of fear. The more it is brushed over, the stronger and the more unyielding it becomes. Fear may make people dim, but that does not make headstrong foolishness any more intelligent!

This is why it is particularly important for organizations to create "spaces" for dealing with fear – this could be in coaching pairs or swapping experiences in teams. This is often less a matter of inventing something new than of considering where opportunities already exist in the company to deal with fear productively (areas of protected communication, since fear maximally tolerates the size of a small group). Fear needs small and familiar islands of communication. What is critical is how and what managers communicate. A speech in which a manager says "Today I need to inform you about something I'm doing for the first time in my career. It concerns the fact that we see ourselves forced to reduce personnel. I've spent quite a few sleepless nights over this and I can tell you that if this news creates anxiety among you, you have my full understanding. We have thought this decision through carefully and are certain ..." is already a big step towards making fear discussable. It connects the factual situation with its personal/emotional implications and by doing so, provides a living example of how figures, tasks and emotions can be integrated.

But in addition to addressing the personal perspective, it is also necessary to clarify whether there is too much fear or rather too much of a feeling of security in the organization, and to intervene accordingly – by either dampening fear or increasing it.

2. Anger, aggression: Not like this!
Function: Aggression helps people to draw boundaries as well as to defend, to preserve, to expand – or even more to conquer new areas of identity for themselves. Aggressiveness can also serve to fend off one's own latent "forbidden" feelings, such as sorrow.

Dynamics, logic: Anger and aggression are feelings that act quickly. They arise suddenly, but can also quickly blow over. They concentrate energy on a specific focus and cause a "power surge". If a certain degree of basic tension is already prevalent, the notorious last straw is often enough to spark off outbursts and further escalation. Aggression has a distancing effect – the others steer clear. When aggression arises, it means change is being taken seriously and personally. Aggression means: This is about me, about my own personal future. Change does not become concrete until it is confronted personally. Aggression has its unpleasant sides, but it is necessary for transformation.

What needs to be done?
The more aggressive impulses are suppressed, the more explosive the outburst. Anger and aggravation also frequently arise when the past is dealt with dismissively (*"Was everything we've been doing up to now only wrong?"*). If the past is appropriately acknowledged, personal self-esteem is preserved. Aggression in the change process – often dealt with under the term "resistance" – is necessary because it makes negotiation processes between preservation and change possible. In this tightrope act, the aim is to show understanding, build bridges, and make the link to positive mutual experiences, but also to outline future scenar-

ios and take a stand. In this stage, we often work with our model "dialogue in dissent" for negotiating with stakeholders. Mediation tools are equally helpful.

3. Sorrow, disappointment: Nothing will ever be the same!
Function: Sorrow helps to resolve, to overcome losses, to gradually dissolve old bonds, to say goodbye and make room for the new.

Dynamics, logic: When we are sad, we are looking back, thinking about what is over and gone, about bonds that have been dissolved. Sorrow means concentrating on what is past and what is lost. Sorrow needs time. Whereas anger and aggression work quickly, sorrow is a slow feeling. Often this slowing down is exactly what is needed before an unexpected breakthrough, which then suddenly brings optimism, energy and new perspectives into the picture.

What needs to be done?
Sorrow is a silent feeling and is often hard to recognize. In this situation, it is important to allow time and – if the sorrow is very deep – to ensure a stable daily routine. Rituals provide support and security. Emotional presence and offering communication are supportive measures. It is necessary to acknowledge, accept and hold the past in high esteem so that it can be released, enabling new developments to emerge. It is a matter of consciously shaping and giving direction to the process of bidding farewell and beginning anew. Throwing a farewell party may seem exaggerated, but a mutually planned and arranged event to say goodbye to the past often achieves remarkable effects.

The advantage of such interventions is that the past is held in high esteem – this is something organizations rarely do. In practical reality, the subtle message often reads: *"The way we organized things before was totally wrong and outdated."* The way change is communicated is one of the most critical success factors in change processes. Writing one's own history as a story of continuous development goes a long way towards overcoming attachment to the old ways. Then it also becomes possible to say: *"We were on the wrong track there, that was not ideal – still, it was an important step and has made it possible for us to now move on in this direction"*; or: *"Five years ago, that was exactly the right thing to do – now, if we reposition ourselves, we can build on that."*

4. Buoyant optimism, joy and courage: Let's get down to business!
Function: Thinking creatively and open-mindedly – being 'in the flow' of things – always needs a positive undertone. This does not necessarily have to be ecstatic delight, but an attitude of approval in the sense of *"We are planning something new here, and that suits me just fine"; "This is good, this is what I want!"* A widespread sense of something new being in the air energizes and is infectious. Feelings act like floodgates – they open or close ways of thinking. Optimistic spirits and joy open up different ways of thinking, whereas fear constricts and blocks them.

Dynamics, logic: A sense of new beginning helps to reconcile the past with the future, is forward looking and widens perspectives. There is, however, a potential danger in the one-sided idealization of the new and different by "change enthusiasts" at the expense of what is worth preserving.

What needs to be done?
Buoyant optimism and joy, when present, should be strengthened and encouraged, and its positive effects should be made visible in routines and symbols. For instance, a manager pursuing an ambitious growth program decided that whenever a division of the business achieved operation in the black, he would repaint its building – an original gesture clear for everyone to see. Optimism and joy generate the mindset, common interest, verve and power needed to push forward energy-taxing processes.

Each of these phases in the logic of feelings provides various opportunities for intervening and steering emotions or their contexts in the change process. In every phase, as we have seen, there are possible interventions that are productive and others that tend to be obstructive.

3. Interventions: What are the main points to consider?
Shaking things up: At the start of any change process it is absolutely necessary to awaken interest among those involved in order to break out of the previous routines and patterns. This means "shaking things up"! Interest is the fuel that recharges and energizes various feelings. How can this be achieved? Foremost, it is necessary to make the "case for action" – the motives and rationale – clear and transparent, and to communicate this with intensity, e.g., *"If we do not do this, we will have (problem X) in five years."*

Orientation: Just as necessary as awakening interest is providing orientation on where things are heading, what the vision is and what position management is taking.

Talk the walk: "Talk the walk" is the counter-position to "walk the talk" (practice what you preach!), as often quoted in the realm of management. In view of the complexity and turbulences of change, this becomes less and less possible, as so many things repeatedly undergo change along the way. Hence, it is more honest and more productive to say: "Yes, we basically want to move in this direction, and we will see where this path leads us. What will remain fundamentally stable on this route is: Our overall image, our direction, the process, communication and a high degree of transparency. We will speak openly about how and where we are in the process, and when we change our course." On the other hand, if a manager commits him or herself to "walking the talk", it restricts employees, generates doubts on credibility and fosters negative feelings: fears that block progress, cause frustration etc. In a manner of speaking, "walk the talk" remains rooted in the old image that managers can always prescribe exactly what needs to be done and where things are headed. This is not realistic when dealing with transformation.

Spiral of basic feelings: As a manager, being familiar with the phase model shown above helps to change one's own image of change. Feelings suddenly appear "normal", they are allowed to exist and are part of the situation. They cannot be deliberately conjured up, or made to disappear. Reaching the desired degree of enthusiasm requires going through phases of fear and sorrow beforehand. These are not a disturbing factor, but rather a motor for change. Or to put it differently: "No effect without emotion."

Initial messages are crucial: Critical, unstable situations – as the initial situations of change processes inevitably are – call for a high degree of sensitivity and receptivity on the part of managers. Careful consideration of the following questions: "How can I shape the initial communication of this change project?"; "What is the fundamental, emotional message I am conveying with this project?" is a crucial first step to future success.

CHAPTER 6

NEW CHANGE CHALLENGES

Since our first edition was released, change managers have had to cope with a different world. Two topics are especially urgent today:

The first regards the existing business: How can we protect our business, become more robust, and manage the unexpected? The first article on resilience will give you some ideas.

The second regards the seemingly pressing need for radical innovation: Do we really need to innovate now? What are we putting in danger? Do we have the right conditions to realize innovative ideas? The second article on the pitfalls of innovation will give you some direction on when to pass on innovation.

1. Article I: Cheating the Coincidence

Cheating the Coincidence – Mastering the Unexpected through Resilience

Barbara Heitger, Annika Serfass

The article was first published in German in the "REVUE für postheroisches management", June 2010.

Coincidences happen unexpectedly. Surprised by the financial crisis, overwhelmed by a large order and continuously changing conditions, coincidences can crush some (individuals, organizations, market participants) whilst inspiring others. "Resilience" as a trait can make it possible to deal constructively with unexpected events, to overcome setbacks, and to discover formerly unrecognized potential. Tackling the challenges of tomorrow, can provide assistance with the situations faced today.

The term "resilience" originated in the natural sciences. It refers to the ability of a material to resume its original shape after it has been deformed by immense pressure. In the field of developmental psychology, this term is primarily used in reference to children who, in spite of appalling circumstances and traumatic experiences, do not fall into depression or develop an addiction, but instead manage to develop strong and well-rounded personalities.

Every living creature and every existing organization is resilient to a certain degree – otherwise they would not be able to survive; however, the prevalence of this characteristic is subject to immense fluctuations.

Promoting resilience as a quality within organizations is a task for management: It must be integrated into strategy development, organizational development, operational performance, into the leadership structures and the usage of resources (finances, knowledge and network capital). Dean Becker, the president and CEO of Adaptiv Learning Systems, even claims that "more than education, more than experience, more than training, a person's level of resilience determines who succeeds and who fails. That's true in the cancer ward, it's true in the Olympics, and it's true in the boardroom".[37]

A team of consultants from Heitger Consulting has worked intensively on the subject of resilience and the opportunities offered by its implementation in management and consulting.[38]

Individual resilience

A "resilient" person has developed a particular attitude towards the challenges of life. For this reason it is very difficult to accurately define resilience. Often, an entire set of indicators are used in order to describe resilience as an "overall phenomenon". Especially in the U.S. – which has had a longer history of research conducted on resilience – a number of concepts have been developed to "measure" individual resilience.[39]

---

[37] Quoted from: Coutu, Diane: "How Resilience Works" in Harvard Business Review, 2002.

[38] Team members are: Andreas Bernstorff, Manfred Bouda, Pascale Grün, Barbara Heitger, Klaus-Jürgen Hütten, Judith Kölblinger, Philipp Rafelsberger, Stephan Rey, Annika Serfass and Sigrid Viehweg.

[39] On www.resiliencescale.com you can take a short online-test developed by Gail Wagnild and Heather Young 15 years ago, which is still used for research purposes today. The transfer of the scale to a German sample has been conducted by Jörg Schumacher et. al. 2004: "The Resilience Scale – A questionnaire acquiring mental resistance as a personal characteristic".

We have partially based the following chapter on research conducted by Andrew Shatté, Karen Reivich and Martin Seligman from the University of Pennsylvania, and otherwise upon the findings of numerous other developmental psychologists.[40]

The aspects supporting a resilient character can roughly be divided into three areas: Social, factual and emotional aspects.

Social aspects – to empathize, to adapt and to establish networks:
Empathy as a character trait can help to provide a wider perspective that goes beyond the common viewpoint. Resilient individuals have a high situational **adaptive capacity** because they try to understand different perspectives and have the ability to adjust to given circumstances. Moreover, resilient individuals create their own **stable social network**, through which they receive support, advice, and feedback. Such a network enables them to deal with difficult situations, since they are able to acknowledge their own limitations. Assessing the abilities of others correctly, enables them to select the most suitable competences to assist.

Emotional aspects – realism, self-esteem, confidence and humor:
Resilient people evaluate their environment in a **realistic manner** and **accept** unchangeable conditions, instead of repressing them. They perceive setbacks, losses and excessive demands as an inevitable part of life, but without "permitting" these to determine their future. They usually deal with turbulences in a composed manner. They consider stress to be a positive challenge that does not cause any sustained damage. Without having a confident belief in a "better"/ different future, there would be no resilience. Resilient individuals believe in "succeeding next time" after having faced a defeat. They obtain their **self-confidence** by having mastered previous difficulties and challenges. They trust their own abilities, and especially the meaningfulness of their actions encourages them to bravely face the future. Above all, it is important not to forget to keep a sense of **humor!**

---

[40] Worthwhile mentioning are Ann Masten, who researches intensively in this area, and Emmy Werner, who conducted one of the first long-term studies on this topic.

Factual aspects – analytical, future- and solutions-oriented:
Logical thinking, accurate observation skills, and the ability to identify causes (and consequences) are well-developed attributes of a resilient person. In short, a resilient person has an analytical aptitude. This is an ability that they also use to develop sound **future** scenarios. They prepare for possible occurrences and play them out in their minds beforehand. Thus, they have a multitude of perspectives and choices to act upon, which they can put into use whenever it is required. Resilient people are often **solutions-oriented** and have a clear head for knowing what they can influence and on what they need to focus their energy on. They use resources that they can access. Instead of becoming passive and victimizing themselves, resilient people become highly engaged. Several resilient people are aware of the extent to which they can take action and the extent to which there is room for development. By having experienced certain situations in which they took **active control**, it facilitates them to assume **responsibility**.

Similarly as with the human immune system, resilience is a condition that transforms over the course of a life. The extent to which these abilities are ultimately developed depends on various factors: Genetic factors; conditions at home; relationships with non-family members; conditions at school and interaction with people of the same age; affiliation to established groups (sports clubs, communal groups, scouts and the like); and involvement with the cultural environment. In the field of developmental psychology, research is currently being conducted into the influence that risks and protective factors have on the mental health and stability of children.[41]

Furthermore, "being resilient" is not a moral nor ethical category. Trusting one's own abilities is not automatically linked to culturally accepted behavior. This applies to people as well as to organizations. For example, 'Philip Morris' demonstrates a high organizational resilience[42], but is nevertheless negatively associated for being a tobacco company.

---

[41] See, for example: Ungar, M., Brown, M., Liebenberg, L., Othman, R., Kwong, W. M., Armstrong, M., and Gilgun, J.: "Unique Pathways to Resilience across Cultures"; Adolescence 42; 2004.

[42] As for instance; the value of adults' personal responsibility. For further corporate values see: Coutu, Diane: "How Resilience Works" in Harvard Business Review, 2002.

Organizational resilience

Not all companies and organizations are equally well-equipped for unexpected situations. Often, managers believe that they know more or less what challenges their company will face in the future and how people will respond to them. However, the events of recent years have proven that this is a very risky stance to adopt.[43] The more complex the environment becomes, the more likely it will be that an organization will be confronted with surprises. We argue that the extent of an organization's resilience determines whether an organization will survive or be overcome by an unfortunate (or fortunate!) chance occurrence.

It is arguable whether concepts from the field of psychology can be applied to an organizational context. Nevertheless, resilient organizations certainly demonstrate similar capabilities to resilient individuals.

Even so, an organization does not automatically become resilient by exclusively hiring resilient individuals. The art – as always, one may be tempted to say – lies in the organizational design, the processes and structures, and in the self-awareness or self-control of the system. In what way do especially resilient companies differ from less resilient ones?[44]

Agility and taking initiative when it concerns information:
Flexibility and taking initiative characterize the routines of resilient organizations: In this way, staff members pro-actively gather information and weigh out the implications of one decision with other possible alternatives. This applies to internally generated information as well as to information generated in relevant environments. There is no shame in disclosing bad news. In order to be agile, it is crucial to not simply "wait and see" how things turn out. In a resilient organization, managers and employees are able to react upon the first sign of imminent turbulences by setting priorities and involving the relevant people in a quick, targeted, and flexible manner. Information hot spots are a useful institution. Nokia, for example, has a "head troubleshooter" that follows important but latent themes on its radar and pounces on every diversion.

---

[43] Cf.: Coutu, Diane; Weick, Karl: "Sense and Reliability", Harvard Business Review 2002.

[44] The following part relates to the named sources and the results of the discussions during our pioneering workshop about resilience in January 2010. Especially Sutcliffe and Weick did enlightening research work: Weick, Karl; Sutcliffe, Kathleen: "Managing the Unexpected"; Jossey-Bass, San Francisco, 2001.

Communication – direct, personal and with attention to differences:
Communication takes place in a direct manner and, if possible, with personal contact. Through a high level of trust, everyone may contribute his/her own viewpoint and discuss it in a controversial fashion. As a result, differences and discrepancies are tackled in a respectful way. An institutionalized, regular exchange between key staff members ensures a high degree of interaction, which improves the quality of an organization's self-perception and ability to improvise.

Leadership – decision-making capabilities at the place of occurrence:
Managers develop the viewpoint that contradictions and tensions are welcomed. They are capable of bringing staff members that have long years of work experience and those with extensive improvisational capabilities to work effectively with one another. When there are unforeseen turbulences, decision-making power and responsibility shift to that part of the organization at which the right competences are located to manage the situation and to take action. As a result, the leadership structures abandon some of their direct control.

A company can only do this because every employee in a resilient organization is aware of their own responsibility and contribution to the overall success of the company. Staff members act independently within their division and can do so with minimal intervention by their managers. Changes of many organizational structures – away from vertical structures, but towards networks – have made them more agile and adaptable. Resilient companies are connected on various levels. A clear allocation of responsibility (in a centralized or decentralized direction) is not possible.

The relationship with the company – purpose, meaning and trust:
Every single person knows their own contribution to reaching the aspirations of the company and thereby derives an individual purpose in working for that company. This induces a sense of affiliation and commitment that reflects in concrete action. Due to their association with the corporate values, staff members proactively engage in the development of their organization.

Managers are considered to be credible and enjoy a high level of trust. They are also very conscious of their function as a role model. Emotions are seen as part of the organizational life; to ignore these in times of a crisis could dramatically worsen the situation. Positive emotions can greatly enhance efficiency.

Finding solutions – practicing improvisation:
Teams are systematically prepared to practice how to improvise solutions. For instance, this can be done by repeatedly going through various possible scenarios. The more possible alternative options an organization acknowledges, the better it can respond to unforeseen occurrences and stand its ground in a complex surrounding. People react according to their usual behavior when they are under immense pressure. By habitually analyzing alternative solutions, you can learn to more easily improvise in turbulent situations. This does not mean that planning should become obsolete in an organization; it merely means that these are not suited to master unexpected situations.

Mistakes – concentrating on how it came about:
Resilient organizations – especially those that guarantee that they are highly reliable[45] – have a positive attitude regarding errors. Staff members are allowed to make mistakes without having to expect reprisals. In a number of organizations, recently emerged problems are identified as rapidly as they can and, if possible, the guilty party is made responsible in order to free the rest of the organization from any blame, while resilient organizations instead learn from their mistakes for further development. Resilient organizations investigate issues meticulously, to discover how the error could have happened in the first place, and are not satisfied with overly simplified, one-sided explanations. Mistakes support the learning process of organizations when considered as only the symptoms of more fundamental problems, and therefore improve the structures and processes of organizations.

Staff members – networking and interaction between generalists and experts:
Resilient organizations pursue the highest possible diversity in their staff composition: A multitude of perspectives, assumptions and attitudes minimize the blind spots of an organization, even if this should involve an arduous integration process. The flexibility in the roles of employees is systematically strengthened through educational programs, cross-level training and job rotation. This generates an understanding of the functional interdependencies between different parts of the company and thereby increases the resilience of the organization.

---

[45] For more details about the culture of mistakes in highly reliable organizations, see: Weick, Karl; Sutcliffe, Kathleen: "Managing the Unexpected"; Jossey-Bass, San Francisco, 2001.

Staff members with highly specialized expert knowledge and experiences receive a high degree of recognition in the company and, when required, are given a high degree of decision-making responsibility.

However, generalists are employed for key positions, since they are capable of changing their perspectives quickly and getting the right specialist on board.

(Self-)reflection – organizing new perspectives:
Our view of organizations is that they create their very own worldview from which they derive their own expectations for promising endeavors. However, a danger can emerge for an organization when the re-interpretations of externally-derived information exclusively strengthen existing expectations and assumptions. In especially resilient companies, different functional areas continuously question accustomed processes and structures after intense observation. Employees and managers do not settle for simplified explanations of cases of malfunction. In a dialogue they reflect together upon assumptions and blind spots. Corporate self-confidence is used to improve actions and reactions in certain situations.

Awareness of purpose and values – creates meaning for the running of daily business and at a personal level:
Belief in the meaningfulness of one's own actions is a key characteristic of resilient individuals and can be transferred to an organizational level. Most of the long-standing successful companies have firmly established corporate values. The purpose of a company is known by every employee and features prominently in its vision, mission and strategy. Naturally, these go hand in hand and are not formulated arbitrarily. Once again, resilience does not fit into an ethic or moral category: Experienced values do not even have to be accepted within the surrounding cultural environment as long as they enhance a higher level of purpose within the organization.

Awareness of what makes the organization "tick" – knowing and safeguarding revenue drivers and core processes:
The most important revenue drivers and core processes of an organization are commonly known and transparent. Top management also pays a lot of attention to them and incorporates the expert knowledge of the operational sectors into their decision-making. In case of a disruption, financial reserves for central value-enhancing processes are very close at hand or at least readily avail-

able. These resources (material, financial, know-how, well-established relations) are in opposition to the maxim of pure cost reduction, but outweigh the risk of shortages in core value-enhancing processes. Moreover, there are programs that ensure the sustainability of core processes. Flexible structures and strategies are installed, contingency plans are developed, and employees are trained in cases of malfunction to maintain the performance level at the "heart" of the organization.

Awareness of risks and vulnerabilities – minimizing risks and promoting flexibility:
In steady times it is important to identify and comprehend potential weaknesses and dangers in the core areas. As suggested by Yossi Steffi, one way in which this can be achieved is by creating a vulnerability-map.[46] Raising awareness of **vulnerabilities in the operational business processes** (malfunctions in the production process, stand-stills in the logistics chain, loss of key personnel, etc.), **strategic vulnerabilities** (product development process, customer and supplier relations, public image, etc.), **financial vulnerabilities** (credit-worthiness, liquidity, financial crisis, etc.), and **vulnerabilities due to external risks** (sabotage, natural disasters, liabilities, etc.), help to distinctly classify potential dangers and prepare countermeasures. The management team and the employees can recognize the constraints that have been caused by these vulnerabilities and tackle them proactively.

Awareness of relevant environments – establishing stakeholder monitoring:
Resilient companies are aware of their embeddedness and the interdependencies that result from it – in spite of their size and the extent of their market power. The risks due to these dependencies are defined and the majority of them are linked to possible countermeasures. The establishment of long-standing, stable costumer and supplier relations is fundamental and a top priority. If an unexpected risk or opportunity should present itself, organizations can use their relations with customers and suppliers to establish new, quick, and flexible solutions. Moreover, the markets are being continuously monitored in search of alternatives. The influence of frequently overlooked stakeholders that may be damaging to the company, are also taken into consideration. Realizing

---

[46] In the book: Sheffi, Yossi: "The Resilient Enterprise. Overcoming Vulnerability for Competitive Advantage"; the MIT Press, Cambridge, London, 2007.

the role of the company within the bigger picture can provide an extended perspective of existing interdependencies and restrictions.

Strategic resilience
Strategy work will change in the future if companies want to be successful in the long run – when turbulences have a sizeable impact. There is hardly any sector anymore that can work with long-term planning horizons; profound changes in sector-specific conditions, in customer preferences or radical innovations by competitors are becoming more and more common. In order to face the turbulences in a resilient way, companies are adjusting to the idea of planning for the near foreseeable future. This implies disregarding an "ultimate goal" and to engage thoroughly with the current situation at hand, in order to derive the greatest possible benefits.

Strategy work will address the following questions: What is the stable core of the strategy? What is our strategic focus? What is supposed to remain flexible? A map will be designed for the flexible parts: An analysis of the current potential of the situation.[47] In this way, attention will only be paid to the currently available potential, and not to the desired or planned potentials.

In each situation there are factors on which you can rely or even fully depend upon. In the pursuit of strategic objectives, these factors should be identified and put into use. On the basis of this diagram (i.e., depending on the support or limitation of identified factors) follows a play-to-win strategy (goal: Market leadership) or a play-not-to-lose strategy (goal: Remaining competitive in the market).

If a PNTL strategy is chosen, it means: To continue, to "wait and see", and to keep an eye on the situation until it changes – and it will definitely change.

If you pursue a PTW strategy, it means that you are committed to creating radical strategic innovations, since evolutionary developments fall short of expectations! For this, continuous contact with stakeholders is a requirement. Numerous different strategic "experiments" create opportunities to test chances

---

[47] Situational potentials are well described in Francois Jullien's book "Lecture in Front of Managers about the Effectiveness and Efficiency in China and in the West", Merve Verlag Berlin, 2006.

and risks. Top management accepts that incurred losses and failures of several of these experiments are unavoidable. One possible way in which to generate promising experiments is with the so-called "learning journey"[48]. Innovative impulses with regard to strategic core questions are generated, reflected upon and experienced in intensive dialogues together with other innovative companies. The participants are engaged with the question: How do other successful companies deal with similar developments, in order to maintain market leadership and remain successful for another ten years? A thorough understanding of the drivers of similar companies, and not mechanical benchmarking, are of key importance and sought in intense "off-the-record" discussions with top managers to gain conclusive insights. The ultimate goal of the journey is to understand the effectiveness and the prerequisites of strategic innovation and to jointly develop new ideas and dynamism to be implemented in one's company.

By focusing on currently available potential, the classic strategic question can be answered on whether the formulation of the strategy should be based on core competences or diversification. Core competences provide a focus and competitive advantages by energetically generating a distinct individual profile. In contrast, diversification offers diverse docking options for the needs of customers and can thereby compensate for sector-specific turbulences with successes in other areas – possibly with the risk of attaining too high a variety.

Both approaches can contribute to strategic resilience, or possibly restrain it – depending on the internal and external constraints of the situation. At its core, strategic resilience can be attained by various different alternatives, flexibility, caution, and by the acceptance and usage of the current situation.

Someone who is aware of the risks can bypass them and is better prepared
The benefits of resilience become especially visible in turbulent times – when a chance occurrence strikes – but it is also a skill that an organization needs to continuously work on.[49]

---

[48] One of our projects – a Learning Journey with the KWS SAAT AG, launched five innovative initiatives which resulted in an immense motivation concerning those new priorities within the management team.

[49] We call the five phases of this continuous process: Reduction, readiness, response, recovery and renewal.

In order to prepare for turbulences, awareness rises and risks are acknowledged and prioritized – the vulnerability of an organization is reduced as a whole.

As a next step, measures are taken to prepare for any eventualities, members of the organization are trained, and flexible structures and strategies are implemented.

If an unexpected turbulence occurs, there are various different approaches and priorities depending on the nature of the turbulence (e.g., a strategy, revenue or liquidity crisis, a sizeable order, a natural disaster, etc.). An overview of the extent of the possible consequences is established and the necessary operational measures are taken.

The next phase involves stabilization and the quickest possible return to day-to-day business. To effectively master a turbulence, the parties involved must intensively tackle the matter at hand.

After having overcome the turbulence, the final phase consists of an evaluation of the lessons learned: The potential for renewal that had become apparent through the unexpected event, the effectiveness of measures that were taken, and the extent of the actual consequences. The opportunity of innovations to emerge after a turbulent incident – new products or business models, new core processes and monitoring concepts – are prioritized and implemented. Further findings are integrated into the formulation of the organization and determine the approach of preparing for future unforeseen and surprising occurrences.

In the end, resilience means to be prepared for a chance event before it actually occurs.

Bibliography
We use many sources in our resilience research. The present article refers mainly to the following:

Chorn, Norman
    HR as Partners in Organizational Development, Centre for Strategy Development, Sydney, January, 2009.

Coutu, Diane
    How Resilience Works; in: Harvard Business Review; No. 5, 2002.

Coutu, Diane; Weick, Karl
  Sense and Reliability, in: Harvard Business Review; No. 4, 2003.

Dufresne, Ronald; Clair, Judith
  Moving beyond Media Feast and Frenzy: Imagining Possibilities for Hyper-Resilience Arising From Scandalous Organizational Crisis; in: Law and Contemporary Problems, Vol. 71:201, 2008.

Hamel, Gary; Välikangas, Liisa
  The Quest for Resilience; in: Harvard Business Review; No. 9, 2003.

Jullien, François
  Vortrag vor Managern über Wirksamkeit und Effizienz in China und im Westen, Merve Verlag, Berlin, Juli 2006.

Shatté, Andrew; Reivich, Karen
  The Resilience Factor, Broadway Books, New York, 2003.

Sheffi, Yossi
  The Resilient Enterprise. Overcoming Vulnerability for Competitive Advantage; the MIT Press, Cambridge, London, 2007.

Somers, Scott
  Measuring Resilience Potential: An Adaptive Strategy for Organizational Crisis Planning; in: Journal of Contingencies and Crisis Management, Vol. 17 No. 1, 2009.

Starr, Randy; Newfrock, Jim; Delurey, Michael
  Enterprise Resilience: Managing Risk in the Networked Economy; in: Strategy + Business, Issue 30, 2003.

Ungar, M., Brown, M., Liebenberg, L., Othman, R., Kwong, W. M., Armstrong, M., and Gilgun, J.
  Unique Pathways to Resilience Across Cultures; Adolescence 42; 2004.

Weick, Karl; Sutcliffe, Kathleen
  Managing the Unexpected. Assuring High Performance in an Age of Complexity; Jossey-Bass, San Francisco, 2001.

2. Article II: Let It Be ...

Let It Be ...
Seven Reasons Why Innovation Might Not Be Right for You

Barbara Heitger, Annika Serfass

Innovations make the world go round. They promote superior total shareholder return[50], redefine industries[51], change consumer behavior and peoples' perceptions of "how things are done". They make all our lives easier, longer, more efficient, and more enjoyable. Innovation has become THE buzzword of the decade, making creativity and innovation the top-agenda items for CEOs all over the world.[52]

And:

Innovation sucks. It's irritating, time-consuming, and you can never be sure whether you will actually make money with it – this is proven by failure rates of about 70%[53] for consumer products. Moreover, only 55% of senior executives are satisfied with the financial return on their innovation expenses.[54]

There are simply too many "ifs" involved. There are too many tools, too many different people involved, too many different underlying dynamics, far too unpredictable consumers within target groups, and too many clever competitors in an overall too complex world. And even if you do everything right: innovation still cannot be forced into existence.

---

[50] BCG 2010 Senior Executive Innovation Survey: An annual TSR premium of 12,4% over the last 3 years, and 2% over the last 10 years (Asians are doing much better, while Europeans lag behind).

[51] See for example: "Blue Ocean Strategy" by W. C. Kim and R. Mauborgne; 2005.

[52] E.g. IBM Global CEO Study: Capitalizing on Complexity, 2010; McKinsey Global Survey: Leadership Through the Crisis and After, 2009; IBM CHRO Study 2010.

[53] In Germany 2010, based on a study of GFK and Serviceplan.

[54] BCG 2010 Senior Executive Innovation Survey, although it has risen from 43% in 2008.

The organizational requirements for "breakthrough[55] innovation" have been described very aptly and thoroughly in an abundance of books, articles and models. However, innovation must not be an end in itself! We believe that there are reasons – very good reasons – not to try and be the most innovative company on the block. We shall now explain when it might be best to give a miss on radical innovation.

1) The price to pay

Several traits stabilize a system by promoting efficiency, endurance, effective usage of resources, and a sense of belonging. Such traits include the superiority of those with higher success rates, those with a higher output, those with an extensive skill set, and those with a higher degree of commitment.[56] The tricky part is that the "new" needs privileges compared to the "old" in order to get the chance to grow. Mostly, it is necessary that other people are hired for this new, other paradigms are introduced, together with a different set of rules. The principle here is an antithesis of the norm; it even negates it. This often leads to frustration for those who are currently doing an exceptional job and represent the pillars of the company. Consequently, a preference of the new can become a dangerous destabilizing factor for the corporate culture and identity, as well as for internal processes and efficiency. Innovations are this "new", they replace something that may have existed for a long time. People need a minimum frame to depend upon (including seniority rules), so therefore when your organization is already busy with 15 different projects to promote change from PMI to matrix, do not add innovation on top of these. You have to say your farewell to the "old", so that the staff members – and the organization as a whole – can properly move on. A truly innovative culture implies just that: Finding appreciative ways of "saying goodbye" to old structures, processes, etc. that have enabled successes so far, in order to have the room to maneuver and establish a readiness for new and unknown ventures.

---

[55] Or "radical", or "disruptive" innovation. Which are all three different from evolutionary innovative steps (which are not an object of this article).
[56] Sparrer, Insa & Varga von Kibéd, Matthias: "Ganz im Gegenteil", 200, p. 169/170.

> **Reflect on:**
>
> - Are high performers receiving the sort of appreciation they need?
> - Is there a balanced combination between stable "old" features and exciting "new" ventures?
> - How do we address the upcoming end of an era for our company (e.g., shifting from fixed-line network business to mobile network business)?
> - How daring and clear is the organization in creating protective incubators for innovation?

2) Don't eat yourself up

There are a number of successful firms that promote the idea that you have to force yourself to be innovative. The Austrian chocolate producer Zotter kills some of its best-selling products every year to "make room for the potential of the others"[57]. In other industries, self-cannibalization is essential for survival. Imagine phone providers only ever sticking to their fixed-line networks. However, self-cannibalization might not make you fat, but dead. Have a look at your customer base: Who are they? Are they trendsetters? Fast followers? Or the long tail? By knowing your customer base, you can make an informed guess on how your customers would respond if you were to deprive them of their favorite product. Are they loyal to the product, the underlying technology, or the brand itself? Also, pay attention to the shifts in your industry: Is your core technology gradually becoming obsolete? How much longer can you stick with it whilst developing a new cannibalizing business? It is true that unconventional methods such as self-cannibalization can push you beyond your boundaries, but you should only use this approach when you are absolutely certain that your customers will remain loyal to your brand or when your product/service is becoming obsolete. Make sure to involve some representatives of your customer segments and some unconventional thinkers into your decision-making process.

---

[57] Interview with the founder Josef Zotter by A. Kausl in: IMP Perspectives Management Journal "Geschäftslogiken der Zukunft", 2010/11, S. 85–99.

> **Reflect on:**
>
> – Who are the most loyal customers and which segments do they belong to?
> – What do they value about our products?
> – How would different customer segments respond to replacements and how would they respond if we do not push for innovations?
> – How and when do we decide to stop producing/offering a product/service?
> – Is our business model or core technology threatened by replacement and is a profound change therefore necessary?

3) Take a stand

Yes, brand evangelists are always delighted when a new version of some gadget is available for purchase. However, there are also many consumers who are not thrilled by products that are stubbornly marketed as innovation, but only add a bogus value to their user experience. It is a widespread phenomenon that during a long growth period, "innovation" is often only a marketing assertion, while the underlying business models, structures and systems are primarily copied or scaled up. The outcomes are so-called "bells and whistles". Rear wings and rims for your car, fragranced toilet paper, or added nutrients your body will not digest, are just a few examples of non-functional add-ons.

These "innovations" can bring in some cash, but they will never revolutionize an industry or turn around a struggling organization. Giving in to the pressures for innovation does not make you more innovative. The answer to "how can we think outside the box?" is not to: "Think harder!" It is also not to: "Be creative!" It takes a lot more to make an entire organization truly innovative. If you wish to step in Whirlpool's shoes and make innovation a core competence, you must completely transform your entire organization.[58]

Do not miss the point of being different. All in all, you do not have to follow a misguided "play-to-win" strategy. Sometimes, "play-not-to-lose" can go a long way. So take advantage of your current market position.

---

[58] See: N. Tennant-Snyder and D. Duarte: "Strategic Innovation", 2003.

> **Reflect on:**
>
> – What sort of added value does the product provide?
> – How many resources are assigned for "bells and whistles" and how many are assigned for true innovation?
> – Does the workforce have the necessary abilities for (semi-)radical innovation?
> – How big is the need of the company for (semi-)radical innovation?
> – What is our core identity – what story do we tell ourselves?

4) Steel isn't Google

And that is a good thing! So-called High Reliability Organizations (HRO) provide a different value to society than the thrill of the new. Working in the emergency room of a hospital, on an aircraft carrier or in a car assembly line implies something altogether different than inventing a new toy.[59] The biggest obstacle to generating returns on investments in innovation is supposedly a "risk-averse" culture.[60] What if such a culture is necessary to ensure the required results?

When "safety comes first", tested and proven models are a requirement. Any divergence from these models is most often not creative, but in fact a highly dangerous mistake that is a result of stupidity, a lack of training, boredom, a lack of concentration, and several other reasons. Such a setting also requires a certain type of employee – one who does not get distracted whilst performing repetitive tasks and focuses on the task at hand. The Center for Creative Leadership[61] differentiates "pioneers" and "builders" when it comes to innovation: A quest for novelty versus a quest for practicality. In HROs there are more builders involved who are perceived as more disciplined, accurate, reliable, efficient, sound, methodical, prudent, dutiful, dependable, and organized.[62] Both "pioneers" and "builders" can be highly creative and can trigger groundbreaking innovation – they simply do so using entirely different approaches: The

---

[59] K. Weick and K. Sutcliffe defined the term HRO and its workings in their book "Managing the Unexpected", 2007.

[60] BCG 2010 Senior Executive Innovation Survey, namely 31%.

[61] CCL, from the reading material of the seminar "Innovation Leadership", 2010.

[62] "Pioneers" are perceived to be spontaneous, energetic, unconventional, catalyst, ingenious, creating dissonance, independent, and capricious risk-takers.

builder works on a single problem relating to his field of expertise until he solves it; the pioneer works on so many as twenty inspiring projects simultaneously by rapidly trying and testing each one.

If your organization is an HRO (or similar to one), use Six Sigma, TQM, and Continuous Improvement to safely adjust your processes. It makes you smarter, more efficient, cost-effective, and more dependable – in creative ways, too. You will keep a firm eye on operations and your staff's in-depth expertise.

Resist havoc; concentrate on taming and moulding wild and weird ideas that work elsewhere to make them suitable for you.

Reflect on:

- How important is reliability (and zero tolerance for mistakes) in our business?
- How adventurous is our industry?
- What is the objective for improvement: Better operations, safer products or providing a new offer to the world?
- What types of people do we mainly employ – "builders" or "pioneers"?

5) The Icarus problem

Too much innovation can become a real problem. Certainly it is not one that many companies face, but it remains a problem nonetheless. Take Enron for example: After 16 years the company became the seventh-largest corporation in the U.S., and then within the same year became the most infamous bankruptcy scandal in U.S. corporate history. During its first 16 years, the company dramatically transformed the energy industry through tireless and continuous innovation. Some of the most noteworthy projects include: The largest gas-run heat and power plant in the world in Teesside, the first weather derivatives transactions, the EnronOnline transaction platform, deregulation efforts, and formulating contracts for gas or power supply with no linkage to specific asset.[63] These were considerable achievements in an industry that resisted change and was mostly determined to maintain the status quo. The energy and drive needed to stretch the boundaries was derived from a corporate culture with very high levels of trust and an attitude of "questioning everything". However,

---

[63] Special report: "Enron: 10 years on", in: Energy Risk, November 2011, p. 23–40.

all the crucial resources – financial assets, skills, etc. – were tied up in the new projects and businesses to fight off the bankruptcy of the company. The bankruptcy was primarily a result of fraudulent accounting practices, but the immense trust of the company in employees also resulted in a waste of large amounts of time and money on bad ideas without being monitored, and excessive creativity. It seems as if Enron had singed its wings while flying past the sun, just as Icarus had done in the ancient myth.

There are quite a number of "innovation junkies" that defy gravity. Most of them are very capable of exploring new possibilities[64], but lack the skills and competences to transform these into organizational knowledge to put them to use and make actual profits from them.

> **Reflect on:**
>
> – How much innovation/ how many "new" developments can the organization sustain? Are we biting off more than we can chew?
> – Innovation efforts are comparable to farming: Are we capable to sew some seeds, cultivate ideas, harvest them, and then let the land lie fallow – all in due time?
> – Is trust backed up by a minimum of "checks and balances"?
> – Do we have the skills to use creative ideas and transform these into profitable businesses?

6) Not well measured – not well managed

The underlying idea of measuring in terms of money – whether it concerns handing out innovation budgets, trying to estimate the amount of units that can be sold, or calculating possible margins for new products – can often be counterproductive in the process of promoting "the right ideas". Plus, management is prone to decide and define rather than allowing open-ended processes. This is the very tricky paradox of innovation: Sustaining an emerging process instead of killing off ideas at an early stage on the one hand, and having a high degree of dedication to the innovation processes on the other hand. Yes, innovation needs extensive dedication! Any true artist can confirm this.[65] There-

---

[64] In the sense of James March's well-known concept: "Exploration and Exploitation in Organizational Learning", 1991.

[65] We like Twyla Tharp: "The Creative Habit", 2003.

fore, you need an apt means of judging and monitoring processes to promote discipline and encourage creativity at the same time. If your company is not able to provide this, then it must be outsourced. For idea generation and prototyping, cooperate with an exciting and creative design firm such as IDEO and make budgeting innovation possible.

> **Reflect on:**
>
> – Does the company have a clear innovation strategy?
> – Are innovation processes in place and known to all?
> – Does innovation monitoring include more than monetary KPIs?
> – Is the organization disciplined enough to develop competitive products from good ideas?

7) Let it go …

You are right to think "the old ways aren't so bad". Actually, you are spot on. Several researches on innovation explain the way in which new ideas gain entry to the market through Darwinism[66]: first, there is a multitude of ideas or options (which are – in a way – spontaneous mutations), most of which are abandoned almost instantly, while others linger for a while longer, and only very few ultimately prevail. Every year, the majority of companies that fail are start-ups. Therefore, most of the shrewd ideas that had been pulled out of the hat never even gain entry to the market, and if they do, it is unlikely they will be very profitable. Tested models and successful products are good; otherwise they would not exist anymore. A lot of the time "tested-and-tried" products trump "new-and-unknown" ones. Everyone knows and has played Monopoly for decades, while new and exciting games are often quickly forgotten. So yes, we should not hang on too strongly to the old days, but we should also not overglorify the new.

Innovation successes are often measured by "customer satisfaction" (45% of companies use this metric) and "overall revenue growth" (used by 40% of companies).[67] Perhaps your customers are already very satisfied. You could further

---

[66] E.g. Robert Sutton in "Weird Ideas that Work", 2001, p. 14/15.
[67] BCG 2010 Senior Executive Innovation Survey.

enhance their satisfaction using measures other than innovation: How about superior service or friendliness?

> **Reflect on:**
>
> – If we should decide not to innovate – what will ensure our successes in the future?
> – What – besides innovation – could really excite our customers?
> – Which attributes of our products have been successful over a long period of time (think of equivalents to companies' core competencies) which truly make them special?
> – Which features of our old products still excite us?

If these seven reasons not to innovate should make you think "Sure, it's hard, but that's no reason not to innovate", then you are no longer contemplating but have already decided to go for innovation and overcome the obstacles. In this case, take a close look at each of the seven possible pitfalls and systematically tackle each of the obstacles to succeed in groundbreaking innovation.

Let us be clear: every person and every company can learn how to radically innovate – but might not necessarily have to. Engage in self-reflection and explore your surroundings to identify the extent of "innovativeness" that suits you, your company, your industry and your customers best.

Bibliography

Books and articles:

Kausl, Alexander
Zotter – Der Unbeugsame, in: IMP Perspectives Management Journal "Geschäftslogiken der Zukunft", 2010/11, S. 85–99.

Kim, Chan; Mauborgne, Renée
Blue Ocean Strategy: How to Create Uncontested Market Space and Make the Competition Irrelevant, Harvard Business Review Press, Boston, 2005.

March, James G.
Exploration and Exploitation in Organizational Learning, in: Organization Science, Vol. 2, No. 1, February 1991, p. 71–87.

Sparrer, Insa; Varga von Kibéd, Matthias
: Ganz im Gegenteil. Tetralemmaarbeit und andere Grundformen systemischer Strukturaufstellungen, Carl-Auer-Verlag, Heidelberg, 2000.

Special report
: Enron: 10 years on, in: Energy Risk, November 2011, p. 23–40.

Sutton, Robert
: Weird Ideas That Work. 11 ½ Practices for Promoting, Managing and Sustaining Innovation, Penguin Books Ltd, London, 2001.

Tennant Snyder, Nancy; Duarte, Deborah L.
: Strategic Innovation. Embedding Innovation as a Core Competency in Your Organization, Jossey-Bass, San Francisco, 2003.

Tharp, Twyla
: The Creative Habit. Learn It and Use It for Life, Simon & Schuster, New York, 2003.

Weick, Karl; Sutcliffe, Kathleen
: Managing the Unexpected: Assuring High Performance in an Age of Complexity, Jossey-Bass, San Francisco, 2007.

Studies and surveys:

Boston Consulting Group
: Innovation 2010. A Return to Prominence – and the Emergence of a New World Order, 2010.

Gesellschaft für Konsumforschung (GfK), Serviceplan
: Studie über die Ursachen von Produktflops bei Fast Moving Consumer Goods, 2010.

IBM
: Capitalizing on Complexity. Insights from the Global Chief Executive Officer Survey, 2010.

IBM
: Working beyond Borders. Insights from the Global Human Resources Executive Officer Survey, 2010.

McKinsey
: Global Survey. Leadership through the Crisis and After, 2009.

CHAPTER 7

CASE STUDIES

CASE I:

my.change, my.chance
The path from standard software selling to solution providing

Alexander Doujak, Barbara Heitger

Introduction

The following case study is closely linked with our work on this book. The two of us had "blocked" three weeks in the beginning of January 2000 to work on the book, hoping to complete essential parts of it. However, *"things never turn out as expected"*.

From our point of view as consultants, this was true for the present case study from the very start. During the Christmas holidays we had lunch with the manager of an international software firm – a provider to one of our customers. At the end of our talk, the manager told us about a restructuring program that was being planned in his company. Other consultants had already been asked for offers, time was running short, and an in-house employee event had already been scheduled. Would we be interested in drawing up a consulting concept? The case roused our interest, and we began to consider under which conditions we could submit an offer.

Our first consideration was that we need direct contact with the senior managers, need to get to know their perception of the project. Interview appointments were quickly arranged, and we spoke with each of the five Steering Committee members. These discussions formed the basis for our proposal. In a meeting, we presented our hypotheses and proposed approach. We saw to it that already in this preliminary stage of making an offer, our way of working together tangibly anticipated the form our common work would take in the later project. The Steering Committee accepted our tender, and things began to move in quick succession – but first, let's take a look at the customer's initial situation.

The initial situation

The customer is an international software company that develops and implements Enterprise Resource Planning (ERP) software. This international parent organization has developed a new structural and process model that is to be implemented in the national units. The transformation will be a fundamental one. A software company that supplies standard software is about to become a Solution Provider that prepares and implements value-oriented solutions in collaboration with its customers. Additional products – mainly internet-based – open up new market segments, but also increase complexity. This means a change of basic position from "ERP market leader" in a saturated market to the position of a provider of new solutions in new market segments. The priority shifts from "acquiring as many new customers as possible" to "expand the customer base providing solutions".

The last year has been a very successful one for the Austrian unit. Further growth is planned for the next year. The market situation is extremely demanding. New providers are pushing their way into the market, particularly in the new segments. The internal template for the reorganization has been arranged in two projects – a Vision Project and a Field Operations Project (FOP) that has developed structures and roles for the new organization. An initial draft of the new organizational structure has been drawn up by the management. This change project is – after the considerable personnel growth and expansion of the range of services in the previous years – the most comprehensive project of its kind in the Austrian unit.

The managers suggest images to describe this initial situation. The following three images are highly significant as illustrations of how demanding and turbulent the change is expected to be:
- "Quiet before the storm"
- "Mountain with a steep, zigzag track leading up – we're standing at the base"
- "Now: principalities. In the future: autonomous cities and municipalities in a common whole"

Project architecture

The first step: decide on project architecture; determine objectives and composition of the project team

The initial phase already anticipates the subsequent dynamics. The basic architecture is resolved in the course of an initial evening and night meeting with the decision-makers (regional managers, the designated new country and project managers). These managers plan the following elements: a Steering Committee consisting of executives from the overriding unit (regional management), a Change Board, in which all managerial personnel from the Austrian organization participates, and a Sounding Board involving all employees.

The staffing of the Change Team, which will control and drive the change process with the project manager as team leader, is a significant, indicatory decision. We select a microcosm approach that aims to represent all the essential trends in the company in the project team. Initial staffing proposals are evaluated according to the following criteria:

- Affiliation with the involved organizational units
- Corporate affiliation (< 1, < 2, > 2 years)
- Basic attitude: progressive/conservative
- FOP know-how: high/average/low

The decision committee votes in a two-stage process: In the first round, each committee member evaluates the candidates based on their individual assessment (point polling) and subsequently the overall image is discussed. Interestingly, the initial decision is considerably modified in the course of this decision-making process. The committee decides for a "well-balanced combination" that symbolically documents the external representation of all forces and perspectives.

From our observer's perspective, we see that fundamental things are decided this evening – in part implicitly: the key players for the upcoming process, essential responsibilities, collaboration and decision-making configurations. And last but not least, the standing of the consultants. The discussion of the "microcosm project team approach" generates acceptance which, in a system with immense consulting know-how of its own, is no small matter.

The second step: setting phases and appointing the future management team

In the next stage, a phase model with concrete milestones is prepared and passed by the decision-making group. This is the second crucial decision-making process, which takes place in a second night meeting. The basic considerations for this are:

Phase	Time-Frame	Content
1. "Flirting": **Information**	February	– **Beginning of the project on Feb. 1st** – Everyone can talk to everyone else: 　– New positions 　– Organizational model, roles 　– Possibilities of new teams – Form of information: 　– Unstructured 　– 3 h FOP trainings for each member of staff
2. "Engagement": **Decision on team-members**	March	– Rules of the game start on March 1st, 2001 – Organizational units promoting themselves – Employees make an application – Managers put together their team – New organization is functional and implemented starting on April 1st
3. "Wedding": **Teambuilding**	April–June	– Kickoff for the sections/teams – Developing strategies and objectives – Clarifying the tasks of each member of staff – Planning of budget, expenses, revenues – Planning of customer activities – Deepening of the FOP roles and their collaboration
4. "Marriage": **Optimization**	July–December	– Deepening of the FOP idea – Transferring the FOP objective into the market – Putting FOP roles and processes into practice – Optimizing the entire organization – **Project closure on December 31st**

This results in the following overall image, which shows that the tempo at the beginning of the process is much faster than in the later phases. The concentration of the meetings of the main panels (Steering Committee, Change Board and Sounding Board) around the milestones is also noteworthy. It shows that making, communicating and implementing decisions rapidly is a necessity from the very start.

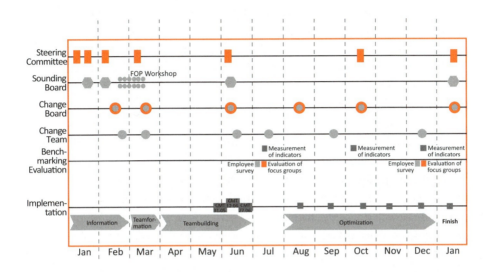

Key success factors for the implementation process
1. Energetic implementation of the "solution provider" vision
2. A high level of initiative, promotion of autonomy
3. Fast, simple, pragmatic
4. Providing security, orientation and continuity (internally to employees; externally to customers)
5. The right people in the right places
6. Business plus emotion (combining the logics of figures and feelings)
7. Overall view, clear change architecture and simultaneous flexibility
8. Lasting change, not just initial successes (achievements; no "scorched earth" policy)
9. Making future managerial staff responsible for the change in their areas, and establishing a network among them
10. Timing meetings of the Change Team, Change Board, Steering Committee and Sounding Board in close succession – to strengthens rapid feedback and the integration of suggestions

"Flirting": Company meeting; the information phase begins

The objective of this phase is to communicate the "why" and "where to" of "solution providing", to develop a common image, and to win over and activate the employees for this route. The overall project kickoff is on February 1st in the company meeting for all employees. As a microcosm of the change process, it includes all the basic elements that characterize the overall process. The client's fundamental decisions are presented, focusing on vision, personnel decisions on top management staffing, introducing the project team and explaining how the change will proceed.

The project team then holds information workshops for all employees, in which the basic characteristics of the FOP organization are presented, while feedback and questions regarding the current employee situation arise from the interactive setting. In doing this, the Change Team obtains the necessary "traction"; the direct dialogue strengthens their position. The workshops clearly show that there are diverse approaches to the topic of FOP and solution providing, particularly in regard to the configuration of new roles. A number of personnel decisions by the managers contribute to the emotional strain. Pressure within the company increases, the "open" situation is causing insecurity for many employees, particularly regarding personal perspectives.

An Intranet platform installed for the topic of change takes off well initially, but is shut down by the Steering Committee after an escalation in which employees are personally attacked.

"Getting engaged": The team-finding phase

The FOP concept foresees quantitative and qualitative reinforcement, particularly of the market-oriented teams (four branch-specific "segments") in order to ensure that the solution-providing approach can be implemented. The plan is to staff the new positions internally, external recruitment is not an issue until the second stage. The objective in this phase is: *"The right people in the right place – via a process that is both interesting and transparent for everyone and exploits the company's corporate culture of taking initiative and entrepreneurial action."*

The basic principle is: "Internal market" with clear ground rules. The new managerial personnel advertise new positions, and employees can submit applications. As a support measure, assessments are carried out as demand arises (employees or managers) – for employee orientation or as a basis for decision-making. The response varies widely throughout the different departments.

The Change Team, as the "process architect", sets up a few ground rules for this temporary phase (March 1–31), and acts as an "information hub". For instance, one essential rule is that each employee is allowed to apply for only *one* new job. The ground rules are decided upon with the management in a meeting of the Change Board at the beginning of February. Response to this event is highly ambivalent in the aftermath, showing that people have differing degrees of commitment and differing expectations of one another. Again, decision-making is carried out in two stages. After basic agreements have been reached between the employees concerned and supervisors, the results of all decisions is reported to the "Trio Team", an ad hoc decision-making panel of the Steering Committee. The "Trio Team" makes final decisions in cases where management were unable to reach consensus, and issues the overall personnel plan as a fair and reasonable distribution of resources. Only in three cases does it become necessary to revise a decision by the "Trio Team", confirming the initial assumption that – *"we have known our people for a long time, 80% of the personnel decisions are practically made already"*. By the end of March, managerial personnel have staffed their teams, with the exception of a few positions that require external recruitment. Attention is focused almost entirely on personnel decisions, overshadowing both internal clarification of processes and roles and external communication. However, each employee, having made his or her own personal decision, has strengthened commitment to his/her individual position.

"Wedding": Kickoff phase in departments and teams

The organization is "ready to fire" (original quote from our client) on April 1st. On March 29th there have been meetings of the Steering Committee, the Change Board, and the Sounding Board with the participation of all employees. In a cascade procedure, the essential points are coordinated, refined and examined from various perspectives in order to ensure the effectiveness of the implementation. In the Change Board, managerial personnel focus particularly on the new structure's feasibility in their respective areas. Diverse assessments of the situation are presented in a spatial constellation that makes them visible and addressable in a controversial way.

The highlight of the employee event (Sounding Board) is an analogous presentation of the new processes to all involved employees, in which concrete scenarios are enacted. An interactive Q&A game focuses on dialogue between the new country manager and newly formed teams. One question in particular concerns everyone: *"How much is actually going to change?"* The teams that have experienced personnel changes, especially a change of manager, expect the most radical future change.

The new teams – particularly in the branch-oriented sectors – begin with team-building workshops. Some of these are only rudimentarily staffed. The Change Team conducts an initial evaluation, which reveals that individual stakeholders' understanding of the reasons to change is relatively high (70–80%), although not everyone has a clear understanding of his or her individual contribution to the project. External communication still shows gaps.

The Change Team increasingly finds itself in a monitoring and controlling role. The new line managers assume the role of "Change Drivers".

"Marriage": Optimization in departments, initial evaluation
Once the staffing of the new positions has been clarified, focus moves to internal structure and process. The Country Management Team of the new organization slowly begins to take form, with the effect that two Country Management Team members assume a dual role in the Change Team. This illustrates the gradual handover of the change responsibility from the Change Team to the Country Management Team (CMT). Managers have to adjust to the new business model and its management, and do so by "diving into the deep end". Not only the team, the business model and the operative objectives are also new: The new CMT also represents a new generation of management. The previous senior managers are now concentrating on growth in the new region. Some CMT members receive support in the form of individual consulting.

A qualitative evaluation is carried out in group and individual interviews. The interviews are taken very seriously, a fact expressed in punctuality and full attendance. In mid-June, the results are presented to the Change Board.

Three trends are clearly discernible:
- Winner: *"I've been advocating a strategy-change in this direction for the past two years."*

- Offended: *"We were the best on the market with our old strategy. Why does there always have to be a change?"*
- Ostrich: *"Well, I've already lived through many changes in the company, but in the end, everything always stays the same. This one will pass, too."*

Positive and critical voices are more or less in balance.

The following hypotheses regarding the as-is situation are discussed by the Change Board:
- Not everyone in the company is feeling the change yet. The perception of change depends on the degree of involvement in the change process.
- The new structure is perceived as a burden, since closure on the old structure has not been entirely completed. Many people harbour the hope that a return to the old structure will be possible at the end of the year.
- Senior management is perceived as failing to set an example for the new corporate culture. Many employees are irritated by the arrival of a new management level. (*"Since the new management's been staffed, the number of large BMWs in the garage is increasing by the week."* Although this statement is not based on facts, it is symptomatic for the basic feeling of many employees.).

Results	
How important is the project for our future success?	min. 40% max. 100% Ø 70%
What do you think our company's position is in terms of goal achievement in the overall my.change project?	min. 20% max. 50% Ø 40%
What effect do you think my.change has on customer relations? (50% stands for unchanged, 50% for negative, 50% for positive)	min. 50% max. 75% Ø 60%
What effect do you think my.change has on partner relations? (50% stands for unchanged, 50% for negative, 50% for positive)	min. 25% max. 40% Ø 30%

Results (cont.)
Positive voices Information policy for the change process was very good Survival strategy: No further successes without this new course "Lines of business"-thinking is shrinking New teams are experienced positively A lot of people had the chance to talk with each other
Critical voices Downsizing wave as a risk Old responsibilities are a barrier to the practice of new roles Resource problems Customers/partners not involved enough Communication was not good The tasks of Business Development have not been clarified Executives are not accepted

Implementation crisis and slow handover of responsibility from project to line

The project is slowly reaching high-altitude strain. Most of the energy lies in identity formation of teams and customer-oriented activities. The Change Team, which giving up its role as main agent and advisor and taking on a controlling function, is feeling somewhat degraded by this transition. Its members lack confidence in the new management structure's ability to push forward "their" change project and to ensure consistent implementation. Furthermore, although the evaluation results have been registered and ostensibly understood, there is no evidence of activities being organized as a consequence of this. "Hot topics" – such as the lack of acceptance for managerial personnel in some areas – are being hushed up. A "stoplight model" for controlling implementation activities, which is logical content-wise, is "shot down" by management. Furthermore, the new structure has yet to yield "star projects". Some of the examples presented are rated as "cosmetic changes". There are shortcomings in operative implementation. Upon reflection, it becomes clear that the reasons for this are primarily structure-related. The Change Board has lost implementation energy, which has shifted to the CMT. But the CMT is more than over-burdened with its new responsibilities, and a new model needs to be found for clearly demonstrating the shift of responsibility from the change project to the line.

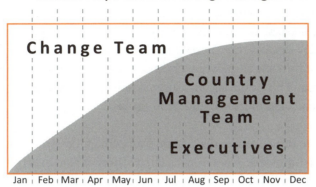

Entities responsible for change management

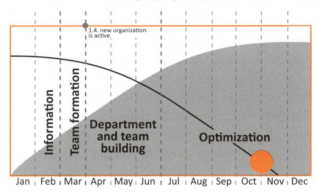

Change project phases

— Level of activity and importance of the change team for the project.
— Level of activity and importance of Country Management and new executives in the change project.

An exemplary implementation in one of the sectors

In one of the sectors, the new "solution providing" strategy is implemented on a market-related basis. There are two directions of impact. For key accounts, executive contacts are consistently maintained in order to establish "solution providing" at the level of top customers. For the second target group of traditional contacts, IT managers, a "Customer Parliament" is organized. The objective is to firmly establish "solution providing" among the operative customer contacts, and to collaborate on further concept development. An innovative event is planned, with the idea of enabling a direct, personal dialogue among all relevant customers. For the customers, this creates an improved basis both for collaboration with the company and for an exchange of views with other users. The event's protocol, which mimics a parliamentary session, guarantees direct, unfiltered customer feedback. Like citizens in a parliamentary session, the employees are allowed to listen only but not to participate in discussions. The customers discuss their perception of the collaboration with a frankness that shocks quite a few employees. The main feedback is that solution providing has by no means hit home among the customers, and that there are numerous ways in which collaboration could be improved.

The results are processed, and a customer-specific follow-up is agreed upon in a subsequent Employee Conference. The Customer Parliament has a rousing effect, both internally and externally. New projects emerge from the aftermath of the Customer Parliament discussion and customer commitment increases.

Closure of the Change Team and handover to the line sector
The handover to the line sector takes longer than initially planned. Several "honor laps" have yet to be run. The objective "project conclusion by the end of December" proves too daunting. At first, ambivalence is felt within the Change Team itself toward letting go and handing over complete responsibility to the line managers. Following preliminary discussions with the Country Manager, the Steering Committee also makes an initial attempt to commit the project team to maintaining responsibility for "sustainable anchoring". The basic question is: *"How can we establish clear responsibility in the line organization for the FOP implementation?"* At first, there is talk of establishing a staff position for "corporate development". The ultimate decision is for a variant that plans for a CMT manager taking (part-time) responsibility for corporate development. The responsibility of this function lies in monitoring and driving the change process, as well as supporting the Country Manager in this connection. This decision creates stability and clarity for the further consistent management of the change process, with emphasis on fine-tuning and anchoring in daily business.

The Country Management Team is up and running
In November, things are ready to go. The Change Team members hand over their work packages – yellow post parcels highlight the symbolic act – to the managers and CMT; this "ritual" reinforces the official stepping down of the Change Team. A mirror on each parcel emphasizes the necessity of keen self-observation in FOP implementation. The subsequent CMT workshop is held under the banner of focusing, prioritizing and improving the work of the team. Twenty-four "priority" topics are proposed during preparations for the meet-

ing. Our intervention consists in classifying these into portfolios and establishing an observer panel that monitors the team's working method. The results of this self-analysis show that the team's working mode needs improvement, and that it is in need of structuring, so that it can co-ordinate with other teams to increase its efficiency. The Country Management Team needs to carry out its various functions (strategy work, change management and corporate development, control of operative business) in a more differentiated fashion.

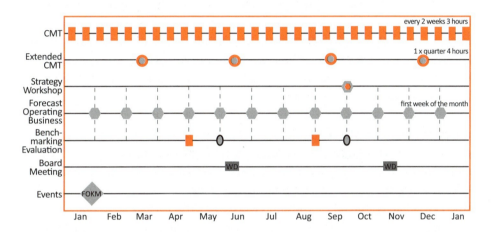

The final qualitative evaluation
A final qualitative evaluation is carried out in January of the following year. The setting is the same as in June. Group and individual interviews are carried out by in-house consultants regarding fundamental questions such as: *"What is the current mood regarding the change process, the new structure and the topic of solution providing?"*; *"What has changed in comparison with the spring of 2001?"*; *"How well are we positioned for the future?"*. The following results are presented to the Country Management Team in February:

The overall assessment of the new structure is basically positive. Working in sectors makes it possible to concentrate more effectively on one's own responsibilities. There are clear contact partners for customer inquiries. (*"Now I know who to pass them on to."*).

Working in sectors has been accepted. The irritation that was felt in the spring has for the most part disappeared. The lack of clarity that still remains concerning the new processes has ceased to be a major cause for concern, since focus is now more on tasks in one's own sector and not so much on the processes.

However, the new structure is still a cause for discomfort in cases where an individual's contribution or precise tasks remain unclear, or where uncertainty is still felt about possessing the required competencies and the hierarchy and bureaucracy are perceived as becoming more pronounced. (A recurrent image is: *"People are looking up, trying to climb the ladder by hanging on to the coattails of the person in front of them."*).

Insofar as the change process is primarily equated with the implementation of the new structure, it is considered to be complete. The new processes are known. But they are still not really being carried out. Process design and clarification of new roles in daily business are – apart from one's own immediate environment – considered to be management's responsibility (*"This still needs fine-tuning; this is an issue for management."*).

Discussion of questions regarding change of identity and the corporate culture is still at an early stage. One aspect is particularly important: One of the core values of the company is to be competent, to exude confidence. In the course of the switch to solution providing, this self-image of competency changes dramatically. The technical consultant (who always "knows better" than the customers) has become a solutions consultant (who collaborates with the customers: *"I have to ask the customers?!"*). This still triggers a great deal of anxiety.

The completion of the first year of solution providing also marks the conclusion of our description of the process. One thing should be added that was an essential success factor: Despite restructuring, the main business objectives for the year were achieved. The project ended a month earlier than planned and its completion was deemed very successful in evaluation discussions with the Steering Committee and the Country Manager.

Our contribution as consultants in the sense of "development partners" of the client
- Intense diagnosis and intervention work with the Change Team
- Moderation and design development for Change Boards and large-scale Sounding Board events (> 200 employees)
- Kickoff workshops in the departments
- On-demand individual consulting and coaching of managers
- Strategy work with individual teams

- Concept, moderation and evaluation of the Customer Parliament
- Training workshops in which the new self-image of "solution consultant" was put to the test and enriched with change management know-how
- Evaluation (through consultants who were otherwise not involved in the project, strengthening the external perspective)

Special features of our collaboration with the client in this case were: high speed and mutual flexibility. The "acid tests" in the beginning and the intense contact in the acquisition and planning phases that arose from "off the bat" architecture work lay the foundation for considerable openness and frankness in consultant-customer interaction. The diversity of our role was also unusual for us. We were (specialist) consultants for change architectures and processes, and as systemic consultants we developed designs, moderated events, contributed external perspectives and strengthened the system's self-control mechanisms. We acted as personal consultants for the individual support of key staff. As trainers in the change management workshop, we contributed ideas for the organization of customer projects. Evaluation was the one area where we found separation from personnel important. This unusual versatility of roles worked very well in this project, since our client (also in the consulting business) has considerable competence and experience with flexibility of roles. Moreover, we arranged our own co-operation so that one of us was more strongly involved than the other, enabling us to exploit our different proximity/distance to the client in our work together. We had a great deal of fun working on this project through all its highs and lows in what we experienced as a clear partnership with the client from start to implementation.

Lessons learned

On the change map, this case study falls under the heading "Renewal". What conclusions can we draw from this case regarding hard cuts and new growth?

Hard cuts

It is very difficult to change organizations during a phase of great success. The necessity to establish or mutually prepare hard cuts is an essential condition for achievement – not only at the start, but also continually throughout the course of the process. Rapid personnel decisions in the beginning (in this case, the decisions of senior management) may have a polarizing effect, but they also provide orientation. The rapid change from top-down decisions to broad bottom-up involvement (over the stages "flirt", "getting engaged" and "wedding") mobilizes a great deal of change energy.

Personal communication by the Change Team and executive staff is crucial in the phase of unclear responsibilities. The interactive information and feedback workshops – with the intense involvement of the Change Team – were instrumental in the employees' acceptance of the overall process.

The length of the transition phase (the temporary phase of parting from the previous structure and making way for the new) varies for individual target groups. This is why the acceptance of hard cuts takes varying lengths of time and the general mood remains ambivalent over a long period.

New growth
New growth requires verifiable initial business successes. Acceptance is substantially boosted by not selling cosmetic changes as "quick wins".

Organizational change "from the outside to the inside" generates energy. Early integration of customers (e.g., within the framework of a Customer Parliament) yields important innovative impulses, both for the company and for the customers.

In our observation, it was particularly the competitive situation in new market segments and the ambitious objectives (< 50% turnover from the new product) that were essential change drivers for new growth.

Overall direction
Anchoring business goals in the mandate for change projects steers them clearly in the direction of implementation and spans a structural bridge to the line. In this case, this "experiment" was successful; we feel that the question whether or not to do this needs to be rethought for every project.

The continuous co-operation and reflection on the overall direction of the process with the clients and key individuals enhances process security and the coupling of client and consultant systems.

An early modification to the project architecture, the handover of the project to the line, proved successful in this case. Expressed in an image: Change projects are "midwives, not nannies" of changes.

> **CASE II:**
>
> ## A 130-year-old company becomes Internet leader
> *Alexander Doujak, Erwin Lebic, Maria Rosiczky*
>
> **The initial situation**
> An Austrian service company with a long-standing tradition in the information processing industry is on the verge of a radical change. The company has a dominant market position and is market leader in Austria. The public image is outstanding: The company's reputation for respectability, trustworthiness and professionalism are an important basis of its success.

Key data

The company is organized as an incorporated society, with 20,000 members, 360 employees, and generates (with ten domestic and foreign investments) a turnover of approximately 35 million Euros. Its employees issue information on approximately 5 million financial ratings, handle over 100,000 debt collection cases and support approximately 90,000 creditors in over 5,000 court proceedings per annum.

The last decades have been marked by the strong personal presence of the managing director, who plays an important role in the company's outward representation. However, his tenure is coming to an end, and two further managing directors have been appointed to manage this transition phase together with him in a team of three. The corporate environment is undergoing radical change, and increasing internationalization in the industry poses a new and major challenge. New legal provisions are challenging the company's market dominance. And last but not least, young employees in middle management are determinedly demanding a change of corporate processes and management style, creating further pressure. Numerous initiative projects are pending; integrating these projects and handling them with clear focus is vital.

In this phase, corporate management drafts a change project. We are called in as consultants. Interestingly, we had been in contact with the company three years before, without it having lead to collaboration. The managing directors still remember that we turned down an offer at that time in the opinion that there was no chance for an integrated overall process. Now, the situation seems to have changed.

The objectives

The goal is to develop and implement a program for sustainable organizational development with respect to strategy, structure and corporate culture. The orientation towards implementation is an essential success factor for our client; the change project should therefore aim for concrete results and involve all the employees on an ongoing basis. Most change project objectives run along these lines. What is unique about this project is the organization's strong orientation towards innovation, which is expressed by its vast number of innovation projects.

On our change map, this case can most fittingly be positioned under the title "mobilization". The aim is to boost the perception of the necessity for change within the organization and to raise the capacity for change in both individuals and system.

The project architecture

The starting phase

The two new managing directors in the team take on the function of project sponsors, meaning that they make final decisions and determine the overall strategy. The first step of our work involves intense discussions of the clients' personal perspective, but also of the perspective for the whole enterprise's further development. This is one of the mainstays for the entire process. In the conclusion of this first sequence, the steering group, comprised of representatives from the various corporate areas, is nominated. The objective is to establish an optimally representative cross-section of the entire enterprise in this unusually large group – a total of 22 employees, including the managing directors. The size of the group reflects the central objective of integrating employees on a broad basis and giving them the opportunity to play an active part in shaping the company's future. Moreover, the steering group is meant to symbolize the future management culture.

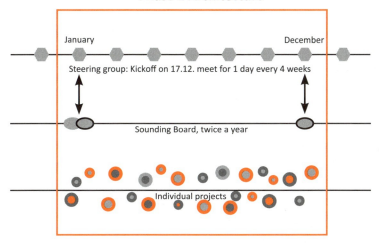

On the level of content, main emphases are determined in an initial workshop based on the basic model "Strategy – Structure – Culture", in which filtering out and prioritizing the essential projects from the abundance of proposals proves particularly challenging. This is accomplished in two loops. The project are decided upon on the basis of a "filter model". The first filter is the "Strategy Fit", the strategic value of the respective project. The next filter is the "Resource Fit", i.e., feasibility in relation to available personnel resources. The third filter is the "Cost Benefit Fit", the project's budgetary soundness based on an investment calculation. The fourth and final "fit" is the temporal prioritization of the individual projects.

Each member of the steering group leads one project, meaning that responsibility is shared very broadly among the employees. Over 80% of the projects contribute to the main direction of impact: working more closely with the Internet. This initial phase is highly energy-charged and constructive. A spirit of buoyant optimism arises, and feedback from the individual projects is very encouraging.

The first four steering group meetings – held over a whole day on a monthly basis –focus on the project reports, but also on the implications of the project results for the overall development process. Another component of these meetings is self-reflection, with steering group members providing personal feedback regarding their own strengths and weaknesses as managers and their expectations of the others. The managing directors participate in all of these meetings. This requires some persuasion, but in the end they arrive at the conclusion that they cannot "delegate" this very fundamental corporate change. Their participation serves to successfully convey the seriousness of the present change project: There have already been numerous, similar initiatives in the past, but this time, the directors' consistent participation ensures the project's lasting strategic priority.

The crowning achievement of the first half-year is the meeting of the Sounding Board with the participation of all employees. During preparations for this event, the concern arises that operations would come to a standstill if all employees were to attend, leading to the decision to arrange the Sounding Board in two sessions. The setting and structure of this large-scale event are geared toward a high level of interaction. To start with, all participants briefly share their points of view and expectations in groups. Then, after an introductory lecture and a discussion, a "trade fair" is simulated, in which all projects display their activities in the marketplace, and the employees wander from one stand to another. Participation is enthusiastic, and commitment is very high. The responses, compiled afterwards in a big exhibition, are quite positive. This is the first event of its kind in the company, and sets an impressive example for how collective change energy can be boosted by large-scale events.

The next major event is an employee outing, which is also used as an occasion to address further collective development on an emotional level.

Project lifeline
These highs are followed in the autumn by a few lows. A number of incidents indicate that some employees are hanging back in a cautious, wait and see position. The planning process for the following year turns out to be a negative low point. Although this is not an "official" part of the project, it does have an impact on the steering team, as all of its members are affected. In addition, new strategic concerns arise at this time that make high demands on the managing directors' attention. The Supervisory Board is re-commissioned, and the discussion of potential investments or international collaborations is charged with turmoil.

Since these topics have not yet been communicated widely at this early stage, but nevertheless demand a great deal of management's energy, the impression arises that they have "retreated to the ivory tower" or are no longer commited to the steering group's issues and projects. In a steering group meeting, it becomes very clear that the speed and priorities of the team of managing directors and the rest of the group are widely divergent. An outsourcing project affecting the IT department sets off further irritation. Two members leave the steering group, as they now belong to another company.

> *Due to the great number of projects, discussions of operative matters predominate in the steering group. More and more, the "overall direction" fades from view: The participants are aware that several overriding strategic projects are running in the background. One of these projects concerns hiving-off of the largest part of the company, but as this cannot be discussed openly, it leads to many feeling that they have lost their connection to the company's "vital nerve". Accordingly, attentiveness for the overall process declines.*

In a further meeting of the steering group, a new organizational chart is presented, leading to another major irritation: some of the members have not been designated for managerial functions, which is taken in with much ambivalence and interpreted by the responsible personnel manager in hindsight as a very negative personal experience.

In a critical vein, one could also say that the evaluation of the progress of projects was overly positive in the initial phase, making it inevitable that this initial evaluation had to be revised for several projects at a later point.

The second Sounding Board and an important workshop
The last phase of the first year is marked by a second Sounding Board, to which the majority of employees are invited. This Sounding Board is once again awaited with suspense, expectations naturally running very high due to the success of the first. On the whole, this event is also rated as successful. One important feature is a Q&A session with the managing director conducted in the form of a hearing (see the chapter "Interventions" for details on its design), which is marked by very open communication about pending projects and the overall situation. The project market is attended with interest, but also shows that such events can suffer from inflation – the attraction of absolute novelty is gone.

The highlight of the second half-year is a workshop dealing with the fusion and hiving-off of two business areas. The background: The whole company is organized and structured along traditional lines as an association. However, in order to make international investments possible, it is now necessary to consolidate and spin off individual areas as partnerships. Naturally, this means a shift in dynamics, requiring a new clarification of interfaces and processes and the development of a new identity. Rumors – and also fears – arise to the effect that there is a sellout in the offing and that the spin-off and subsequent sale of this section is necessary in order to secure the enterprise as a whole. Job security and relative stability had been the organization's mainstream values up to now, which explains the high level of irritation. On the first day of the workshop, the managing directors present the general conditions and the basic strategy, followed by a discussion. This takes place in a very open atmosphere, which raises the confidence of those involved and creates a constructive mood. On the second day, in the absence of the managing directors, the structure and main contents of the project are discussed. The discussion crystallizes around working out an overall vision for the change. It becomes clear that the spin-offs, which are proceeding according to a relatively clear vision, are putting pressure on the remaining parts of the business to redefine their goals as well, i.e., the question of elaborating a vision to guide these other areas – or all employees of the company – arises. This is presented in short role plays prepared by the participants. Each group presents a "worst case" and a "best case" scenario.

In this way, the participants give expression to underlying fears and misgivings, and identify opportunities and potentials offered by the new constellation. Individual personal perspectives become comprehensible and it becomes possible to discuss them constructively.

Conclusion and outlook

The first phase of this change process ends with a concluding workshop. The members of the steering group are asked to bring along an object that symbolizes the change process. Together, the participants present and discuss the life history of the project, and a very congruent outlook on the process emerges.

The next phase, after a year characterized by projects, is dedicated to tackling structural changes, increasingly aligning all product divisions to e-business, and developing a consistent strategy for all areas. On our change map, this project now occupies the position of corporate renewal.

The architecture of the second phase is adapted accordingly, as illustrated by the following overview:

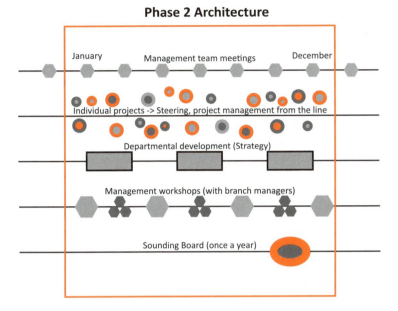

Lessons learned

In this case, the hard cuts consisted mainly of structural changes – i.e., the outsourcing of part of the IT section and the spin-off of two central business areas.

In retrospect, one can say on a critical note that while the first spin-off was thoroughly and meticulously planned, its implementation was accompanied by a great deal of commotion and emotional upheaval throughout the organization. Based on this experience, the second spin-off process was drafted differently, and was more inclusive of the employees.

The following can be learned from this case study:
- In the case of spin-offs (according to strategic clarifications), personnel decisions (*Who will stay with the company? Who will leave and needs to look for a new job?*) must be given maximum priority. Lengthy decision-making periods can cause a severe decline in productivity.

- Large-scale events with the participation of all employees are a particularly efficient lever for shaping processes if they make room not only for the discussion of substance and structure, but also for expressing emotions.
- Executive management plays a pivotal role by providing the employees with a means of orientation. Physical presence is one of the most important responsibilities in phases of radical upheaval.

In terms of the targeted "new growth", the project proved to be a complete success. From the structural perspective, this was achieved by means of a project portfolio that compiled and brought into focus the most important innovation projects. In the course of the project's implementation it became possible to integrate and develop numerous innovative aspects.

The substantive goal of the change, the development of Internet products, was also achieved, strengthening and expanding the company's market position in Austria. The organization is now one of the largest New Economy or Internet companies.

In this respect, the following lessons can be learned from this case study:
- Projects are a suitable means of rousing an organization from its "Sleeping Beauty" state if this is achieved within the framework of a comprehensive program.
- The participation of "young" executives or key individuals who represent the company's future is especially important. This unsettles the established order and provides an important impetus for development. We feel that competition among project managers was an essential success factor.
- How the selection process for projects is carried out is crucial. If strategic priorities are clearly demonstrated in the planning and prioritization of the projects, this can lay the foundations for a new phase in the enterprise's overall development.
- However, project work only represents a first step. After this "upheaval", focus must shift to anchoring new growth in the line.

Overall steering
The commitment and presence of the managing directors in the main steering groups and large-scale events is a critical success factor.

In this respect, the following lessons can be learned from this case study:

In most cases, it cannot be taken for granted that managing directors participate in every important event. For the employees, however, this is one of the strongest signals for the importance of the process and the performance of all individuals. For the responsible project authorities, this means: *"Stay firm and insist on participation – it pays off!"*

This aspect can be carried even further by establishing projects in which managing directors actively participate (and do not merely "delegate").

CASE III:

Live and let die
Alexander Doujak

Introduction
An Austria based enterprise, the world market leader in its product segment, came under immense pressure to streamline and reorganize due to declining world market prices: the currencies of its main competitors experienced a devaluation of over 20%. The company rose to the challenge and went public. Since then, the group has pursued an international growth strategy.

The initial situation
The following points briefly summarize the initial situation in terms of project management:

- Project management is a familiar instrument in the enterprise
- There are many projects in the individual corporate divisions
- Concentration on individual projects is prevalent
- Connection to the overall corporate strategy is secondary
- There is a lack of organized debate covering all projects in the executive committees
- Due to fierce competition, there is a high degree of pressure for action

In concrete terms, project portfolios are the obvious instrument for implementing an "*Un:balanced Transformation*". However, "normal" project management – focused on operations – will not suffice for this. The situation calls for strategic management thinking and action.

The problem is identified in an initial workshop with the steering group, in which all of the boards and the managing directors of the individual companies are represented. This group works out the objectives for a comprehensive project portfolio. The basic tenor is: "*We need to streamline, but at the same time create the conditions for new growth. This will require conducting more projects and coordinating them accordingly."*

In this company, the integration of streamlining and growth does not run as an additional project, but is rather undertaken by means of changes in the controlling of the project portfolio. A new communication architecture is established: "Market circles" to discuss projects that move internationalization forward, Project Planning Committee (PPC) circles for product innovation projects, and a "quality offensive", which concentrates on projects to increase productivity. This enables a periodic alignment of projects and direct communication between project leaders and the relevant decision-makers. The newly conceived management of the project portfolio proves to be an essential means of implementing the "*Un:balanced Transformation*".

An important precondition for this is that this project portfolio really includes all strategically important company activities, in contrast to a "normal" one which in practice usually only involves individual aspects. The important point is that the portfolio be directly connected with the formulation and implementation of corporate strategy. Only if the board and the managing directors continually reexamine this connection (which generally is not the case), can one speak of a project portfolio in the sense of an "*Un:balanced Transformation*".

The objectives
In light of the above considerations, the objectives are as follows:
- The project portfolio is closely linked with the groups' strategic thrust. The projects are an essential component of strategy implementation. This becomes all the more important as seemingly contradictory projects emerge, since both directions of impact – streamlining *and* growth – are simultaneously implemented in "*Un:balanced Transformation*".
- The individual projects work independently towards set goals on the basis of a defined mandate, coordinated in the steering group.
- The intense focus on one individual project is supplemented with an overall view – "overall" can relate to the entirety of corporate projects or to specific areas (strategic business units or corporate processes such as innovation, technical value creation, marketing or supportive processes).
- Establishing rigid structures between the individual projects – which would question their autonomy and limit the organization's versatility – is *not* an objective.

- Since development and streamlining are simultaneous goals, both aspects need to be integrated in the projects (e.g., for production relocation projects), and determine the coordination of projects (e.g., streamlining projects and projects concerning corporate culture).

These objectives require going beyond conventional multi-project structures. As one executive director described it: *"We want an internal project market, not a planned economy. This means a balancing act between the interests of the overall enterprise and those of the individual projects."*

The structure of the project portfolio

Concretely, a distinction is made between a comprehensive portfolio and the portfolios of individual strategic business segments. This maintains the manageability of the overall system while at the same time not undermining the autonomy of the business segments in their "own" domain. Each of the comprehensive projects are based in one of the business areas which assumes the official control in this case. A few projects are managed by the board (e.g., IPO).

Instruments applied for the presentation of project portfolios

As mentioned above, a network is often not perceived as such. This means that an initial task is making the individual projects visible, in order to set them in relation to each other. This sounds easy in theory, but in practice often means tedious analysis and exigent prioritizing. Often, a first analysis reveals an astronomical number of projects – perhaps 100 or more.

This analysis provides an overall picture of all existing projects in the company, enabling the identification of similarities and differences – the basis for recognizing potential synergies or conflicts. Ideally, the coordination of the projects is decided in an event at which all important participants (clients/project leaders) are represented.

- **Project lists, project databases**

  For presentation purposes, it may be useful at first to simply list all projects and group them according to various criteria. As things progress, these lists can be upgraded to a database accessible to employees. In our case, this means:

Project number	Name	Project leader/client/ management	Responsible strategic business segment	Objectives	Contribution to TOP 1–5	Project type

Listing the projects

A few basic principles, not to be taken for granted in practice:
- The projects should be successively numbered to enable systematic filing.
- The project name should be included in the mandate to prevent single projects running under different names in the company.
- The project managers, those assigning the projects internally and the steering committee members should be appointed according to a fixed, standard organizational procedure.
- Since a strategic business segment is in charge of most projects, this needs to be specified.
- The objectives should be determined based on the project task and remain stable – unless the steering group decides otherwise in special cases.
- The individual projects support the implementation of strategic objectives: This connection must be clearly defined.

Clustering of projects

Building on the initial step of simply listing individual projects and classifying them according to various criteria, one can, in a next step, filter out relevant similarities and differences and compile these into groups or clusters.

A graphic presentation of these groups gives a clearer picture of the overall analysis. This bundling of projects into groups is particularly useful for identifying common elements that can provide a basis for coupling projects "of the same kind". Since the groups overlap and several projects constitute subsets of various groups, different levels of common interest can be derived from this overview. The following diagram clusters projects according to strategic TOP objectives for one year: 1 = Customer orientation; 2 = Development of corporate culture; 3 = Result orientation; 4 = Kickoff IPO; 5 = Improve communication.

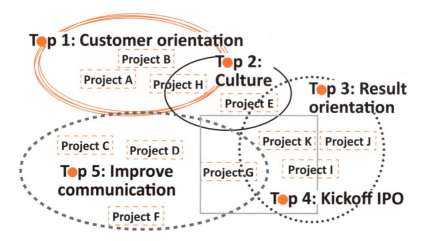

Project portfolios

Drawing up project portfolios, in which the individual projects are brought into relation to each other, is an important tool for presenting projects and analyzing the whole spectrum of projects. This facilitates the prioritizing of projects and determining the allocation of resources, management modalities and the selection of a project manager. Three examples for portfolio presentation are as follows:

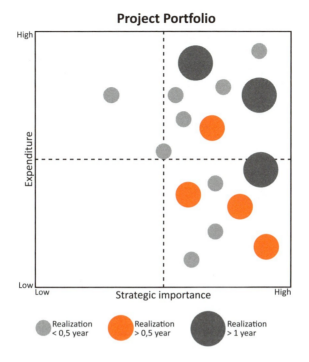

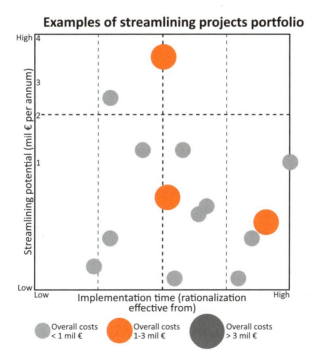

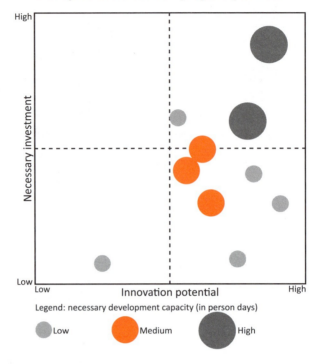

Arrangement in phases

A further relevant aspect in the analysis of points in common and differences is the timing of projects in terms of project phases. This applies primarily to repetitive projects, for which a clear phase outline can be standardized. For instance, a possible phase outline of research and development projects would be classification into: "start", "milestones 1–4" and "finish".

Analysis of dependencies

After the project network has been made visible with the help of various tools, it becomes necessary to examine the relationships between the individual projects. Criteria need to be defined for evaluating these relationships. This is done by examining the levels on which the projects interlink.

Levels of coupling

The analysis of dependencies can also rely on differentiation and a listing of factual, social and temporal levels.

This listing can be understood as a checklist for the analysis of potential dependencies. It can record qualitative information on relationships between individual projects, which, when translated into a diagram, results in specific patterns.

Level of coupling	Example
Scope dimension Strategies	Targets Tasks Resources Methods …
Social dimension	Organization Project type Environments …

Strategic controlling

The conventional concept of multi-project management treats controlling primarily as the central administration and control of project data and information.

The controlling approach presented here is geared less towards central control and more towards building relationships between individual projects and organizing (communication) spaces for their overall coordination – as shown in the illustration of communication architecture at the beginning of this case study.

Management of couplings

The methods described in the previous section serve to identify reciprocal influences between projects and potential for dependencies. This also brings potential synergies and conflicts to light. Comparing this potential with the actual coupling of projects raises the question of which projects should be coupled more intensely – and where more slack would be advisable.

For instance, it may be functional to link two projects more closely via a common infrastructure or staff pools if their objectives complement each other, since merely coupling via common defined objectives would be too weak to have a coordinating effect. In the following, we would like to show a few examples that could serve as possible starting points for project coupling. In sum: Strategic controlling means the establishment of structures and relationships between projects.

Examples for project couplings

Dimension	Examples for project interlinking
Scope Dimension	**Objectives/Strategies** – Formulate same or complementary strategies, objectives – Make success criteria interdependent **Tasks** – Define same/complementary task area – Make results interdependent **Resources** – Employ same/complementary know-how (management, technology) – Establish mutual capital flow – Utilization of the same infrastructure – Common offices, workspaces – Personnel flow (e.g., vocational training in various projects) **Methods** – Same documentation structure/standards – Software – Planning methods – Controlling methods
Social Dimension	**Organization** – Allocate projects in the same organizational area – Multiple responsibilities – Interdependent personnel appraisal, bonus systems – Establish communication structures, same report and control paths **Environments** – Coordinate conjoint customer communication – Coordinate conjoint supplier communication – Further conjoint communication with external environments
Temporal Dimension	– Define start, end, milestone and permanent dependencies

Organizational integration

The strategic coordination of projects is best done within the framework of overall communication structures, also often called Steering Committees. Their competencies include:

- Assigning individual projects (definition and conclusion/termination, specification of fundamental strategies, strategic controlling)
- Acting as the "final authority" for regulating the relationships between individual projects (determination of priorities, decision-making in conflicts, decisions on project coupling)

Hierarchical classification depends on the projects' size or scope. If a project relates to the company as a whole, it should be managed at the top level. Sector-specific networks can also be situated in individual functional areas, such as strategic business fields or functional areas such as marketing or engineering. In the example described here, control lies with the central management team, in which all board and managing directors and the main functional areas of the group are represented.

Lessons learned

Improved management of the project portfolio leads to better allocation of scarce resources and increases the efficiency of necessary short-term measures towards overcoming a current crisis. It also reinforces the corporation's strategic orientation and stabilizes the situation by having the line move the change forward itself, instead of setting up a separate change architecture. In this case, the corporate crisis was overcome, the corporation successfully went public one record year followed the other.

Most important of all might be the management capability of how to manage the corporation in tough times.

Steering groups

Lessons learned for hard cuts/new growth:
- **Anchoring lasting change in line management:**

  In order to initiate a change process with hard cuts and new growth, a specially constituted change team is not absolutely necessary. Sometimes success can depend much more on anchoring the process in line management from the beginning. A comprehensive project portfolio is an essential resource for implementing "*Un:balanced Transformation*".

- **Work on hard cuts and new growth simultaneously:**

  Even in times of economic hardship, it is important to initiate growth projects and not focus only on streamlining. In this case study, procurement and production costs in the core business needed to be cut – by means of factory closures and "go east" relocations, while simultaneously, new investments had to be made – in new products and internationalization steps.

- **Implement consistently:**

    It is important to maintain continuity in handling the project portfolio (in the beginning, all projects are attractive, up to the point where it becomes clear that resources are scarce, things are not running as expected, etc.)
- **Involve managerial staff:** For top management this means …
    - … taking enough time for this steering task – sending a clear signal about how important it really is – and remaining available to participate in the negotiations that become necessary time and again
    - … keeping an eye on the various requirements of streamlining projects (Where is the most potential for quick streamlining?) and growth projects (Where is the highest potential for growth and innovation? Do we have the resources to allow innovation to "mature"?).
    - … remembering that the big picture needs be kept in sight at all times (individual projects often absorb all of the sponsor's attention).
    - … providing back-up support to the project managers and being a living example of reliability and consistency in dealing with information, decisions, etc.
    - … involving themselves in the big picture (even if a project is not running in their particular business segment). This is often very hard to enforce, as it contradicts the logic of line responsibility.

Corporate development is more of a jungle expedition than a straight one-way street!

> **CASE IV:**
>
> **An unlikely couple?**
> **Technical consulting and systemic consulting**
> **in the project:**
> **"Old masters on new paths"**
> Barbara Heitger
>
> *"We are the old masters"* or *"We are the company's high-end manufacturer"*: This is how the company – let's call it "Meister Inc." (*"Meister": German term for certified expert craftsman*) – described itself in its search for an external consultant for its project of radical repositioning. In the following, we will describe the phases of this repositioning from its conception to its implementation: its architecture, its development and the assumptions and hypotheses on which we based our interventions. A special feature of this project was the integration of technical expert and systemic consulting.

The initial situation

Meister Inc., a medium-sized enterprise in a corporate group, is specialized in making customized versions of machinery developed and produced by the corporate group. No matter what wishes clients may have for machinery specifications that deviate from serial productions, the employees of Meister Inc. are able to fulfill them. They deliver top quality precision work, which for them is a matter of great pride. Everyone is familiar with the product in its entire complexity. However, the base line of customization and small series production for special machines is creating problems in profit performance. Meister Inc.'s corporate group division is operating in the red, and has to initiate a radical turnaround program – cost cutting, strategic repositioning and business process redesign. Although the marginal losses of Meister Inc. do not play a great role in the corporate group, it, too, feels the pressure to change. Throughout the whole corporate group, the profit goals and consistent strategy implementation set by the new executive board are being taken seriously as pivotal criteria of success. The management of Meister Inc. has recognized the necessity for change and developed a vision and a strategy with the following emphases:

- Focus on small series production of special machinery instead of customized single-order production
- Distinct profit improvement through sales growth and higher productivity (via redesign of selected core processes)
- Utilization of its core competencies in construction, manufacturing and assembly of special machinery for the development, production and marketing of small series (foster entrepreneurial and sales orientation)

All three strategic directions of impact are to be integrated in one change initiative. Two past attempts to start such a project have failed to fulfill the management's expectations. The current project tender highlights the importance of consultants being able to cover the technical and methodical dimensions (business process redesign and optimization: BPO) as well as implementation-oriented change consulting (integration of strategy, organizational and people orientation in one overall process).

This is the essential information we receive from our first telephone conversation with the managing director. He also points out that the management team of the business is itself in a generational change, that the development of a special machine for small series production is near completion, and that the corporate group has repeatedly questioned Meister Inc.'s viability in the past, without, however, having drawn any consequences – the company has seen only minimal change in the past years. The CEO defines himself as our client and, as project manager, the responsible authority for controlling, HR and organization, being member of the board as well.

Our initial hypotheses as consultants
- Technical and change management competencies need to be distinguished and combined in this project. For this reason, I call in a co-operation partner as BPO expert: although primarily a technical consultant, he is also very interested in systemic work.
- The planned project comprises hard cuts (cost reduction, possible staff downsizing, loss of old "master identity" by changing to series production, fewer resources in development and construction, etc.) and new growth – both quantitative and qualitative: generational handover, greater turnover and annual production, innovations through series production in know-how, structures, processes, stronger sales & market orientation.

- The contradictory dynamics of these change objectives and the impending generational change make for great challenges for executive management, both in initiating and controlling changes, and in undergoing radical changes themselves.
- At the same time, the variety and difficulty of the objectives are so high that prioritization and focusing seem urgently necessary.
- This is why it is important to elicit executive management's perspectives and priorities for the change in the next step in order to develop a tailor-made offer.
- In terms of process, it is important for our client to already experience our working methods in the acquisition phase, enabling us to test whether and how co-operation in the interaction of technical and process consultation with Meister Inc. can best succeed.

In order to do this, we propose working in tandem (BPO and change management consultant) with the the board of management (five people, including the CEO as client and project manager) for one half day – for a retroactive fee in the event of subsequent co-operation, and otherwise without costs for Meister Inc.

The project architecture

The initial discussion – preliminary phase and acquisition
After brief introductory rounds and clarification of objectives and framework, we ask every member of the management to mark their answers to the following two questions on this matrix:
- How will our environment (market, corporate group, etc.) change in the next 2–5 years? evolutionarily to radically (y-axis)
- In order to ensure future success, how will Meister Inc. have to develop? evolutionarily to radically (x-axis)

Afterwards, we interview each board member, asking systemic questions about the way they positioned their answers (circular questioning, resource-oriented, defining differences). The others listen. We then briefly withdraw in order to propose an initial provisional diagnosis and a rough idea of the objectives, architecture and milestones of the change program. We discuss the pros and contras with the management, and develop our draft programme further on the basis of this exchange.

This diagnosis and the discussion of our initial draft program form the basis for the offer that we now submit. A short time later we are awarded the assignment.

Hypotheses regarding the preliminary phase – why this way and not another?
Our hunches about why the client decides in favor of co-operation with us are:
- We have productively visualized the differences and agreements in the management's views on market development.
- As a result of the setting, the otherwise more operatively oriented team reaches more clarity on change objectives, the necessity to prioritize, as well as the change processes' success and risk potentials.
- We have demonstrated our impartiality as consultants and as well our technical competence (BPO expertise).
- The setting establishes the client system, the consultant system and the common working system, so that an initial successful co-operation is experienced.
- We propose "prioritizing objectives and generating commitment" as a project gateway. This implies that we are aware that BPO and the introduction of series production are not possible without middle management and the "practical experts" of everyday business, and this was clearly recognized by management.

The preliminary objectives for the change project are:
Redesign of the two or three core processes (standardization, cost cutting) where optimization will yield the most results – including piloting, design and introduction

Development of a sound corporate identity as a way of living the new strategy (departure from the "old masters" idea as core identity, commitment to small series production)

Winning the acceptance and commitment of the executive staff in their role as driving force behind the broad implementation of hard cuts and new growth; building up expertise and a common understanding of the change process

Identifying change priorities and strengths that should be preserved (protection from too much change)

Phase one: prioritizing and commitment
The architectural elements in this phase are:

Work with the board of management, particularly on the following topics:
- Prioritize strategy objectives
- Develop stakeholder analysis for strategy implementation
- Change management in terms of hard cuts (streamlining, possible staff downsizing and loss of the "old masters" identity) and new growth (series production, new product and repositioning of distribution and development) – success factors
- Develop a common understanding as to how management will steer the change process – particularly in dealing with "hot potatoes" (staff downsizing, changeover to small series production)
- What do members of the board expect from each other in this venture?
- What personal outlooks – both positive and skeptical – do they share concerning this change? How have they mastered similar changes in their lives so far? (The aim of working through these points is to strengthen the management as a team in their pioneer role, preparing them to deal productively with questions and reactions from their managers and employees.)
- Co-operation and contracts with us as consultants (respective functions of specialist and systemic consultants)
- Input regarding the methodology of business process redesign
- Strategies and major topics for the communication with the corporate board/the supervisory board and management staff

In this phase, we work with the management in two one-day workshops that lay the foundation for further work, as their previous emphasis was strongly division-orientated and focused more on the control of operative daily business.

Further architectural elements in this phase are:
A communication event with all managers about the reasons for the change, its objectives and architecture

Diagnosis:
We conduct qualitative individual and group interviews with (approx. 15) representatives of the involved divisions and levels in order to acquire an understanding of the company's "reality constructions" regarding both themselves and their market and shareholders. Explicitly taking stock of the status quo regarding strategy, leadership, organization and corporate culture in this way helps to accelerate the process of reorientation and allows pros and contras to become visible as early on as possible.

The diagnosis reveals the following central observations and concerns:
- We are going through a phase of upheaval – transition from the status of "old masters" to an uncertain future – with anxiety, hopes and a great need for orientation.
- We are uncertain about what our leverage and leeway in the corporation is, and how our success will be measured (customer retention via special machinery as sales promotion for customers of large-scale standard machinery orders **or** profitable own business in small production series). This means that there is a need for strategy clarification with the parent company.
- We bundle know-how and competencies in a way that is unique in the corporation; we master a high level of technical complexity.
- We need more contact with our end customers and the market if we are to intensify production in small series.
- Steering through informal networks provides a high degree of flexibility, but less transparency concerning processes and figures. If small series production is to work, stable processes, cross-functional co-operation and a different management style are required (generational change from a patriarchal style of management to more self-control and teamwork).
- Several business processes need redesign.

"Goal-setting and commitment" workshop
All interviewees (supervisors and employees from sales, development, production and organization) and the management (a total of approx. 30 people) participate in this workshop. Reflecting on the communicated results of the inter-

views, the participants work in groups and prioritize topics that, from their point of view, need to be addressed so that the strategy can be implemented.

Based on the results of these first working groups, management defines the mandates of a further round of working groups in the presence of all participants. These are tasked to work out a concrete vision of the future: What needs to be changed, what should be kept, what opportunities and pitfalls need to be anticipated and how success can be qualitatively and quantitatively measured.

The results are briefly presented in a plenary meeting and commented, elaborated and developed further in a self-organized "topic market".

Groups representing a cross-section of the working groups "wander the market", visiting each topic board. The executive management works in a group of its own.

This setting involves everyone collectively (the participants experience cross-sector collaboration), and also individually (each participant contributes to each topic).

The essential links among topics become clearer. Having established this basis, we shift the focus from company and strategy implementation to the individual, and propose working in small coaching groups on the question of what "costs and gains" the planned changes are likely to bring for each individual. The third step focuses on the respective functions: In a "negotiation market" the participants are grouped according to divisions (development, sales, production and internal service provider) and work out which contributions to the change process are definitely expected of them, what their stand on this is, and what their needs are. The exchange leads to reciprocal confirmation, but also to clarification or reorientation of expectations on all sides.

In the concluding sequence, the CEO (as initiator and client) summarizes his understanding of the workshop results: which change objectives were confirmed, prioritized, put into concrete terms, or questioned in the workshop. In a Q&A sequence, the participants and the management clarify the next steps: milestones, expectations of each other and mode of communication within the corporation.

- Immediately afterwards, there is **a prioritization and commitment workshop with the management** that has the following agenda:
    - Defining the next loop in strategy development (prioritization, setting demanding but realistic objectives)
    - Deciding on which business processes are to be developed (greatest value creation and feasibility)
    - Preparing a rough draft of core projects and, in particular, planning the next phase

We address these topics by linking the results of the goal-setting workshop with the management's perspective on one hand and our own, external perspective on the other (change management and BPO expertise).

Reflections on the prioritization and commitment phase
The triad "work with the management – interviews/diagnosis – goal-setting workshop" clearly succeeds in winning over experts, internal service providers and managers for the change, and developing a common "sense of urgency" beyond the confines of daily business and one's own division. Interactive work enables the management community to have a direct experience of what the targeted management culture will be like (workshop as a rehearsal stage for the future change) and promotes networking, while also exposing uncertainties and potential losses – thereby pinpointing management issues that will have to be dealt with in the future. We do not, however, succeed in persuading management to decide not only on three business processes in the handling of orders and production for the BPO, but also to include the sales process, which would address the relation to the corporation as a further issue – as the corporation is actually Meister Inc.'s "client", being the sales channel that takes care of the contact to end customers.

The interaction between technical and systemic process consulting has already been established in this phase. The client finds the differentiation between content-related expert inputs and systemic process interventions for architecture and workshop designs to be clear and constructive. However, there is some dispute among the consultants, particularly on the question of how much of the client's workload we should relieve them of by means of input, pre-processing work or finished concepts, and how much self-control and self-development we should enforce – a very interesting and challenging process for both of us, as the integrated coupling of these two functions is an innovative approach. In this phase, we find it essential that, in addition to goal-setting and commitment, the different levels of change become felt: the strategy as the company's future course, the departments (organization and processes), and the individuals. And the first phase was about developing a common understanding regarding success factors for sustainable change and key people to implement it. This does not mean reaching ultimate clarifications, but rather providing initial orientation: inciting and promoting exploration and experimentation in the direction of self-organization for change. This is the central function of the goal-setting workshop in phase one.

Phases two and three: development of prototypes and pilot projects for the new business processes

Planning the workshop with the management
At this point in the project, the company's order situation radically deteriorates. This means that the interaction between "securing daily business/crisis management" and the concretization of the second project phase needs to be clarified in fine-tuning work, first with the client and project manager, and then with the entire management. The pros and contras of continuing the project are the first issue on the agenda, and overall crisis management strategies for business management and then for each department manager are determined.

Only then are "the head and the heart" free for the concretization of the second phase, which starts with input and discussion of methodology, phases, capacities and BPO result criteria.

Processes selected for BPO are stipulated as success criteria and milestones, and the architecture for the second phase is decided upon. We propose variants for processes and change architecture, each with pros and contras, and present our reflections on our work, followed by managers presenting their previously developed "program". These internal and external views of the matter are brought together to produce the following:

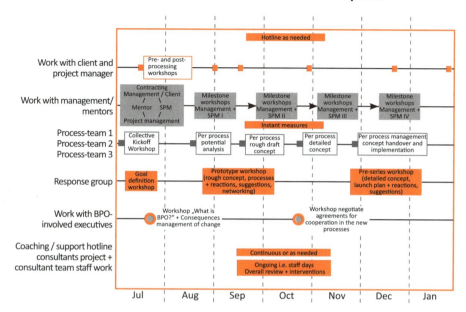

Client functions

(CEO or management board, including project management)

- They make project & milestone decisions.
- They initiate the project.
- They provide the project with strategic alignment, i.e., general objective guidelines.
- They determine the extent and rank the importance of the project in the context of both: business situation and other responsibilities of the company and its employees.
- They decide which resources are available for project implementation.
- They make the decisions affecting external consultant support.
- They visualize project headway and results at regular intervals.
- They involve themselves in the project in their management and role model functions.

"Every member of the management board assumed a mentor function for a subproject."

Functions of mentors

Every management member assumes a mentor function for a subproject or process team, with the exception of the CEO and the general project manager.

- Catalyst function:
  Initiating new ideas, starting new initiatives, encouraging collaboration
- Addressee function:
  Contact point and contact partner for all questions, decisions and consequential problems arising from the respective business process
- Monitor function:
  Taking on, depicting and discussing process-specific debates, actions and decisions in the company in awareness of necessary steps to take
- Management function:
  Preparing and making necessary decisions regarding the process with their colleagues in management, and ensuring their operative implementation
- Controlling function:
  Installing feedback loops in the process and tracking the ongoing change progress: Where it's running smoothly, where problems are arising and how these can be dealt with
- Internal marketing & communication

Functions of the response group

As far as possible, all important trends, structures, stakeholders and differences in the enterprise are represented by key individuals in the response group; it comprises all executive staff and important key players but also workers and front line employees. Its functions are:

- Response and sounding to the work of the process team and management
- Feedback of perceptions of the project from each respective position
- Feedback on project implementation and progress in the individual sectors
- Indication of previous omissions/failures or the need for additional initiatives
- Multiplier function in the company
- Advice and suggestions for client/management, project manager and process teams

Functions of project management

Project management is responsible for the leadership and control of strategic and operative project business and administration (objectives/quality, resources/costs, deadlines). This does not mean that project management carries out the tasks that arise, but that it is accountable for their accomplishment within the set timeframe and with the expected high standard of quality. It executes the decisions and assignments of management with the necessary steps and initiatives. Project management and consultants work together in close co-operation.

Sub-project managers (SPM) and process teams

- The sub-project managers are "contractual partners" with management in the concretization of their project assignment and in the control milestones. They lead the process teams.
- The process teams bear responsibility for the analysis of actual processes and the rough draft of redesigns (prototype for the new business process = Milestone 1). Taking account of ideas coming from the response group and feedback from management, they are responsible for conceptual fine-tuning and testing (piloting the new business process = Milestone 2).

Role and function of the external consultants

We assume responsibility for:

- Technical and methodological input on BPO and change management topics
- Integration of strategic, organizational and personal perspectives
- Implementing success factors for hard cuts and new growth
- Training and methods for the analysis and redesign of business processes
- Setting new ideas in motion (catalyst function)
- Bringing in experience from different companies and sectors
- "Holding up a mirror" to the process (external view) and providing opportunities for reflection
- Addressing delicate, latent issues and dissolving obstacles to development
- Providing security and releasing energy (providing help for self-help, containment)
- Raising awareness for resources and strengths
- Creating space for emotions, working on personal issues

- Ensuring continuity and securing commitment, particularly in support of project manager and subproject managers
- Aligning change processes to the agreed objectives and controlling these at milestones (reviews)
- Providing vital content-related input (e.g., on the topics of corporate culture, corporate management/control, changes to the functions of senior management, organization, the concept of a learning organization, etc.)
- Design- and process know-how: project architecture, design configuration and moderation of meetings, workshops, large-scale events

We are not responsible for:
- Technical, content-related decisions
- Ongoing operative project management

Lessons learned

The architecture aims to anticipate the objectives of the change by requiring continual contracting between the management and the sub-projects (milestone workshops). The process teams work in offices next to the manufacturing area, enabling direct and immediate access to results and the status of discussions (taking advantage of the existent informal communication culture, high level of transparency). The focus on cross-sector and cross-level interaction and the intense integration of all management members as project managers or mentors ensure that everyone comes to grip with the new concepts and that these are well supported.

Our constant collaboration with the management board makes it possible to work on corporate identity, on the management of market turbulences and on issues arising from the change process as a "work in progress".

It is important for the process teams working on new processes as a "nucleus" for BPO aim for streamlining cost cutting and growth (integration!) simultaneously.

The response team is an important counterpart in the prototype and pilot product workshop. As a microcosm of the organization, it acts as a rehearsal stage for the pros and contras of newly configured processes. It tests concepts and pilot projects from the different departments and is a platform for negotiation markets, where future users provide input for practical use. This reveals chances and risks that the process teams often overlook, as their intense work on the subject lessens critical distance. The secret of success is to use support and resistance and skepticism as well to further develop, test and improve redesigned process drafts. While doing so, we develop the intervention "Evaluating pilot projects: check-up for further implementation" (see Chapter 9).

A crucial factor for the successful launching of the second and third phases is the meticulous staffing of process teams and team leaders. A further vital factor are the Contracting Workshops held with the management/mentors and the sub-project leaders. These focus not only on negotiating objectives, tasks, capacities and milestones of subprojects, but also on the question of impending staff reductions and how management will deal with these. This is of great importance for the subproject managers, who are able to express their fear of feeling like traitors, as their jobs involve streamlining measures that affect their colleagues and make them feel guilty.

Our technical consultant works intensely with the process teams alone, enabling them to work out individual steps on their own and pursue the ensuing implementation themselves (help for self-help).

The challenging timing – i.e., the fact that the different elements of the project architecture follow in quick succession – proves to be a substantial accelerator for the project, charting an "unspectacular" route to "streamlining, cost-cutting and new growth", and also establishing the maxim of "negotiating conflicts" in the company.

The interlinking of the elements encourages the taking of responsibility, openness for eventualities, a general atmosphere of progress and a feeling of being "on the road again". This generates more security and confidence, particularly because internal know-how is clearly perceived and utilized by the process teams. The newly developed processes prove more efficiency than what was foreseen in the objectives. The urge and necessity for more market contact and collaboration with the corporation towards further development of marketing and sales have yet to receive more attention, and now need to be pushed forward. In retrospect, it would have been desirable to involve the corporation or customer representatives from the beginning, so that this could have been accomplished at an earlier stage.

The combination of technical consulting, with its intense content-related involvement on the one hand, and systemic process consulting and project management integrating overall control (architecture and process interventions) on the other, required intense work in order to integrate the different basic assumptions (expert versus self-control interventions). We see this case as a pioneering venture that was rewarding for both the client and the consultants.

> **CASE V:**
>
> ## Growth and Renewal through Business Model Innovation
> *Marc Sniukas*
>
> Marc is a principal at Doujak Corporate Development. He can be reached at marc.sniukas@doujak.eu.

The initial situation

Our client, an Austrian group, currently employs around 4,300 people, with annual sales of about € 1 billion. The company operates in four strategic divisions and produces products for the construction and building material industry, the furniture industry, the sporting goods industry, the machinery and generator industry, the aircraft industry, as well as for the solar and energy technology industry.

The owner of this internationally oriented, family-run company wants to diversify and extend the various businesses. In order to finance the creation of new businesses and group divisions, the existing businesses need to double their EBIT margin. In this case, to reach both of these goals, Business Model Innovation becomes a critical matter for the company's corporate development process.

How to get started?

In order to start the process, the topic was introduced and a "Future Space" was held at the annual group meeting, at which the top 120 global managers from various divisions and business units come together. Future Space is a two-day long group event that aims to develop ideas that innovate existing business models and that establish entirely new businesses.

First, we worked together with the newly established Strategic Innovation Office to initiate a process for the Future Space and to formulate how the ideas would be put into practice after the event. The preparation process consisted of four steps (Figure 1):

1. The first step involved a two-hour meeting with the division and business line managers. During this meeting, we established a common view on the owner's objectives regarding how to diversify and raise profitability, and the purpose of the Future Space in this regard. We then outlined a framework to describe the existing business models and agreed on common definitions for a business model and Business Model Innovation.
2. Next, these managers, together with key stakeholders from their respective organizations, described currently used business models. Their discussions were structured and addressed the relevant questions through the assistance of a business model handbook, which we had written especially for this purpose. These descriptions were then sent to the Strategic Innovation Office for a quality check. One-to-one talks also helped to further sharpen the descriptions and clarity of the business models, as well as of the framework we had chosen.
3. In another two-hour meeting, the business unit managers presented their descriptions to the 1st line group managers, which was in fact a dry run for the Future Space. This meeting also helped to further refine and sharpen the descriptions.
4. In the fourth preparation step, the managers researched into key trends that impacted their business and addressed examples of innovative business models. These examples were used for inspiration during the Future Space.

Figure 1 – The Future Space Preparation Process

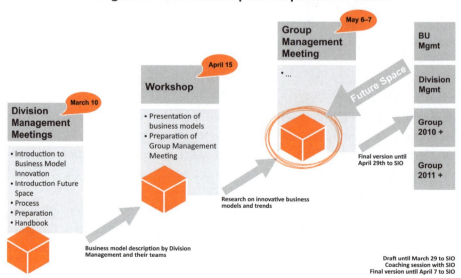

Alongside these discussions, we worked with the Strategic Innovation Office to plan the Future Space, define how ideas would be evaluated, and to reach a decision on which ideas to implement.

The Future Space itself consisted of two days that covered these three steps:
1. **Past & Present:** Employees described the history of the company, transition periods, and major events that had contributed to the development of the current business model presented by the group managers.
2. **Inspiration:** We provided inspiring inputs in keynote speeches and presentations and 16 market places demonstrating cases of innovative business models.
3. **Creation:** This step was guided by our Strategic Innovation Toolbox: A card deck presenting 25 ways of how to reinvent your business model. Teams of 4–5 participants were put together to brainstorm ideas for new business models or ways to innovate existing ones. Our toolbox – the card deck – provided inspiration and guidance for the discussions.

These were the outcomes of the Future Space:
- A total of 251 initial ideas
- 25 ideas for new businesses
- 18 ideas for social businesses (a specific request of the owner)
- 11 ideas for businesses and services that the holding could offer
- 120 ideas to further develop existing divisions and their business
- Business Model Innovation was established as a key objective for the entire group and the importance of this topic was evident to top management
- A common understanding of Business Model Innovation was established
- Discussing current business models of various units helped to further the overall understanding of the whole group

Keeping the momentum: The BMI process & organizational set-up
What to do with all these ideas? How can the selection and implementation be organized?

After the Future Space, the 251 ideas were further discussed in one-on-one meetings with the Strategic Innovation Manager and participants of the event. During this discussion, certain topics and themes emerged that were clustered into potential projects for new business models and new businesses at a group level.

At a half-day workshop the group executive board and the managing directors of the divisions decided upon which ideas to pursue further. Evaluations were conducted using a scorecard which included strategic, organizational, financial, and innovative metrics. Here are a couple of examples:

- On a scale from 0 to 10: How well does the idea fit into our strategy?
- What is the strategic purpose of the idea: Can it help to expand or defend a current business? Does it establish a new business that has already been identified? Or does it lay the foundations for a potential new business?
- Change need and change capabilities? Using the change map described in the second chapter "In the Jungle of Change Concepts".
- Resources and competencies: Which do we need? Which do we have? Which are the ones that need to be built?
- Financial aspects: revenue potential, cost, payback, etc.
- Innovation: How innovative is the new model? Is it one that is known to the company and to the industry? Is it known to the industry and new to the new company? Is it new to the company and to the industry? Is it entirely "new to the world"?
- etc.

Based on the assessment, five group projects were launched, each of which dealt with a specific cluster of the business model and the new business ideas.

For these five projects, we developed a common BMI stage-gate process (Table 1). This entire process not only guaranteed that all projects were managed in a similar manner, but also defined at what point and for which kind of decisions top management became involved.

	Setting the stage	Discovery	Development	Conversion	Commercialization
Description	Project set up. Define and describe project Formal GO	Discovery of opportunities Gain insights	Development of business model concepts Develop business model idea portfolio and evaluate ideas	Conversion of concepts into real-life Testing concepts and receiving market feedback	Implementation and launch Launch new business model

	Setting the stage	Discovery	Development	Conversion	Commercialization
Input	BMI idea	Project brief	Insights from discovery phase First ideas	Business concepts approved for test	Finished and tested Business Model
Tasks	1. Define and build team 2. Define purpose, scope and focus 3. Define goals and metrics 4. Define process and project plan	1. Company Assessment 2. Market Assessment 3. Industry Assessment 4. Future Trends	1. Develop BM portfolio 2. Evaluate BM portfolio	1. Strategy & Business planning 2. Customer tests 3. Technical feasibility 4. Implementation strategy 5. Organizational gap analysis	1. Implementation 2. Start-up/Incubation 3. Acceleration 4. Transition
Output	– Project brief – Project plan – Team is established – Common understanding about the project has been created	– Description AS IS – Description of opportunities – Description of first ideas – Update project planning	– BM idea/option portfolio – Evaluation of ideas – List of assumptions to be tested – Business case for each business model	– Final Business Model evaluation – Strategy is developed – Organizational structure is defined – Partners/Network are defined – Tested Business Model is profitable	

	Setting the stage	Discovery	Development	Conversion	Commercialization
Gates	– Team established – Resources have been committed	– Idea screening – Stop/Go decision – Is the idea still interesting? – Is it worth spending the resources for the next phase?	– Go to testing – Stop/Go decision – Justified to start conversion/testing/experimentation phase? – Budget decision	– Launch decision – Budget approval – Business model is profitable	Launch review (12 months) Business model review Business model optimization Integration into holding

Table 1 – A Business Model Innovation process

Step 1: Setting the stage

The teams for the various projects were chosen based on the experience and insights required from the different company groups. The group-wide projects engaged representatives of the various divisions and business units, including one manager from the Strategic Innovation Office in charge of facilitating the overall process, workshops, and team meetings.

Each team met for a one-day kickoff workshop to:
- Participate in team building exercises to define the roles and responsibilities of team members and how they wished to collaborate.
- Clarify the goals of their project. The general goal for each project was clear: to establish the potential for a new business. This goal was reinforced by the fact that the owner was present at the kickoff workshops. Aside from the overall goal, teams also defined their own goals for their project, which were agreed upon with the project sponsor (usually the owner).
- Define and assign tasks, set the required time frame, and set deadlines based on the overall process.

- Define the objectives the team wanted to reach. Just as with the project plan and deadline setting, these were agreed upon with the project sponsor and steering committee.

Step 2: Discovery
The main purpose of Step 2 was to seek and discover opportunities for new markets, new value propositions, and new ways of doing business. Project team members conducted desk and field research to further elaborate upon the current business model, the industry, the market, and future trends that could offer opportunities. For each of the work packages, we developed specific templates and tools to use. This common set of tools not only supported the teams, but also enabled the members to repeat the process. Furthermore, a set of common tools facilitated reporting, communication, and the comprehension of results. Workshops with key stakeholders, customers and suppliers were conducted to describe customer needs, current offerings and present customer experiences.

Step 3: Development and design
Detailed descriptions for various businesses and their business models were developed, based on the initial ideas and the additional insights gained during the second step. A business case was also developed for each model that included expected financial results. A crucial task in this step was to list all the underlying assumptions of the various business cases, in order to identify how they would be tested and what costs each test would involve. Based on this description, top management could then decide whether to enter the next stage or not and to what extent they were willing to invest.

Step 4: Conversion
The fourth step in the Business Model Innovation process is about putting ideas into practice and to transform them into innovations that can be used in the marketplace. The goal is not to fully launch the Business Model Innovations yet, but to test the ideas within a limited scope in order to determine whether customers like the innovation, accept it, and are willing to pay for it. The assumption list developed in Step 3 provides the basis for the tests in the market. Each of the assumptions needs to be tested in the market to obtain feedback and some real, hard data. The manner in which these tests are conducted, depend on the project and the business model. Currently the projects are at this stage.

Step 5: Commercialization
Once the various business models have been tested and adjusted, the businesses can be launched on a larger scale.

The overall architecture (Table 2) for the five group-wide projects also involves regular status updates and reports to the holding board. These regular updates address the progress of the group-wide projects and those of the individual divisions.

Aside from the group-wide projects, each division and business unit has taken on the responsibility to further develop and implement the ideas that had emerged during the Future Space. Group companies follow the same process and use the same tools. A Business Model Innovation Core Team was set up, in order to ensure learning and the sharing of experiences. This team consists of representatives of all group divisions and meets on a quarterly basis to discuss the progress that had been made and the best practices that were gained. The Core Team also decides on the tools and the support that is required from the Strategic Innovation Office.

In addition to the Core Team, a Strategic Innovation (SI) Team, with all the members of the Strategic Innovation Office and the consultants, meets on a regular basis to review the progress of the various projects and the extent of the overall Business Model Innovation. This team uses the Systemic Loop approach to review interventions, assess the current state of the Business Model Innovation within the company, and define the next interventions on several levels. The SI Team develops new tools based on its own judgment or the recommendations from the Core Team, the Project Teams, or the Board. Furthermore, the SI Team acts as the competence centre for Business Model Innovation within the group.

The SI Team and the Core Team also present the topic at group meetings and the annual innovation meeting. In 2011, the Business Model Innovation approach was presented at the innovation meeting consisting of a larger group of employees that were primarily working for R&D, which effectively introduced the concept to the wider organization.

	Nov 2010	Dez	Q1 2011	Q2	Q3	Q4	2012
SI Team	SI Team Meeting		SI Team Meeting	SI Team Meeting	SI Team Meeting	SI Team Meeting	
Core Team	Core Team Meeting Kickoff	Core Team Meeting	Core Team Meeting	Core Team Meeting	Core Team Meeting	Core Team Meeting	
Board Update			Division 1 Division 2	Division 3 Division 4	Division 1 Division 2	Division 3 Division 4	
Project 1	Setting the stage	Discovery				Development	Conversion
Project 2	Team Kickoff	Setting the stage	Discovery	Development		Conversion	Commercialization
Project 3	Hire Project Manager		Project Manager	Setting the stage	Discovery	Development	Conversion
Project 4	Hire Project Manager		Project Manager	Setting the stage	Discovery	Development	Conversion
Project 5	Hire Project Manager		Project Manager	Setting the stage	Discovery	Development	Conversion

Case V: Growth and Renewal through Business Model Innovation

Table 2 – BMI architecture

Figure 2 shows the overall organizational set up.

Figure 2 – Organizational Set-up

- Strategic Innovation Office
- Steering Committee
- Strategic Innovation Core Team
- Cross Division Project Teams
- Within Division Project Teams

Lessons learned

Although the project is not yet finished, a number of important matters can already be reflected upon:

- **Top management commitment is key:** Each project has a board member as its sponsor, and in three of the five projects the sponsor is the CEO and at the same time the owner. This ensures that the new approach receives the necessary attention and resources.
- **Education is crucial:** Before beginning to work with top management and project members, one should spend at least a day or two to train the members about the concept of Business Model Innovation. This is also valid for workshops with clients, suppliers, and other stakeholders, especially if the intention is to engage them in idea development and brainstorming.
- **The process is not a linear one:** Although I have presented these steps of the process in a sequential manner, as management would prefer it to be, it tends to be far less structured than that in reality. It is often necessary to move backwards and forwards, and to conduct a number of repetitions, modifications and improvements along the way. Business Model Innovation is in its nature a very uncertain terrain, so that trial and error becomes part of the process. This does not only apply to the business model itself, but also to the process of how you develop, design, test, and implement your business model.
- **Going through the process once is not enough:** Teams often think that the completion of a step in the process is sufficient in order to progress.

However, it is not. You need to return to that step and check whether the quality suffices before moving to the next step.
- **Do not waste too much time on planning:** At the end of the day, you need to test your business model in real life in order to discover whether it really functions or not. Put your business model into practice.

> **CASE VI:**
>
> ## On a Treasure Hunt for Innovation
> *Barbara Heitger and Annika Serfass*
>
> This case study will also be published in German in the conference volume "Siehe ich mache alles neu" (Off 21,5). Innovation als strategische Herausforderung in Kirche und Gesellschaft" in the Paulinus Verlag, 2012.
>
> Dark clouds were on the horizon for a large family-run enterprise. But no one had the time to look at the challenges ahead. A "Treasure Hunt" integrated exploration for innovation with daily business.

The initial situation: The world is changing

Today's successes may lead to failures in the future, especially when a company is so successful that all resources are absorbed by the operational business and operational projects.

What is to be done, when a company is in a fully exploitation-mode? What is to be done, when you are stuck in a merciless rat-race with your competitors? What is to be done, when there are dark clouds ahead, but no one has the time to check the weather forecast?

You take a time-out – a special kind of time-out to inspire new on ideas of things to do and how to do them. We call such a time-out a "treasure hunt". In 2008, we initiated a treasure hunt with a North-German family-run business – a heavily R&D-focused global market leader. The outstanding successes and continuous growth of the company apparently prevented all from taking a close look at future challenges. Soon, potential risks were in sight, but no one had found the time to define these challenges or even develop a strategy.

Future challenges

The head of strategy and the director for HR and organizational development initiated the project with us. Could it be possible to equip managers with new ideas and innovative approaches for challenges in a minimum amount of time and without disrupting the day-to-day work? We developed a concept that heavily relied on a precise and thorough diagnosis and preparation, in order to meet this request.

The first step for a successful treasure hunt was to take a close look at those dark clouds: What questions were at their core? What were the true challenges that the company would have to overcome? We established a core-team for the project in order to find the answers to these questions within various different settings. Employee or customer-surveys can provide insights, while "War-Gaming" is another good approach: Hereby a group of employees steps into the shoes of an aggressive competitor – "What would they have to do in order to kick us out?" A third approach was "Green Field Setting": A task group invented a strategy and an organization with the existing resources, but without the restrictions and limitations due to the current organizational design. And there are many more ways to tackle these challenges. The process resulted in the definition of several strategic challenges in the form of questions that needed to be worked on.

In fact, the German hidden champion emerged as an international company at a staggering rate, with suddenly more than 50% of their staff working outside of Germany; but how should one integrate all these people into one corporate culture? Another future challenge involved the experts of bio-engineering, i.e., the lack of them. Who would develop the products in 15 years' time? How could one respond to the changing needs of clients? And what would be the answer to disruptive trends, such as acquisitions and deregulation?

The answers would have to involve something else that the company currently does not employ.

The development of these strategic questions resulted in a form of creative tension and a sense of urgency for innovation as well as motivation to step away from the day-to-day business and to think outside the box.

First recipe for success

– Ambivalence and the operational business absorb time and energy. There is no right time to put strategic uncertainties on the agenda. In spite of that, the organization is very successful.
– Establish a case for action by "War-Gaming", "Green Field Settings", and "Evolutionary Development" by identifying a common understanding of strategic threats and opportunities.
– Create a sense of urgency and a common understanding of the questions that need to be addressed.

The destinations

We searched for companies that faced similar challenges and for successful companies – often hidden champions such as our client – who were interested in an open exchange, instead of a benchmark! Host companies, whether profit or non-profit oriented, can be situated anywhere in the world (depending on the available budget). However, it is much more difficult to visit political parties or government agencies, since they operate with very different restrictions and objectives. It does not have to be the market leader that one pays a visit to. Sometimes, it is much more useful to ask the runner-up company to explain why it is so difficult to become the number one and which obstacles are actually faced on the way to the top. What matters in the end is how honestly one engages in self-reflection.

Second recipe for success

– Establish a small high-quality project team that invests time into the design of the treasure hunt.
– Enhance the attraction of the project, e.g., by initiating an application process for all staff members that wish to participate.
– Put together cross-functional and multi-level teams to jointly go on the journeys.
– Thoroughly prepare each journey with great attention to detail:
  – Formulate four to six strategic research questions that relate to the pre-defined potential threats.
  – Extremely careful selection of companies that will be visited as the sparring partners.
  – Continuous briefings on the teams and visited companies.

3 x 3 x 3 – our recipe for success

Due to the restriction that senior managers cannot be detained for several days, we invented the 3 x 3 x 3 formula: Three management teams would go on a three-day journey, visiting three different companies. These teams were as diverse as possible: cross-functional, cross-hierarchical, and international.

Since managers usually do not have the time to prepare thoroughly, we provided the briefing-sessions for the day during the bus ride, the train ride or the flight, on the way to the companies that were being visited. Once we had arrived, everyone introduced themselves and a prep-talk was held for the day ahead. Then, the work began on the already formulated strategic questions. The teams privately discussed what was troubling them, what obstacles they had to overcome and how they had gone about that. They questioned each other's strategy on how these had dealt with the surrounding environments, stakeholders, structures, and processes. Following this, a tour was conducted of the facilities of the host company since it contributed to the discussions. To round-off the day, there was an exchange on the recently acquired information. It is important to have a good moderator to structure the day. Other than that, this moderator should ask a number of provocative questions to facilitate the discussions, should provide intensive coaching for the participants, and foster a challenging group discussion.

Right after the visit, short and spontaneous videos were made of the highlights and several personal impressions were recorded.

Back on the bus, or the train, or on the plane, the experiences and insights were immediately evaluated. Group discussions, journals, and questionnaires helped to compile the relevant aspects. All participants had their laptops with them and could record their personal impressions on video. Check-lists on the lessons learned for future challenges related these experiences to their own contexts. In order to change the stubborn mindset of participants that often makes them declare "Yes, but this doesn't work in our case", a very capable moderator is required who can instead motivate them to continuously attempt to adapt these newly discovered impressions effectively. The intense work experience of these three days induced a strong sense of belonging for those in the leadership level and also strengthened the commitment to implement these ideas.

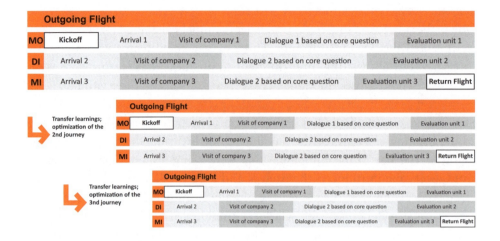

Overall, it is important to understand that the treasure hunt is not like a visit to the museum, where you look at interesting artifacts and copy some of their attributes. It is a quest to comprehend the pre-requisites of strategic innovation, to discover new ideas together, and to generate new energy to incorporate into the company. It was important to the company that the process was completed within a three-day journey.

Third recipe for success

- Prepare the treasure hunt as a challenging adventure that questions the fundamental assumptions of the organizations.
- Create an atmosphere that offers room for openness and challenges for one another.
- Foster co-creation by using the perspectives and knowledge of others for assignment questions.
- Plan for a highly interactive journey but make sure to have a very capable moderator.
- Encourage improvisation and creativity with the notion of venturing into an undiscovered land.

The challenge after the journey

A treasure hunt is not over yet when you get home. Only then does the real challenge begin: A transfer of all the gathered impulses into the organization. A large group event was held with almost the entire leadership-community.

The travelers were questioned by those that had stayed at home: What were the eye-openers? What were the most relevant derived insights? Why and in what way are these relevant to us? All the ideas that had emerged were critically assessed by the management and the board members of the company. It had really paid off! Five innovation-initiatives were implemented.

> **Fourth recipe for success**
>
> – Take into account, the danger of the "not-invented-here-syndrome" during the integration and transfer process, which refers to the risk of rejecting something new simply because it was obtained outside the company.
> – Innovation potential is checked and tested by those who stayed home.
> – Use the outcomes of the treasure hunt to generate engagement among the leadership-community of the company for new innovative initiatives.

The agenda

The development of the journey as a treasure hunt with a clear agenda addressing "Discovery", "Identifying and Understanding", and "Transfer", support the practical relevance of the outcome and simultaneously function as a reality-check for the company:

Discovering
- Create a sense of need for innovation
- The core team has overall process responsibility
- Organizational diagnosis of the core questions
- Preparation of the management team (case studies, expert-articles, ...)
- Kickoff with each travel group to become familiarized with the methodology
- Consistent processing of the content among the core team
- Careful choice & briefing of the visited partners

Finding and Understanding
- Intense exchange during the journey
- Facilitated 'off-the-record' dialogues with the learning journey partners and 'jump in' inspections
- Facilitated group analyses to develop hypotheses and ideas related to the search assignments
- Coaching and challenging provided by external consultants

Discovering
- Intense discussion and assessment on generated ideas & hypotheses with the entire international management team (travelers and non-travelers)
- Learning and development of a 'take-home-agenda' on a personal, individual and organizational level
- Detailed follow-up of the journey
- Innovative initiatives developed through commitment

Raising awareness
Generating curiosity

Fostering inspiration
Understanding levers
Developing new ideas
Gathering new energy

Substantiation and implementation of ideas
Celebration of successes and reinforcement of strengths

Case VI: On a Treasure Hunt for Innovation

The success factors
Focused and well-prepared:
- Create a sense of urgency for the need of innovation
- Careful selection of the future challenges that are being examined to strategically position the treasure hunt
- Make sure to carefully select the host companies
- Thorough preparation and evaluation by the project team
- Smooth journey without any stress but with some creative tension and an atmosphere that creates a sense of adventure
- Analysis of the host companies during and shortly after the visits

Suitable host companies:
- Comparable challenges
- Agreement among the entire project team on the choice of the company
- Access to top-managers and willingness for private discussions

Continuous systemic reflection:
- No simple benchmarking, but developing an understanding of the drivers and pitfalls when compared with one's own situation
- Co-creative dialogue creates leadership teams that are committed to innovative initiatives
- Combination of analytical (What?) and systemic (How?) reflection during the treasure hunt

Quest for resilience
As a result of the project, the company has also strengthened its own resilience – with regard to reacting quickly and being flexible when confronted with its challenges. There is more room for potential and innovation, when some attention is diverted from the day-to-day business and receptiveness towards new discoveries is enhanced. Even several characteristic features of a resilient organization can be constructed by a treasure hunt: The way in which managers became part of a leadership team provides for more direct and open communication; pro-active research for information from different sources became more frequent; the sense of belonging to a strong team and a goal-driven organization stabilized the company; and the search for new perspectives and new

insights makes it possible to gain a more holistic picture of the organizational environment and future challenges.

In the long run
The company's top-management portrayed commitment to the project and verified the argument that even champions must not allow themselves to become complacent if they wish to remain in the leading pack in the long run. As a special prize, the head of personnel development was presented the "Chief Learning Officer Award" for the project in 2010. The prize is awarded annually for innovative projects within the field of organizational development.

Ultimately, the treasure hunt proved to be a turning point for the entire organization – the courage to delve into an unknown world and to explore came quite naturally, while curiosity, fruitful inquiries, attentive listening and challenging one another became distinct features of the corporate culture.

Bibliography

Pichler, Martin
    Nicht kopieren, sondern kapieren, in: wirtschaft + weiterbildung, 09_2010, S. 24–27.

Heitger, Barbara; Antia, Delna
    Resilienz – Innovation per Expedition, in: Personal Manager, Januar 2011, S. 29–31.

Heitger, Barbara; Serfass, Annika
    Dem Zufall ein Schnippchen schlagen – durch Resilienz Unerwartetes meistern, in: REVUE für postheroisches management, Heft 6; 2010, S. 30–37.

CHAPTER 8

THE PHASES OF CHANGE "THINGS NEVER TURN OUT AS EXPECTED"

In this chapter, we will present a phase model developed from the comparison of numerous "life cycles" of change projects we have worked on. The model also incorporates the experiences we have gathered as business partners and managers of the change processes within our own consulting firm.

Our description of the typical "route" taken by a transformation is meant to:
1. provide orientation and suggestions for possible interventions to managers or consultants,
2. provide a checklist – much like aircraft manuals for pilots, who rely on their experience and intuition, but also consult the handbook to make sure they haven't missed anything.

The model is not meant as a list to be worked through from top to bottom. As systemic practitioners, we know that these phases cannot be treated as sequential, linear slots, but that each individual phase shows traces of the others. For example, the persons concerning themselves with "creating an image for the future" will always have an eye to implementation. And when, at a late stage in the change process, it is a matter of consolidating successes, those initial images for the future can re-emerge and be cause for a full-blown controversy. The phases follow an iterative, fractal course, and each individual phase reproduces the others at some level. However, their emphases are by no means interchangeable.

Phase models provide orientation by indicating "universal regularities" and typical dynamics. They are particularly helpful when dealing with the high level of emotional strain that prevails in many transformation processes. They reduce tension, enable comparison and help set milestones.

We have identified five phases in change processes:

1	Interrupt routine – we must change
2	Create images of the future – develop architecture, plan the route
3	Make brave decisions – jump into the deep end
4	Implement consistently – combine desire for the new with broad involvement
5	Master the high-altitude challenge – consolidate successes

Phases 1 and 2 are concerned with letting go of the past and everyday routine – in the conviction that today's success can be tomorrow's failure. An image of the future slowly crystallizes and becomes more defined and tangible in the first implementation steps in Phases 3 and 4. At this point, it becomes vital to replace the existent, no longer adequate problem-solving patterns learned in the past. Phase 4 involves broad implementation and anchorage of change in the company's control system and stabilization of the "new way of doing things". The same goes for Phase 5, but with increasing intensity. These two phases are longer than the previous ones, and it becomes crucial to repeatedly re-fuel the process by creating momentum and maintaining consistency in change management. We place great emphasis on Phases 4 and 5 because many transformation projects concluded prematurely with Phase 3 – which is much too early to ensure lasting changes.

Based on our experience, the phases are not equally long and we work with an assumed ideal-typical proportion of 10:10:20:25:35. This sequence contrasts with many change management concepts and projects, which concentrate chiefly on the change's initial phases and neglect its integration into all corporate systems.

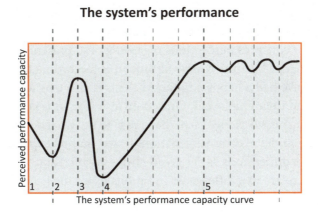

The system's performance capacity curve

In addition to the phases, we have developed a "system curve", which represents the system's perceived ability to perform (vertical axis) as it runs through the phases (horizontal axis).

This ability to perform is made up of three dimensions:
- A past-oriented dimension, which relates to the way the organization views its own history (ancestral gallery, past successes, performance, tradition)
- A present-oriented dimension, based on indicators of present-day success (performance indexes, share price, core competencies, intellectual and innovative capital, a positive corporate culture)
- A future-oriented dimension (future capacity, success potentials, probability of future success, but also the confidence in being able to easily deal with future turbulences)

When assessing the system's perceived capability to perform, it is important to be aware of the resources and achievements of the past and present as well as their potentials for the future. Sharpening self-awareness is important; this means, above all, defining, deciding and prioritizing criteria for one's own performance potential and success.[68]

---

[68] The discussion of multi-perspective models of success evaluation is becoming increasingly important. The concept of the Balanced Scorecard is a highly esteemed solution. Knowledge management measures such as EFQM, due diligence and cultural due diligence processes, benchmarking and best practice comparison are also instruments of self-observation that reach beyond the (necessary) control of daily business.

The Phases of Change

Assessment is always influenced by the specific perspective and emotional situation of the evaluators (see Chapter "The logic of feelings"). It is important to note that this concerns perceptions regarding past, present and future that are subject to change over the course of time. It is (according to Erickson) "never too late to have had a happy childhood". This is also true for companies, their managers and their employees. One could also say: *"It is never too late to have managed a successful change."* – perhaps easy to say when looking back, but not when in the midst of a transformation. Based on our experience, the assessment of these dimensions varies greatly from organization to organization. For instance, there are vast differences in rationales for the necessity to change.

An example:
An energy company is seeing poor figures. Here are three different takes on what is "apparently" the same situation:

Manager A: *"This is a major crisis."*

Manager B: *"The situation looks bad, but is not seriously threatening."*

Manager C: *"This is a normal business cycle, there's no need for additional action."*

The reasons for these positions are just as diverse:

> *"Our capacity for the future is endangered because we can't make the crucial investments."*

> *"The present figures aren't that accurate – they illustrate past problems that we are now solving."*

> *"In the past, we have always managed to react quickly in emergency situations."*

Which reason was assumed for which position? Whatever the case may be, the further procedure is the decided by the position taken. The "negotiation" of such positions is an essential component of any development process.

Typical interpretation of the curve:

Phase 1: Perceptions of the organization's status are quite diverse at the beginning. The assessment of the system's performance sinks, even if the present figures paint a rosy picture. Conflicts arise, particularly regarding which direction to take. The need for action is gradually accepted.

Phase 2: The change is officially made. Images of the future are elaborated, decisions are made regarding the architecture and the route of the change process. Increased trust in the company's future causes the system curve to rise. This "initial euphoria" is intensified by first successes.

Phase 3: The first pilot projects of the transformation bring the extremity of the hard cuts and new growth to light. It becomes clear that the targeted change is radical. Concepts that worked out at the beginning are often turned upside down and reworked after initial practice runs. The assessment of the system's performance diminishes: past competencies are no longer valid, the new situation appears foreign, awkward and artificial. "Inexplicable" misunderstandings often arise, new solutions cannot be implemented or are drawn out, and uncertainty prevails throughout the company (*"Not even the simplest of procedures works anymore."*). This low point is often experienced as highly critical. At the point of transition from Phase 3 to Phase 4 the curve often hits rock-bottom. Just as in learning a new sport, practice is necessary for mastering new techniques, and these can only be acquired by "unlearning" the way things were done before.

Phase 4: A gradual rise in performance is achieved through disciplined practice, commitment, humor and the willingness to try something new – and as a result of the new and the existing systems adapting to one another. The steep rise also helps to leave the memory of strain and disputes behind.

Phase 5: This phase could also be called "management of consolidation and stabilization". By now, the system is consistently performing at a higher level – the change has "materialized". New everyday routines have developed. The new identity has become a matter of course. Even if there are still small "ups and downs", the system settles down.

To conclude this description of our model's dimensions, we believe that each phase is indispensable. Fundamental changes must go through these phases, with all of their highs and lows, in order to take effect. In "real life", such transformations are not a linear process. Detours are often taken, and "honor laps" are run. It is vital to success that these phases are lived through in awareness of their dynamics and emotional content.

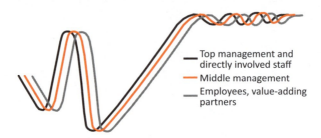

Different target groups go through these phases at different times. The initiators of the change and senior managers go through them first; their emotional assessment of the situation is more progressive and they are more anxious to reach implementation and consolidation than middle management and employees, who get involved later on in the process.

In the following, we describe the individual phases in more detail. We start with a practical example followed by some basic considerations concerning the respective step. Managers and consultants are chiefly interested in implementation, of course. For this reason, we provided change agendas with key strategies for each stage and several ideas for interventions – a mix of tried and true measures and invitations to think out of the box. Some of these interventions – marked by the sign "➔" – are described in more detail in Chapter 9.

Phase 1: Interrupt the routine – we need to change!

?? ➔   What's the situation? An example:
An internationally active consulting firm is more successful than ever. Turnover and operating results have increased steadily over the last years. However, there are divergent assessments of the current situation within the firm. Some think: *"Our business model has proved sound, we should be satisfied."* Others think: *"It's high time for a massive change. We've reached our limits and could make much more out of our brand. The competition is growing faster than we are; we no longer have the right solutions for our customers."* There are strong advocates for both poles; many employees and managers are ambivalent.

Highly varying outlooks on the organization's status and future capacity are typical for this phase. There is no common image – neither of the past, nor of the present or concrete future developments. The situation is usually seen through "department portholes", and the overall panorama tends to be fragmentary and individualized. The energy for change differs from area to area, e.g., from top management to account management (with direct customer contact). Contradictory signals (e.g., customer feedback) are coming from the outside. A discussion arises on whether the right market information is being taken into account on the stakeholder side. The collective mood is ambivalent: The everyday routine exists side-by-side with interest in the new. But there are also anxiety blockades that resist any "upheaval" in the security of everyday business.

Change agenda – what to do?

1. Interrupt the routine: "Change starts with me"

Interrupting the routine means actively encouraging and "rousing" conflicts. It also means consciously provoking destabilization – pulling oneself and the company away from the comfort zone of familiar, everyday routines. A prerequisite for any effective change is that essential key players (particularly, but not only, top management) are personally willing to interrupt these routines, without being able to predict or control the exact direction the change will take. In other words: they must venture onto dangerous territory, allowing the uncertainty of the future to both unsettle and invigorate. One essential lever in this process is the knowledge that everyone involved shares responsibility for the whole, not merely for their own part in the project.

>i< **Possible interventions:**
- Informal and/or official preliminary discussions with internal and external stakeholders: assessment of the situation and future potentials.
- Self-reflection: "Where do I tend to whitewash personal problems and points of criticism?"
- Team building: Top management session on the topic "tension field": "Our overall responsibility ↔ my division's responsibility"

➔ "The change begins with me" (concept see Chapter 9)

➔ Start a vision process with key players (concept see Chapter 9)

2. Evaluate the need for action: "From the outside in"

A change begins and ends with the "organization's business". Change projects that are only inward-oriented, without positive effects on customer and/or supplier relations are not only "useless", but also destroy future initiatives. This is why it is important to systematically import information from the outside – in a way that facilitates emotional acceptance (e.g., with recognized experts in the respective fields, important customer representatives, lead users, …). Successful transformations are driven by intense competition and market, business and customer impulses.

>i< Possible interventions:

- Introduce or strengthen market/customer/benchmarking indexes.
- Due diligence methods (including cultural due diligence)
- Hold a strategy session with key players, with scenario work for "hard cuts".
- Qualitative diagnosis
- Hold a "Customer Parliament" or "fireside talks" with important customers (concept see Chapter 9)

3. Assess change capacity: "Let's test ourselves!"

Not only the need for change, but also the change capacity of an organization is a decisive factor in choosing the right processes and support measures (see Chapter 2: "In the Jungle of Change Concepts"). It is important to reflect on and learn from experience: e.g., *What conceptions of change ideas tend to dominate our behavior during transformations? What were the strengths and weaknesses of previous change projects? How sound is the change management competency of those actively involved? How can we assess change readiness or change fatigue?* We believe that the best way to get a good sense of one's own capacity for change is to carefully review past changes and "non-changes", conduct learning exercises with others and launch small "test balloons".

>i< Possible interventions:

- Project reviews of change projects
- A learning journey on change projects within the own or other companies
- A pilot project to conduct a small change (as a test)
- "Past – Present – Future" (exercise see Chapter 9)

- "Learning Organization" questionnaire with joint evaluation (concept see Chapter 9)
- "Creativity Blockers" (exercise see Chapter 9)

4. Rousing communication: "Open things up – take a position – set signals"
In this phase of great ambivalence it is important to "open things up", to create communicative situations that promote the expression and perception of the various trends coursing through the company. In particular, responsibility lies with senior management to consistently convey the message that things are being "shaken up" and to explain why radical change is necessary. Courage and readiness to take risks are most noticeably exhibited in minor decisions with high symbolic impact – much more so than in "grandiose verbiage". The positions of the individual key players should be made visible – in a respectful dialogue. "Stimulating communication" clarifies contents and transformation objectives and gives initial impulses on the road to change, thus providing orientation and combining cognitive with emotional messages. Whoever communicates has a personal influence on interactions. In addition to written communication and "speeches", interactive settings are necessary – in a group size that allows for "really talking with one another".

>i< Possible interventions:
- Competition Newsletter
- "The Negative News of the Day"/"The Opportunities of the Day" (Intranet webpage)
- Rewards for openness – clear feedback (concept see Chapter 9)
- Take a stand: set up presentations or installations on essential dimensions of change (concept see Chapter 9)
- Eliminate luxury (a minor intervention with far-reaching effects, e.g., changing the company car policy) (concept see Chapter 9)

5. Identify key players: "Finding the best people"
Change does not simply "happen" – it is driven by people (and later by teams). It is now vital to find the key players for the change, people who will accelerate the transformation process and be the pivotal players in the future (solution system instead of problem system). The key players must truly represent all of the organization's important trends. In order to ensure good leverage for an in-

dividual's actions, he or she must be both highly committed to the change and securely anchored in the organization. One danger lies in seeing only the "usual suspects", i.e., experienced project managers or department heads as key players – remember, this is the group responsible for the current status. These staffing decisions are fundamental for success.

The **Forms of Capital Model** (adapted from a model by Pierre Bourdieu) provides decision-making criteria for this scanning process.

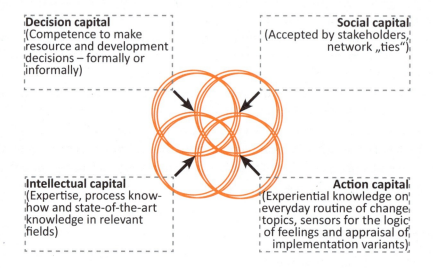

Decision capital
(Competence to make resource and development decisions – formally or informally)

Social capital
(Accepted by stakeholders, network „ties")

Intellectual capital
(Expertise, process know-how and state-of-the-art knowledge in relevant fields)

Action capital
(Experiential knowledge on everyday routine of change topics, sensors for the logic of feelings and appraisal of implementation variants)

>i< **Possible interventions:**
- One-to-one conversations
- Internal market for project management & collaboration (Intranet)
- More intense networking among management
- Analysis of forms of capital (concept see Chapter 9)
- Microcosm analysis/environment analysis (concept see Chapter 9)

Phase 2: Imagine the future – develop architecture, chart the route!

??→ What's going on? An example:

A regional branch of an international IT corporate group has developed a new model for dealing with the market. The reasons for this change are described in a "vision concept" that foresees no longer merely selling off-the-shelf products, but creating individual solutions with the customers. This will mean radically rethinking corporate processes, and a shift in personnel capacities and qualifications. The concept was prepared and presented by a small group. The response to the presentation is that it is "an ivory tower idea" and "totally unrealistic". The management forms a change team among the employees that will be responsible for implementing the change.

The second phase begins with initial concepts or ideas on possible future scenarios. Of course these ideas cannot be implemented on a 1:1 scale – they have yet to be linked to the social system and are often seen as foreign by those concerned. It is often unclear how binding the proposals are, who is supposed to implement them, who will be affected and how. Due to the potential for insecurity at this point, it is vital to create process security – a stable transformation process – particularly to provide those involved with markers and milestones on which they can rely on when developing the ideas and content of the change (vision, strategies, organization models) and to allow these to mature within a stable structure. The involvement of key players – who are highly trusted by the different stakeholder groups – is essential in this phase. The (perceived) performance of the system usually increases in this phase. Future concepts, clear master plans and clear organization provide security – this immediately reduces the perceived "hazard potential". There is a collective feeling of interest, and a high spirit of optimism among those directly involved. This is further strengthened by first successes in the project.

Change agenda – what to do?

1. Vision work: "We are creating a future – a future that matches our company"

A strong vision is an essential energy source for change. We have had good experiences with a resource-oriented approach (*Where do our strengths lie?*), beginning with the key players and their very personal perspective and then integrating "objective" future trends and stakeholder perspectives. This approach works at overcoming perception barriers regarding one's own creative potential (*"I will only be able to change myself if I can also think differently."*). The vision has to be a dream that is both challenging and realistic – and that fits the system. This is all about self-discovery and identity. It is a process that requires both time and room to grow, to ensure that the image of the future (*"What makes us unmistakable, what is our focus?"*) is well-anchored – not only rationally, but also emotionally.

>i< Possible interventions:
- Continue the vision process (see Phase 1)
- Deliberate staffing decisions for persons who "stand for" this future
- Creative groups that describe "utopias that match our world"
- "Quick Wins and Go to Market Workshops 1 + 2" (concept see Chapter 9)
- Symbolic action: "paper basket – museum – showcase" (concept see Chapter 9)

2. Develop strategy and master plan: "Hard cuts and new growth in the 'big picture'"

The most important thing in this phase is to make decisions concerning strategy, organization (structures and processes) and staffing – or at least the staffing procedure – for crucial positions. Also important is deciding on the architecture (Who will participate in the change process, and how?) and the master plan (What is to be provided and when?). As uncertain as the outcome of radical changes may be, a fundamental strategy and a professional master plan increase (subjective) security. Commitment grows, because discussions and deliberations on the change process are now informed by a conception of the future as a path leading to implementation. Thinking and talking are trial runs for "the head and the heart". This is why who takes part in shaping the implementation strategy and master plan and how this process proceeds are important. Investing quality and time now saves a great deal of money and time and prevents unnecessary conflicts in the next phases. Based on our experience, this type of plan is most effective if negotiated directly with the concerned stakeholders. Large-scale "start-up" events have proven helpful for this, as they prevent the ivory tower-effect.

Special attention should be given to the question of how "hot potatoes" (e.g., outsourcing of divisions, fusion of departments, removal of management levels, dismissal or transfer of employees, central personnel decisions) are dealt with. One vital aspect is creating transparency on how these "hot potatoes" are being dealt with. Another is that planning and implementation of these measures – if they are perceived as "hard cuts" – require their own architectural elements and settings in order to meet the demands of "unlearning" and "letting go" (see Chapter 3 on "Hard Cuts" – "drop your tools"). It is important to provide entirely different architectural elements where new growth is required. Splitting up the strategies for hard cuts on the one hand and new growth on the other – with simultaneous overall control – is particularly useful in the case of a "radical repositioning" ("dual change architecture"), since the emotional dynamics of these two emphases are absolutely contrary.

>i< **Possible interventions:**
- Stakeholder Analysis II ("live")
- Large-scale startup event
- Project management master plan (project task, milestones, timetable, costs, resources – careful: do not underestimate!)
- Strategy implementation pilot project (see Chapter 9)
- External "Sparring Partner System" (SPS) for hard cuts (see Chapter 9)
- Strategy retreat with key players (see Chapter 9)

3. Architecture and teams are crucial: "Security through process stability and confidence"

The decision of where the main responsibility for implementation should lie (directly in the management team, in a separate change team or a corporate development department) is of central importance. All other architectural elements should be selected depending on this fundamental decision in order to ensure maximum process security. Teams are essential motors for any change, since they are best able to illustrate and manage their social and content-related complexity. A great diversity of subject matter, knowledge, emotional acceptance and an appropriate depiction of the complexity of the overall system (stakeholder representatives) need to be integrated. When put together correctly and motivated with good incentives, teams are best suited for the integration of knowledge, experience and emotions. The standard principle in staff selection should be: "Team up the best".

The most important functions the change architecture should include are: decision, control, communications, content-related expert work, pilot testing, response and multiplication, evaluation, support and know-how production.

> **>i< Possible interventions:**
> - Selection of architectural elements
> - Management retreat
> - Symbolic authorization of those responsible for implementation
> - Making fundamental architectural decisions: *"Is control located in the management team, change team or in a corporate development department?"* (concept see Chapter 9)
> - Staff selection (e.g., using the Forms of Capital model) (concept see Chapter 9)

4. Communicating in earnest and with transparency: "This is where we want to go" – "This is how we'll get there" – "Business case of the Future"
At this point, it is good to review the initial phase of "rousing communication" to see what has been clarified and achieved since then and to project a new picture the objectives and the route. Communicating visions concisely *and* in a way that transports their emotional content is a major challenge. People can only really identify with the change if they are dealing with it personally and therefore bringing their own personal perspectives and emotionality into the process. The rule of thumb is: *"Someone who is involved in the preparation doesn't need convincing."* The best way to describe the projected results of the transformation is in the form of a Business Case of the Future. In the light of such images of the future, the change acquires usefulness for the stakeholders and starts to make sense. Providing information quickly, launching decentralized initiatives ("hands-on change") and making use of modern information technology ensures that communication is transparent and intense.

Success factors:
- "Emotional" – "vivid" – "concise": this applies to titles, symbols and experience-oriented elements in the communication of the beginning transformation process.
- Interaction: Communication means creating points in common. Speak – listen – understand – question – and react. Having something in common is a necessary prerequisite for beginning a relationship. This means deal-

ing with one's own feelings and reactions as well as those of one's counterpart, i.e., the stakeholder. Feedback is important for flexible, target group-oriented control of the change process.
- Consistent repetition of the most important messages: this highlights their credibility. Letting "deeds speak for themselves" fortifies the message (the role model effect, especially in management, is a great multiplier).

>i< Possible interventions:
- Generate tension and pressure through clear, challenging goals set by executive management
- Introduce an open evaluation/controlling system for change
- Organize decentralized discussion forums with feedback
- Set up a dialogue platform on the Intranet, with "rapid" information (e.g., project telegrams)
- Symbolically communicate the "golden thread" (concept see Chapter 9)

5. Intensifying and spreading change management know-how: "On the art of change"

Change management is an important new management qualification and requires professionalizing. Coaching or ad hoc workshops – but also a network of focused professionalizing activities with training modules, external consultation and activities to support the knowledge transfer – are necessary for providing broad support for the change processes. Concrete know-how that is in close contact with the change process is crucial: The time resources of those responsible for the change are the scarcest commodity in these processes.

>i< Possible interventions:
- Expert forum/pool
- "Train the trainer" concepts for change multipliers
- Individual consulting/coaching for key players
- Internal change management course for decision-makers (high impact parallel to the transformation process doubles the benefit!)
- "Traveling to foreign worlds" (concept see Chapter 9)

Phase 3: Make brave decisions – jump into the deep end!

??→ **What's the situation? An example:**

A globally active mechanical engineering company is in the midst of upheaval. The executive board and management team have developed a concept for the future. The plan is to relocate production to low-wage countries, reduce delivery time by 70% and simultaneously intensify internationalization and increase service quality. Around 30 prioritized implementation projects have been started. The initial successes prove the decision-makers right. It seems to be possible to "adjust" in numerous different areas without losing the overall picture. But then, operative problems increase: Although production test runs were successful, difficulties are cropping up in series production. Delivery times are off because single parts are missing – even the simplest things no longer seem to work.

Now that the central decisions on future, strategy, organization and individuals have been made, focus moves to the initial implementation steps. The greater the change's complexity, the more the design of the process needs to be pro-risk, pro-experiment and adaptable. This also means the exclusion of extensive, "perfect" conceptions of the project that aim for one to one implementation. Much more effective is trying out large-scale projects in small test runs and learning from these experiments.

An initial euphoria among those involved is typical for this phase – just as typical as the following disillusionment. "Monstrosities" occur, which on closer examination turn out to be misunderstandings or misinterpretations – these are understandable reactions to fear, or aggressive tendencies meant to protect established identities or "conquer" new fields. Resistance arises with the increasing realization of what elements of the former identity will be kept and what elements will be developed.

Change agenda – what to do?

1. Plan and implement quick wins: "Using the trampoline"

"Quick Wins" is an often-used term, but in practice, the results rarely meet basic requirements:

- **"Quick"** means right after the launch of the change, and with surprising speed
- **"Win"** means a lasting, noticeable improvement for several process stakeholders

Quick successes are a very effective way to raise the credibility of change. They also have a considerable external and internal effect, generating energy and motivation for the further transformation ("motor effect"). But from the very beginning, they also necessitate hard work, courage and above-average performance. The "dramaturgy" of the initial successes (timing, interactions and expected benefits for various stakeholders) should be well thought through, to prevent energy from going up in smoke after an initial burst of enthusiasm.

> **>i< Possible interventions:**
- Resource planning
- "Salvation of Sisyphus" – solution of an old, previously unsolved problem
- Quick-win competitions: e.g., "colorful houses" – *"Whoever shows operation in the black first will have their office building repainted."*
- Quick-win portfolio: rating ideas according to their implementation times/benefit/expenditure (concept see Chapter 9)
- Stakeholder impact analysis: examine the effect activities have on individual stakeholders to get a feeling for external perception (concept see Chapter 9)

2. Set signals for hard cuts: "Challenging and unpleasant things first – but with support measures – true to the theme: 'clear, but sincere!'"

Hard cuts are draining – both for the organization and their personnel. In our opinion, a "double strategy" is suitable for successfully overcoming this process. Active communication and clear implementation of hard cuts on the one hand, but support measures for all those affected on the other. Attempts have occasionally been made to make the "true extent" of hard cuts known only bit by bit, but this undermines credibility and gives rise to continual further speculation (*"What's coming next?"*). Sometimes those affected are left in the lurch – this can apply both to those who leave or to those who experience the change as a loss or derogation, as well as to their managers. This phase model gives orientation for the stage of "bearing bad news"[69] provides insight on what is important to consider.

Even for the winners, or those who stay on, "hard cuts" are not easy. Typical reactions include the "survivor syndrome" (see "Hard Cuts" in Chapter 3:

---

[69] C.f. Königswieser, 1985, p. 52 et seqq.

"Un:balanced Transformation"). Declining morale, mistrust in management, guilt and de-motivation are the most frequent negative consequences if this process is not managed proactively and with intense communication. What employees need now are support measures that they can modify for their individual use – and above all, the tangible presence of management. Since hard cuts change personal identity, relationships and the system all at once, it is also important to offer means for symbolically processing this.

>i< **Possible interventions:**
- Self-organization of the farewell
- Information systems for recording achievement and feedback
- Key account strategy work with customers
- Support workshop for "the other front" and coaching sessions
- Balance preservation and change: hold the past and everyone's contributions in esteem/offer means for symbolically processing the change
- Hotline
- The "management team speech" (concept see Chapter 9)

3. Fostering growth and innovation: "Incentives and loose reigns"

Qualitatively oriented, spontaneous generic growth cannot be forced – it sprouts where there is desire for innovation and fertile ground, where people bring their experience, know-how and energy into play, encouraged by strong incentives. This phase is all about "planting the seedlings" and providing the necessary space, resources and incentives for them to grow. Important ideas often come from outside – although there is always hesitance to cooperate with customers, suppliers and value-adding partners at such an "early" phase. Getting innovative ideas to take root in transformation processes is anything but trivial: it is a matter of breaking down the perception barriers of the former everyday routine, coming up with something new and exciting, protecting ideas, allowing them to mature and then testing them (see "New Growth" in Chapter 3: "Un:balanced Transformation").

>i< **Possible interventions:**
- Set aside special areas/labs for experiments
- Pilot projects with value-adding partners (customers, suppliers)
- Intensifying innovative potential in the team (concept see Chapter 9)
- Changing the general framework (concept see Chapter 9)

- "Future cabaret": scenes from the future (concept see Chapter 9)
- "Innovation markets" (concept see Chapter 9)

4. Working with the opposition: "With the opposition – not against it!"
"Opposition" to organizational changes is common – approaches to confronting this problem vary. Managers and consultants sometimes consider it necessary to assert "their solution" – and derogate whoever opposes it.

The alternative is working "with" and not "against" the opposition – seeing whether and how the opposition's energy can be utilized. It has often been shown that not taking known opposition (synonym: the works council) into account shortens the concept phase, but prolongs or diminishes the effectiveness of implementation. Change situations are necessarily ridden with contradictions and ambivalences. Appreciating this and working with opposition is arduous and costs energy, as it means that change concepts one has already established are, once again, up for negotiation. The first step is to understand the opposition: "*Under what circumstances would they cooperate?*" The answer to this question often opens up new options, since opposition arises from concrete concerns: "*What is going to stay the same, what is going to change?*" Or more specifically: "*What am I going to gain/lose?*" The good news: If opposition emerges, it means that change is being taken seriously, and the confrontation between continuity and change is becoming tangible. The bad news: Opposition means conflict, and a position has to be taken on how conflicting interests and the "allocation of the change budget" are to be negotiated. Opposition is being made use of positively when negotiation among the stakeholders intensifies implementation.

>i< **Possible interventions:**
- Inclusion of key players in the project architecture
- Events with an open, dialogue-oriented format, such as "opposition – acceptance – new creation"
- Paradoxical interventions such as "scapegoat search" or "winner-loser solution"
- Workshop: "Conveying shocking news"
- Dealing with contradictions: cost/benefit (concept see Chapter 9)

5. Using evaluation as a motor: "Widespread, stimulating – with consequences"

By evaluation we mean the pointed, consistent and continuous assessment of transformation. Evaluation goes beyond control that focuses on indicators and result criteria for objectives. It provides orientation not only concerning the status of target indicators and performance indexes, but also concerning the overall effect of the transformation process on the system. This is why professional methods (qualitative and quantitative tools, group interviews, mini questionnaires) and the impartiality of the evaluators are crucial. *"You get what you measure!"* What and how we measure and evaluate influences both actions and results in transformation processes. In order to evaluate where one stands, one must not only have clear pre-determined criteria for measuring results but also take into account "feedback loops and side effects" that were not included in the original equation. Evaluation provides valuable information for the control of "work in progress". The effort is worthwhile, especially if it provides prompt, efficient, incisive and interactive feedback to those managing the transformation. Evaluation is an intervention in itself. It provides information for process control and is a motor for the targeted transformation. Therefore, initiating evaluation is a top priority.

>i< Possible interventions:

- Reviews of senior management
- Evaluation of management accounting
- Open, qualitative individual/group interviews, with subsequent feedback to those concerned and follow-up measures
- Change barometer
- "Stand up or remain seated" (concept see Chapter 9)
- "Mini-evaluation-change status" (concept see Chapter 9)

Phase 4: Implement change consistently

??→ What's the situation? An example:

A traditional, somewhat antiquated information service provider has blossomed into a prime Internet provider. In the course of numerous projects, employees also work on securing and expanding the company's strong market position on the Internet. After a very good start and considerable employee interest, numerous projects begin to falter. There are various, in individual cases quite plausible reasons for this. The project management group is exhausted, and the board is sending conflicting signals. In a management group crisis meeting on the subject: *"Discontinue or proceed with new energy?"*, the managers decide to continue, but in a more consistent, determined fashion. In order to focus resources, three projects are "cancelled" and another five are postponed until the next year. As a result, there is sufficient energy for the remaining activities.

The initial euphoria has vanished – the setbacks are acutely felt. What now? An often (unofficially and officially) posed question at the start of this phase is: *"Should we quit or carry on?"* Candid discussion has a liberating effect on those involved. Once the bubble of enthusiasm has burst, it is a matter of scrutinizing the started projects and pursuing them consistently and according to clearly set priorities. Active communication provides important support (*"We're sticking with it!"*).

Middle managers – as the mentors or multipliers responsible for implementation – are now at the epicenter of change. The effects of the change spread; further quick wins have a bolstering effect; more and more projects are concluded. The perceived performance of the system experiences a surge. At the same time, a great deal of identity work is necessary – the transformation is far from concluded.

The various target groups often find themselves in completely divergent states. Senior management is usually impatient, since the change, in the abstract sense, is "over with". Those who participated in pilot projects are still involved. The implementers are in the midst of their work, and some of the affected persons still need to be won over and integrated. On the timeline, this phase is clearly longer than its predecessors, and demands a great deal of endurance from those involved.

Change agenda – what to do?

1. Push forward implementation activities and projects consistently: "Like the legendary 'Baron Munchhausen', pull yourself up out of troubled waters by your own hair"

The pilots projects have been evaluated, implementation across the board has been planned, and the projects for this are ready to go. Disillusionment and realism dominate the general mood. It is clear that a great deal of "fine-tuning" is called for, as well as training and practice. The danger of "change fatigue" is lurking around the bend. The desire to turn back increases – back to the old ways that were familiar and could be followed with self-confidence. The new has been tried out, but still seems alien in everyday business. Everyone has now been informed about the new strategy and organization, and all personnel decisions have been made. The road to the top is clear but steep. The challenge is to get there under one's own steam. In this phase, transparency on the status of change for all those involved is critical. Incentive systems intensify implementation; concentration is focused on effective partial successes. It is important to ensure that decision-making paths for over-arching measures are short and efficient. An emotionally effective overview of the situation needs to be provided at regular intervals. Effective leadership – particularly among middle management, which is driving the transformation – is called for. Project management instruments are a prerequisite, but do not decide the game. Now, after the pilot projects and the first trials are over, it is time to implement the change on a broad basis.

> >i< **Possible interventions:**
> - Implementation control: "traffic lights"
> - Project portfolio (see case study "Live and let die" in Chapter 6)
> - Evaluate pilot projects – check possibilities for further implementation (concept see Chapter 9)
> - Symbolic action: "paper basket – museum – showcase" (concept see Chapter 9)
> - Symbolic implementation of the overall results (e.g., a "rising column" at the main entrance) (concept see Chapter 9)

2. Constantly adapting the architecture: "Nothing is permanent!"

Combining desire for the new with broad involvement is important for architecture and design in this phase. This makes it necessary to renew the change architecture. The following principles are helpful when designing interventions:
- Create incentives for implementing projects aligned as closely as possible to the (new) business process or business model.
- Professional overall change management integrates hard cuts and new growth into a single implementation process.
- Strengthen incentives and implementation competence for middle management.

- Major events build networks among those involved and facilitate a combination of co-operation and competition in implementation.
- The "Ace Pilots" who ran the pilot projects are available as consultants, experts and providers of ideas.
- In simulation workshops, new processes/models can be tested on a broad basis, pros and contras discussed and feedback processed for fine-tuning the new models/concepts. This is managed by those responsible for implementation.
- Intense training and qualification offensives give employees the competence and know-how they require for implementation.
- Meaningful customer activities and successes create a pull-effect for the business and provide motivation for the broad implementation of the change.
- Planning quick wins and implementing them in the day-to-day business generates energy for the "performance surge" in this phase.
- Evaluation is necessary, since many turbulences are to be reckoned with in this phase.

>i< Possible interventions:
- Overlapping project teams
- Phase architectures with clear handovers
- Rotation principle in the board of directors
- Project manager switch
- Handover of responsibility from project team to management team, i.e., from project to the line (concept see Chapter 9)

3. Winning over those who remain neutral or skeptical: "From the team to the organization"

A change process can also be described as a continuous alternation of "opening" and "closing" working modes. What do we mean by this? At the beginning of Phase 4, the decision has to be made: *"Do we continue, proceed on a broad basis, or not?"* This decision is made within the circle of those involved and those who worked on and tested the pilots. After this bottleneck, the broad implementation of change moves up on the list of priorities. Stakeholders – many of whom may still view the process neutrally or skeptically – are now the focus of attention. All those involved up to now act as multipliers. Here again, it is a matter of finding a balance between persuasion on the one hand and dealing with contradictions and negotiating solutions on the other.

> **>i<** **Possible interventions:**
> - "Stakeholder Analysis IV" with clear target group strategies
> - "Open house" days
> - Work on personal perspectives in the new context
> - From the outside inwards: "Customer Parliament" (concept see Chapter 9)
> - Comprehensive project work (concept see Chapter 9)

4. Adapting systems step by step: "Good systems save energy"
Most change processes have a project and team-oriented "set-up". This generates a great deal of energy and facilitates adequate treatment of the change's overall complexity.

In order to anchor change throughout the organization, the systems that determine the person-organization relation are now gradually adapted: systems for business control, controlling systems, HR or incentive and salary systems, communication systems, etc. Which steps are taken first varies from organization to organization. The system with the greatest leverage and the greatest amount of attention needs to be identified, then adapted. This necessitates intense diagnostic work in management accounting, and the involvement of internal or external experts.

> **>i<** **Possible interventions/approaches:**
> - MBO (management by objectives) and incentive systems
> - Wage and salary systems
> - MIS/IT systems
> - Personnel development/career development
> - Strategy process
> - Planning and budgeting process, management accounting systems
> - "Meeting check-up" (concept see Chapter 9)

5. Continuing the process of learning and improving qualifications for the transformation: "Take a look behind your own scenes and build competencies"
This stage involves learning and acquiring the qualifications and competencies necessary for the realization of change (e.g., leadership competence, technical

and process knowledge, IT know-how, market expertise, social competence, languages and intercultural knowledge). Based on our experience, the importance of these qualifications for success is often underestimated. Target group orientation, "business proximity" and experiential learning are success factors ("learning on the job", on-site super-user and coaching concepts, high-impact workshops and training). A great deal of energy is invested in implementation. Whether it has been meaningfully employed and which of the new solution and action models is the most effective needs to be evaluated, also in terms of quality. This increases efficiency, overcomes perception barriers and creates impulses for further "fine-tuning". Evaluations are by no means process decelerators; they improve efficacy, but also release strain and enable a deeper understanding for the change among those involved (deliberate "identity work").

Possible interventions:
- Multiplier and super-user models
- *"If we were to start from scratch now…"*
- Project database
- Target group-specific qualification initiatives
- "Learning on the job" with support
- Project manager exchange group: meta-control principles
- Regular study groups (e.g., "study trios") (concept see Chapter 9)

Phase 5: Master the high-altitude challenge – consolidate success

What's the situation? An example:
An international commercial and private bank has pursued extensive reorganization projects since undergoing a merger. The majority of these have been concluded, but several critical projects are still on the agenda, among them market and synergy projects. For many employees, the transformation is finished, but numerous open questions still remain in "everyday operations". Coordination between all the systems of the fusion partners has yet to be accomplished, specifications are often contradictory. A stable new corporate culture is out of the question at the moment. The executive board conducts a review and sets up a new project office.

The fifth phase is the longest on the timeline, and the most decisive – even if not the most exciting – phase. After the phases of strong project orientation and surface implementation, the focus shifts to broadly based system integration and "in-depth" anchoring. The transformation is gradually becoming reality, is no longer a foreign concept, and is anchored in the corporate culture, everyday routine and, above all, in management (multiplier for anchoring). Many employees have already been integrated. Nevertheless, there are still major differences in the approach to new things. A few ups and downs are experienced; slowly, the system's performance stabilizes at a higher level. Now it is a matter of integrating *all* systems and *all* employees, or anchoring "the new spirit" in day-to-day business. The conclusion of the transformation needs to be thought through and planned with "dramaturgical" skill.

Change agenda – what to do?

1. Attuning management systems: "Integration on all levels"
Initial steps have already been taken in Phase 4, and those system changes that attracted the greatest attention/sensitivity for change have been accelerated. Now it is a matter of continuation and adaptation to the system in the interest of overall consistency. The fundamental question is: Does the business model match the management systems (e.g., planning, management accounting and control), the HR system (target agreement, task-competence-responsibility, incentive and salary models, career development) and the communication architecture? Creative, new solutions – which can also have a simplifying effect – are called for. Who should take care of this? A combination of system experts, decision-makers and users.

>i<   **Possible interventions:**
- Analysis of systems/business instruments
- Management team meeting → system check
- Scenario: If an employee optimizes "in conformity with the system", what are the results?
- The "system lemon" of the month
- What do we get rid of? (concept see Chapter 9)

2. Changing the company culture: Integrating behavior, norms and values in daily business: "Awareness generates new opportunities"

Corporate culture comprises mental images, assumptions, values and norms that characterize behavior in the company and provide orientation. Often, it is not even a matter of conscious awareness, but rather something like a "glossary of common practice". Culture can only be influenced slowly, only to a minimal degree, and never directly. Raising awareness for expressions of corporate culture is the first step in cultural change. This can be managed by external diagnosis – often combined with internal activities, e.g., research teams trained in methodology, who conduct diagnoses on their own. The processing of diagnosis in open, dialogue-oriented settings constitutes a good basis for further developmental activities. This phase is about creating incentives for cultural change that will stabilize and secure the transformation in the future.

>i< **Possible interventions:**
- Success stories of positive cultural elements, visible sanctions and examples for unproductive elements
- Role models
- External cultural diagnosis
- Symbolic integration: symbols for the new
- "Values Diamond"
- Company culture research team (concept see Chapter 9)

3. Continuing widespread training: "Practice, practice, practice!"

Transformation-specific training sessions cannot be bought off the rack from seminar providers. They are tailor-made, target group-oriented programs, the aim of which is to build up the know-how and qualifications necessary for carrying out the targeted implementation, and to test behavior in interaction with others (e.g., in simulations). Knowledge transfer in the organization is not only a training topic, but above all a management task ("learning on the job", superuser, learning platforms via Intranet/Internet).

>i< **Possible interventions:**
- Combination of team-oriented and comprehensive events
- Preparation and follow-up of training events with the supervisors: "transfer check"
- Learning platform on the Intranet

- Central large-scale events
- Regular study groups (e.g., study trios) (concept see Chapter 9)

4. Venturing out: "Leave the stable: The fortune of the earth is to be found on the back of horses"

Successful change is always market and result-effective. Phases of intense inward orientation are also necessary in transformation processes. While Phases 3 and 4 are more concerned with isolated initiatives involving contacts with customers and partners (e.g., focus groups, "Customer Parliaments" and pilot projects), now intense and consistent external orientation is called for. The new has become routine, confidence has been regained, and now it is time to set sail – at full tilt.

- We have had good experiences with an early integration of customers and value-adding partners into the change process – for several reasons.
- Many processes can only be optimized along the entire value-creation chain (key terms: supply chain management or customer relationship management).
- Partial optimizations do not yield much – customers and value-adding partners change with the company.
- Customer and supplier loyalty increases.
- The image of "openness and professionalism" has a high empathy value.
- New ideas emerge and are implemented around the same time.
- "Moving outwards" has an inwardly strengthening effect (feedback).

>i< Possible interventions:
- Supply chain project
- "Stakeholder Analysis IV" with target group strategy
- PR/media work – "live" integration of journalists
- Community events
- Key account events (concept see Chapter 9)

5. Shifting focus to leadership and concluding the transformation: "Making the inspiring move to a new performance level"

One can plan and control many things with systems and structures. But if leadership is lacking, any change can become technocratic and "heartless". Enthusiasm is an emotional dimension. Changes are most effective if the employees "want" them – and do not "have to endure" them! In addition to vision and architecture, leadership is an essential lever in this context. And by this, we do not mean the ability to motivate "on the surface". We mean knowing how to lead a group of people so that every single person feels that they are "in good hands", and that the group as a whole can be moved to achieve outstanding performance. The renaissance of leadership is an indication that personality development is once again gaining importance in the management world. How managers themselves feel in transformation processes is decisive for how they act outwardly. A strong sense of self and social competence are of much more importance for success than cognitive management skills. The transformation comes to a clear conclusion with the transfer of responsibility to those "directing" day-to-day business. For transformation management, this is a time for substantial evaluation and review: *"What did we achieve, how was the quality of change management?"* In emotional terms, this once again concerns "leaving the old", but now with justified confidence in the future: The transformation is successful and is becoming a part of the company's history. Pride in the collective achievement and an atmosphere of celebration characterize the conclusion.

>i< Possible interventions:
- Incentive systems → leadership
- Training: change leadership for top managerial personnel
- Self-experience, group dynamics for managerial personnel
- "Peer-to-peer counseling"
- Coaching
- What do we get rid of? (concept see Chapter 9)
- Transformation conclusion event (concept see Chapter 9)

Phase model overview

Phase 1: Interrupt the routine – we need to change! (P. 238)
1. Interrupt the routine: "Change starts with me"
2. Evaluate the need for action: "From the outside in"
3. Assess change capacity "Let's test ourselves!"
4. Rousing communication: "Open things up – take a position – set signals"
5. Identify key players: "Finding the best people"

Phase 2: Imagine the future – develop architecture, chart the route! (P. 243)
1. Vision work: "We are creating a future – a future that matches our company"
2. Develop strategy and master plan: "Hard cuts and new growth in the big picture"
3. Architecture and teams are crucial: "Security through process stability and confidence"
4. Communicating in earnest and with transparency: "This is where we want to go" – "This is how we'll get there" – "Business case of the future"
5. Intensifying and spreading change management know-how: "On the art of change"

Phase 3: Make brave decisions – jump into the deep end! (P. 248)
1. Plan and implement quick wins: "Using the trampoline"
2. Set signals for hard cuts: "Challenging and unpleasant things first – but with support measures – true to the theme: 'clear but sincere!'"
3. Fostering growth and innovation: "Incentives and loose reigns"
4. Working with the opposition: "With the opposition – not against it!"
5. Using evaluation as a motor: "Widespread, stimulating – with consequences"

Phase 4: Implement change consistently (P. 252)
1. Push forward implementation activities and projects consistently: "Like the legendary 'Baron Munchhausen', pull yourself up out of troubled waters by your own hair"
2. Constantly adapting the architecture: "Nothing is permanent"
3. Winning over those who remain neutral and skeptical: "From the team to the organization"
4. Adapting systems step by step: "Good systems save energy"
5. Continuing the process of learning and improving qualifications for the transformation: "Take a look behind your own scenes and build competencies"

Phase 5: Master the high-altitude challenge – consolidate successes (P. 257)
1. Attuning management systems: "Integration on all levels"
2. Changing the company culture: integrating behavior, norms and values in daily business: "Awareness generates new opportunities"
3. Continuing widespread training; "Practice, practice, practice!"
4. Venturing out: "Leave the stable: The fortune of the earth is to be found on the backs of horses"
5. Shifting focus to leadership and concluding the transformation: "Making the inspiring move to a new performance level"

CHAPTER 9

INTERVENTIONS, DESIGNS, ARCHITECTURES

Introduction

This chapter offers a selection of examples for managers and consultants of how change processes can be organized. They focus on the pro-active management of hard cuts and new growth, and their overall control within the scope of the presented model framework.

An additional dimension, which we ourselves value very highly because we are convinced of its effectiveness, is the dimension of "reflection" and "thinking out of the box". We have also included a few examples of this.

We consider the following to be the "building blocks" of change:
- Elements of change architectures (example: establishment of an external sparring partner system)
- The design of events (example: a "Customer Parliament" or focus group)
- Interventions that managers and consultants can apply in the course of processes (example: "eliminate luxury")

These examples are intended as suggestions for you as a manager or consultant, as an opportunity to think about different possible approaches in more concrete terms. In this sense, the following section resembles a cookbook – as with cooking, concrete implementation naturally depends on the available ingredients, the cooking method and – last but not least – on the state of mind, experience and competence of the chef.

PHASE 1 INTERVENTIONS: THE CHANGE BEGINS WITH ME

When to use it:

The enterprise is facing a major change. This will entail hard cuts and new growth. Focus is on the management team as initiator.

What it achieves:

In a retreat meeting, personal experiences are linked with the upcoming challenges. The managers discuss the company's overall situation. Understanding is deepened through comparison with personal experience.

How to proceed:

1. **Individual work:** dealing with change personally
   In individual work, each manager considers:
   - Where have I experienced hard cuts and new growth in my own life?
   - What phases ("ups/downs") have I experienced?
   - Where have I actively shaped the course of events, where have I let things develop?
   - What stabilized, what provided impetus and energy?
   - What would I do the same way today, what would I do differently?
   - How did I handle the transition phase?
   - How did I consolidate "new growth"?
2. **A-B-C-exchange:** Three participants form an A-B-C-group. The exchange takes place as follows: A interviews B; C observes; then B interviews C; A observes. Finally, C interviews A; B observes.
   Together, they then form hypotheses and discuss the "main thread" that unites their personal experiences.
3. **Follow-up:** The "main threads" are exchanged in the plenary session; followed by a collective discussion of the consequences to be drawn for the forthcoming change.

What you need:

- Undisturbed workplaces for groups of three
- Plenary – circle of chairs

Our comment:
This exercise is good for the opening evening of a kickoff session.

STARTING A VISION PROCESS WITH KEY PLAYERS

When to use it:
It is clear that the organization must change. The "old" vision or business model is no longer consistent. It is unclear where the journey should lead; the ideas on this are highly diverse.

What it achieves:
The "key players" reflect on the company's future: a collective process, in which individual perspectives, market developments and stakeholder interests all have a part to play. The emerging "vision" is attractive, stimulating and a source of orientation for those involved. This raises commitment.

How to proceed:
In preparation for the first meeting, the participants consider which questions "move" them and which issues should be worked on. Everyone brings along a "symbol" (small object) that stands for his or her aspirations for the future.

Step 1: The workshop starts with the presentation of the symbols. The participants first place their object – without giving an explanation – in the middle of the group (circle of chairs). The other participants associate ideas on the possible meaning of the object, followed by an explanation by its "owner".

Step 2: Mixed working groups evaluate the symbols from different perspectives (e.g., market/customers/processes, organization/financial dimension/innovation, learning).

The groups formulate some preliminary guiding principles and topics/questions for further work.

Step 3: The results of the individual groups are combined into an initial draft; parallel to this, a thematic landscape begins to take shape, which will also be the object of further discussion. Decisions are made as to who should do this, and how.

Step 4: Cross-section groups work on a preliminary "slogan" to summarize the findings up to this point. The results of the various brainstorming sessions are presented, but deliberately not consolidated or decided on yet. An array of results should be maintained.

Step 5: A date is set for a follow-up, and working groups are established (What are our next steps? What will the results be? How do we organize ourselves?).

What you need:
- Circle of chairs
- 4 pinboards
- A tablecloth (as a backdrop for the symbols)
- A digital camera (photos of the symbols)

Our comment:
By selecting a symbol, the participants work on their individual holistic outlook on the topic.

"CUSTOMER PARLIAMENT" 1

When to use it:
The internal view of the customers is characterized by stereotypes. There is little direct analysis of the market that is directly relevant for the organization.

What it achieves:
Benefit for the customers:
- Exchange of views with other customers
- Attractiveness of the event; novelty
- Information gain

Internal benefit:
- Empathetic observation and experience of customers
- Strategy work becomes more defined and accurate
- The basic idea: investment in selective customer retention instead of widespread advertising (Topic: relationship quality)
- "Customer Parliament": customer's opinions are asked for; dialogue instead of one-way communication via advertising
- An event with innovative character
- Direct, personal addressing of all relevant customers

How to proceed:
Step 1: Preliminary phase
- Selection of customers (current/"historic"/prospective)
- Invitation of those selected
- "Selection of customer representatives" – possibly several representatives per major customer
- "Marketing" for the parliament with a questionnaire, reminder, etc.

Step 2: Day one: "Customer Parliament"
- Basic idea: The parliamentarians debate, withdraw for fraction meetings, and – after a general debate – adopt a "law" or an ordinance for dealing with customers.
- Employees are "only" observers – journalists or photographers – and do not actively participate in the discussion at all.

- The customers are divided into groups ("fractions") according to relevant criteria
- Allocation of roles (president, secretary, etc.)
- Initiatory debate with determination of topics
- Afterwards: "fraction meetings" (group work)
- General debate
- Passing of law or ordinance
- Documentation of the events (employees as journalists); possibly with film professionals

Step 3: Day 2: Employee Retreat
- Reflection on the previous day's results
- Business management: effect on our general strategy
- Groups: effects on our concrete project strategies
- Agreement for post-session phase: each customer should be personally contacted

Step 4: Follow-up phase
- Each participant is personally addressed (general info and a section specially for him or her)
- Film on CD
- Customer newspaper

What you need:

Location
- General requirement: plenary hall to accommodate all participants (room not too large in relation to the number of participants: this creates a better atmosphere)
- Side rooms for "fraction meetings"
- Alternative 1: in the local parliament itself, possibly in a conference room
- Alternative 2: in the vicinity of the parliament; start with a visit to the parliament
- Alternative 3: in a municipal parliament, state parliament, etc.
- Alternative 4: building with a round floor plan

Our comment:

A video of the event can be used very effectively for managers/employees who could not attend this event.

PAST – PRESENT – FUTURE

When to use it:
The change project is on the brink of reaching a crucial milestone. The images of past, present and future are diverse.

What it achieves:
The managers get a feeling for the various realities of their organization. It becomes clear that there is an interconnection between past, present and future; additional options for further action emerge (e.g., acknowledging the past in order to give shape to the future).

How to proceed:
Step 1: Form 3 working groups (past/present/future) in one room by random group assignment.

Step 2: First individual work, then brainstorming in the respective working group (past/present/future) on the central questions:
1. How do we feel as past, present and future in relation to the other two groups (spontaneous images, then hypotheses)?
2. What are our concerns:
   - What are we proud of?
   - What is questionable?
   - What is clear?
   - How is the balance of "give & take"?
3. Which questions do we have for the other groups?

Step 3: Two groups pose questions to the third. The third group answers from its temporal perspective. This is continued in turn.

Step 4: Reflection in the respective groups: *What are the "do's" and "don'ts" for the change process?*

Step 5: Exchange in cross-section groups: *What should we pay attention to during the change process?*

What you need:
- Room with a circle of chairs
- 3 pinboards
- 1 flipchart

Our comment:
An intervention for creative thinking – also suitable for managers!

"LEARNING ORGANIZATION" QUESTIONNAIRE

When to use it:
The organization's capacity for change is up for debate. There are various, polarized perceptions.

What it achieves:
The participants critically examine the current situation and how it differs from the targeted future. Diagnostic capability increases; the common general perception provides first indications for possible future actions.

How to proceed:
Step 1: In a preparatory session, participants fill out the following questionnaire:

Questionnaire	Today 1 2 3 4 5	Future target 1 2 3 4 5
1. Our management has a clear vision of the company's meaning, values and purpose.	☐☐☐☐☐	☐☐☐☐☐
2. The vision has been successfully communicated and is understood and shared by everyone.	☐☐☐☐☐	☐☐☐☐☐
3. Our company is special – the employees are proud to work here.	☐☐☐☐☐	☐☐☐☐☐
4. Our management is accepted by the employees. Management practices what they preach.	☐☐☐☐☐	☐☐☐☐☐
5. We regularly exchange our impressions of the market in order to develop strategies together.	☐☐☐☐☐	☐☐☐☐☐
6. We have a clear idea of how to realize our vision.	☐☐☐☐☐	☐☐☐☐☐
7. We set challenging and venturous goals in order to continue developing.	☐☐☐☐☐	☐☐☐☐☐
8. Every employee is aware of the importance of his or her contribution to the company's success.	☐☐☐☐☐	☐☐☐☐☐
9. We measure our results and progress effectively.	☐☐☐☐☐	☐☐☐☐☐
10. These results are quickly and broadly communicated and processed.	☐☐☐☐☐	☐☐☐☐☐

Questionnaire (cont.)	Today 1 2 3 4 5	Future target 1 2 3 4 5
11. We invest time for comprehensive communication (exchanging experiences, feedback, IT systems, future scenarios).	☐☐☐☐☐	☐☐☐☐☐
12. We are very familiar with our internal and external customers' needs and problems.	☐☐☐☐☐	☐☐☐☐☐
13. Our customers participate in the development and design of our products and services. This is also true for other value-adding partners (suppliers, co-operation partners).	☐☐☐☐☐	☐☐☐☐☐
14. The company's activities are oriented to the customer's needs and not to those of management.	☐☐☐☐☐	☐☐☐☐☐
15. We continuously learn from the best practices and pioneering experiences of companies that perform better than us in vital areas.	☐☐☐☐☐	☐☐☐☐☐
16. We quickly identify successful methods and practices in parts of our company and utilize them in other areas.	☐☐☐☐☐	☐☐☐☐☐
17. Our staff communicates good ideas for the company's success quickly and directly.	☐☐☐☐☐	☐☐☐☐☐
18. Training and advancement are actively supported by the working environment.	☐☐☐☐☐	☐☐☐☐☐
19. We take on new challenges even if we do not know how to solve them yet.	☐☐☐☐☐	☐☐☐☐☐
20. We are resourceful and ready to try out new solutions, but we maintain our company's core business.	☐☐☐☐☐	☐☐☐☐☐
21. We highlight achievements, but do not penalize mistakes.	☐☐☐☐☐	☐☐☐☐☐
22. We promote self-responsibility and entrepreneurial action in individual employees and teams (empowerment). Risks that must be avoided are clearly communicated.	☐☐☐☐☐	☐☐☐☐☐
23. Our incentive systems are result- and development-oriented.	☐☐☐☐☐	☐☐☐☐☐
24. We are action-oriented and implement ideas, we are proud of our achievements and abilities.	☐☐☐☐☐	☐☐☐☐☐
25. We enjoy the work that we do.	☐☐☐☐☐	☐☐☐☐☐

Step 2: Participants meet in a retreat. Moderators present the results of the questionnaire, which they have evaluated beforehand.

Step 3: Groups process the results and establish a picture of the as-is situation: *What confirms our image? What is surprising? What hypotheses do we have on the results?*

Step 4: The different groups exchange results, then return to their groups to work on the topics: *Where do we see important differences? What hypotheses do we have on this? What conclusions can we draw?*

Step 5: In a plenary session, participants consolidate results and establish a list of "to do's".

Step 6: As a conclusion: a symbolic representation of the initial situation. The moderators draw (or tape) a line on the floor.

The participants place symbols that stand for individual activities on the line between "as is" and "target state".

What you need:
- Masking tape
- Room with chairs
- 3 to 5 pinboards
- 2 flipcharts

Our comment:
The conclusion is a particularly effective way to bring the key messages across.

CREATIVITY BLOCKERS

When to use it:
Everyday implementation is dominated by routine. The employees and executives are hardly generating any new ideas for changes and improvements.

What it achieves:
The managers recognize what is standing in the way of development and creativity in their organization. This gives them an idea where to begin making improvements.

How to proceed:
In preparation for the event, the managers, each with a selected employee, receive a small notebook with the request to write down all the situations in which they experience creativity being blocked.

Step 1: The managers position themselves on a scale, for instance: "I have experienced x situations in which the creativity of our organization or the employees and managerial personnel was inhibited."

Parallel to this, the employees position themselves on the same scale:

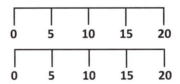

Step 2: Processing in groups. Formation of groups based on scale position. Employees and managerial staff work separately. The group members interview each other – key questions are:
- What was characteristic for these situations?
- Who was involved, and how?
- Under which conditions did these situations occur?

Afterwards they form hypotheses – central topics:
- Where are consistencies to be found (the emeging pattern)?
- Where are the greatest differences?
- What do we think the results of the other groups will be?

Step 3: The groups present their outcomes, and the others react.

Step 4: Formation of "implementation pairs" (manager and employee).

These pairs work on the questions:
- What are our main findings?
- What can we ourselves do to break down inhibiting factors?
- What can we solve comprehensively?

Step 5: Exchange and discussion of the comprehensive issues.

Step 6: Symbolic conclusion: The Top 10 inhibiting factors are written down and then collectively "destroyed".

What you need:
- Notebooks for the participants
- A large room
- Masking tape
- 4 pinboards

Our comment:
Candid exchange between manager and employee is a pivotal success factor here.

ILLUSTRATING THE NECESSITY FOR HARD CUTS: ELIMINATE LUXURY

When to use it:
The necessity for fundamental change (hard cuts) has yet to become a "reality" in the perception of many stakeholders (management, employees, …).

What it achieves:
Routine is interrupted and a strong, provocative signal is sent. Employees and managerial personnel discuss the reasons behind this. "Hard cuts" become a topic in the organization.

How to proceed:
Preparation: In preparation for the management or board meeting, all participants are asked to generate ideas for short-term measures to do away with "luxury".

Meeting:
Step 1: The ideas are documented in a brainstorming session. They are then rated according to the following criteria:

- Effectiveness: *How many employees will we reach with this?*
- Substantial relevance: *How well does this illustrate the direction of the hard cuts?*
- Feasibility and timing: *How quickly can the idea be put into action?*

Step 2: The short-listed proposals are discussed in the plenary assembly. Those responsible decide on implementations.

Step 3: In order to simulate the effect, role play conversations are now enacted among employees (groups of two to four, depending on the number of participants). The group task: "React to the information you just heard on immediate measures". The conversations are held in turn; the other participants listen.

Step 4: The groups process the role-play.
- What assumptions can we now make about employee reactions?
- What recommendations can we derive for our communication strategy?

Step 5: Exchange and decision on communication strategy.

What you need:
- Facilitator (can also be a participant)
- Circle of chairs (flexibility!)
- Flipcharts for documentation

Our comment:
A few practical examples:
- The company car policy is changed.
- And even if the discussion gets controversial: A freeze on the procurement of office materials causes employees to focus intensely on the topic of "reducing costs": It is important to make clear that this is intended merely as a signal for the overall cost-reduction program (intervention in the direction of "Un:balanced Transformation").

"TAKE A STAND": CONSTELLATIONS ON ESSENTIAL CHANGE DIMENSIONS

When to use it:
The organization's key players meet at central events. In addition to a consideration of concrete operative matters, these events always also include joint diagnostic work and a discussion of the strategy for change.

What it achieves:
Different standpoints become discernible and discussable. Personal positioning shows that every single person is concerned. Success factors are consolidated and evaluated.

How to proceed:
The basic principle is the same in all constellations. The moderators explain the scale, and each participant prepares a personal assessment of the situation. Afterwards, everyone is called upon to "take a stand" – i.e., to position themselves in the room according to the terms of the scale. The scales are laid out on the floor with masking tape.

The following questions and quadrants have proven successful in our work:

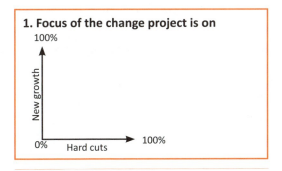

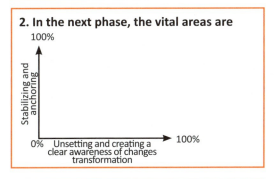

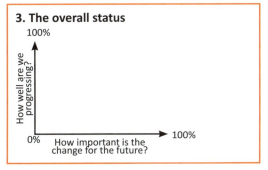

The selection of axes can be changed, but "sensitive issues" must be addressed.

The processing of the results can be done while participants are standing (the moderator interviews the individual participants) or alternatively in deep drive groups.

A possible way of doing this:
   a) Participants are grouped according to similarity. They make comments on the diagnosis, and state which priorities they envisage.
   b) Exchange
      – Inner circle with representatives of the individual groups
      – Facilitator/consultant interviews
   c) Mixed groups discuss afterwards
      – Lessons learned
      – Project ideas
      – Implementations for daily business

What you need:
- Facilitator
- Large room without chairs
- Flipcharts for documentation
- Masking tape

Our comment:
Well-suited for introductory or closing sessions!

ENVIRONMENTAL ANALYSIS

When to use it:
This intervention is particularly helpful at the beginning of projects to raise awareness as early on as possible among those involved of the influences of diverse relevant environments.

This exercise often reveals surprising, completely new perspectives, which then flow into and enrich further work. The environmental analysis can also be very useful in acute crisis situations, and for an effective conclusion of projects.

What it achieves:
The complexity and interconnection of the change project's environment is made visible. Potential conflict, but also possibilities for co-operation are recognized early on. Strategies for giving shape to these relationships are developed, and concrete action plans are prepared.

How to proceed:
Step 1: In a brainstorming session, participants write down a list of relevant environments/stakeholders (flipchart).

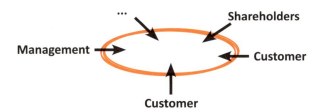

Step 2: For each environment, groups analyze:
- What is the significance of this environment for the project?
- How near/far is it to the change?
- What expectations does the respective environment have in terms of hard cuts/new growth?
- What expectations does the change initiative have towards the environment?
- What potentials and conflicts can result in terms of hard cuts/new growth?
- What do we conclude from this?

Step 3: Each group presents its results; the other groups give their feedback. The compatibility of individual proposals is examined, and activities are agreed upon in the closing plenary meeting.

What you need:
- Pinboard
- Facilitation material
- Flipcharts

Our comment:
Environmental analysis strengthens the external perspective, particularly at the beginning of a change.

ANALYSIS OF FORMS OF CAPITAL

When to use it:
As part of its strategy to intensify change, management has deployed teams to address various questions. These now need to be staffed – or there is a need to diagnose how effective the staffing has been.

What it achieves:
The team members become aware of the resources they contribute. The strategic implementation & results-oriented aspects of project work are reinforced.

How to proceed:
The composition of teams can be decided on or examined with the help of the following criteria:

- **Decision-making capital:**
  The competence to decide formally or informally on resources and developments
- **Social capital:**
  Acceptance with stakeholders, "network ties"
- **Intellectual capital:**
  Expertise, process know-how, state-of-the-art knowledge in relevant fields
- **Action capital:**
  Tacit knowledge of the everyday routines relevant to the change, a good sense of the "logic of feelings" and ability to appraise different implementation variants

As a rule, a well-functioning group is distinguished by the fact that in addition to the type of human capital relevant to its particular task, the other types of capital are also represented. In this exercise, the project teams gather in an initial, constituting meeting in order to determine individual contributions and resources and also the composition of the whole.

Step 1: Each person considers individually: *"What resources in terms of implementation of hard cuts/new growth can I contribute to the project?"*

Step 2: The neighbors interview each other on the essential results.

Step 3: Together, they present the results (after the others have "speculated" on what the resources may be). The results are documented.

Step 4: The team discusses its composition: *"Where do our strengths lie? Do we need reinforcement?"* Consequences/decisions are derived from this.

What you need:
- Flipchart

Our comment:
This can also be used as a decision-making aid in the initial setting-up of teams.

PHASE 2 INTERVENTIONS: QUICK WINS AND "GO TO MARKET" WORKSHOP 1

When to use it:
In the preparation of an implementation strategy for the merging of enterprises or corporate divisions entailing both hard cuts and innovation/new growth.

What it achieves:
Familiarization with different perspectives; strengthening of external orientation in post-merger integration.

How to proceed:
Participants are: salespersons/project managers/employees with contact to key customers of both enterprises.

Step 1: Working groups (always formed according to previous corporate affiliation) prepare the following:
- Images of ourselves:
    - What is unique about us/our success?
    - How do we perceive our customers (+/–)?
    - What specific resources do we have?
    - What must now be renewed/changed?
- Images of the others, rumors, statements (+/–) – everything goes, overplaying is better than understating

Step 2: Exchange in a plenary session

An observer group (including a consultant) from both firms/divisions is determined beforehand.

Per group:
- The others' image of us – and then our image of ourselves

Step 3: The observers move into an inner circle; the moderator (second consultant) interviews:
- Reflections on the images
- Resulting opportunities and risks

Step 4: Mixed groups continue working

The central questions are: What are the results:
  a) for

– customers	+/– (first priority!!)
– managerial staff	+/–
– employees	+/–
– partners	+/–

  b) in relation to the overall strategy: *What do we want to achieve/maintain with customers in the next three to six months?*
  c) with regard to "hot potatoes" and critical questions?

Step 5: In a plenary session:
- Exchange and summarize, clarify questions, prioritize
- Whom do we address concerning the implementation steps?
- In what areas do we make a contribution of our own?

Step 6: Individual work

Each participant selects two high-potential customers (in terms of yield/innovation/turnover growth/role as opinion-makers).

Step 7: Each participant selects a partner from the other company for the development of customer discussions or new contacts.

Step 8: Duos develop an interview guide for joint customer discussions on the basis of previous work.

Objective:
- Customer retention/loyalty
- Joint appearance that demonstrates integration and customer orientation
- Develop "quick wins" and strategic projects from customer inputs

Step 9: Discussion of/commitment to: common language rules concerning objectives/procedures/ground rules and feedback to customers

Step 10: Role-play practice, in particular: beginning conversations; addressing sensitive issues during discussions; concluding discussions

Step 11: Setting dates and determining an evaluation system for the discussions

What you need:
- Workshop room
- Flipcharts for documentation

Our comment:
With customer contacts, the "hot potatoes" of change are tackled from the very beginning; integration via customer discussions in "tandem".

QUICK WINS AND "GO TO MARKET" WORKSHOP 2

When to use it:
Customer interviews have been conducted; the interview pairs have documented and roughly evaluated the results.

What it achieves:
The results are compiled. An initial prioritization of implementation steps is prepared by all those involved. Outward orientation increases.

How to proceed:
Step 1: Pairs are teamed up with other pairs to interview each other on the achieved results.

Step 2: Each of the two working groups (four interview pairs) prepare a summary.
1. From the customer's viewpoint:
   – Success factors for customer retention/"added value" of our merger
   – Pitfalls
   – Opportunities for quick wins
2. Priorities: What have we realized?
3. New questions/"hot potatoes"

Step 3: "Flash snapshots" in a plenary session: three highlights from each working group.

Step 4: The results are presented in a "market" situation.

Step 5: Working groups prepare activity proposals (projects, initiatives and ideas) on the basis of the overall image that has emerged. These are presented in the final plenary session.

Step 6: Commitment is established with the management or the client, who join the workshop. Results are voted and decided upon in an inner circle.

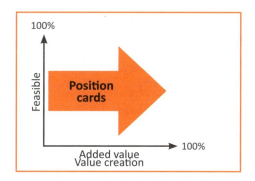

What you need:
- Pinboards for the "market"
- Flipchart
- Facilitation material

Our comment:
Success is ultimately decided by customers; post-merger integration via collaborative customer activity and market-related initiatives and projects.

EXTERNAL SPARRING PARTNER SYSTEM (SPS) FOR HARD CUTS

When to use it:
Hard cuts are looming on the horizon. The responsible managers want to gather complementary perspectives that will help them prepare a comprehensive implementation strategy.

What it achieves:
Establish an external Sparring Partner System (SPS) with impartial, uninvolved persons, whose task is to contribute a complementary, polarizing external perspective. This broadens the spectrum of implementation options.

How to proceed:
Step 1: SPS conducts interviews with managers on the main issue:
Which hard cuts are necessary and why?
The interviews are conducted publicly, audible for everyone present.

Step 2: SPS forms hypotheses:
What if we were to consistently interpret the "hard cuts project" as its opposite – as an "opportunities project" (consistently address resources and potentials)?

Step 3: Managers react

Step 4: Mixed groups (SPS + managers) discuss suggestions for giving shape to the hard cuts.

Step 5: Collective summarization and decision on how to proceed.

What you need:
- Room without tables
- Facilitation material

Our comment:
Our thesis is: A focus on deficits (weaknesses, failures, etc.) leads to streamlining; a focus on potentials and strengths awakens forward-looking optimism.

This kind of work can also be done in support of consultant teams.

STRATEGY RETREAT WITH KEY PLAYERS

When to use it:
The company has extensive experience (both positive and negative) with strategy processes. It has now arrived at a further crossroads, and instruments and processes for strategy planning have not yet been decided on.

What it achieves:
The sensibility for strategic models and different forms of strategy development processes increases. The preliminary phase leads to a reflection of previous strategies, as well as their implementation and consequences. The key players recognize the essential strategic options. The main emphases become more consistent due to the exchange of experience and opinions. The workshop brings about a change of behavior in day-to-day business.

How to proceed:

Preparation:
The managers are asked to "dig up" essential strategy papers from the past years and to write an evolutionary history (from their point of view) up to now.

Workshop:
Step 1: The participants gather in front of a large wall. Bit by bit, the individual strategy papers are briefly presented, their preparation process is described, and the subsequent business development is outlined. The procedure starts with the oldest paper; the others follow in chronological order.

Step 2: Groups evaluate the overall image:

Group 1: *Which strategies were the most successful?*

Group 2: *Which models were most convincing?*

Group 3: *Which development processes were most effective?*

Step 3: A group of delegates summarizes the results and prepares a recommendation, which includes the strategy themes (relating to the current situation), suitable models and developmental processes.

Step 4: The observers react; afterwards the results are collectively summarized.

Step 5: Strategy topics from the stakeholder viewpoint: The participants form stakeholder groups. The essential strategic corporate issues are prepared from their respective viewpoints.

Central questions:
- What are the pivotal strategic questions for us as …?
- Where do we see – from our perspectives – the necessity for hard cuts?
- From our point of view, where should new growth be initiated or promoted?

Step 6: A group of delegates exchanges results (inner circle); the observers are asked to scrutinize the recommendations for practical and implemental relevance.

Step 7: The observers provide feedback in the plenum; central strategic questions are collectively defined.

Step 8: The questions are now worked out in small groups:
- What is the initial situation?
- Which objectives (non-objectives) are to be achieved?
- What approach/method (see Step 4) do we consider sensible in this case?
- What does the timeline look like (milestones)?
- Whom must we involve, what resources are required?

The respective results are compiled on a flipchart or in electronic format.

Step 9: In the plenum, the detailed plans are combined; collective preparation of the master plan. Those responsible summarize the essential results and next steps.

Step 10: In a closing constellation (everyone positions themselves in the room according to their appraisal), the following dimensions are examined:

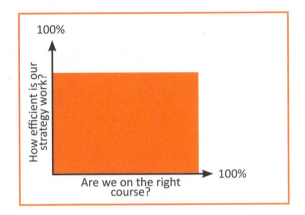

What you need:
- A large wall and a laptop with projector
- Post-its
- Facilitation material
- Masking tape

Our comment:
You should plan with at least 1.5 days for this demanding workshop.

STRUCTURE DECISION – WHO SHOULD DRIVE THE CHANGE: MANAGEMENT TEAM, CHANGE TEAM OR CORPORATE DEVELOPMENT DEPARTMENT?

When to use it:
The change objectives are clear, but the allocation of responsibility for the change has yet to be determined:
- to the management team (line)?
- to a temporary change team (project)?
- to a corporate development department (staff)?

What it achieves:
The decision-makers discuss the advantages and disadvantages of these alternatives. The decision becomes more deliberate, its effect on the organization more clearly defined.

How to proceed:
Step 1: The three options – management team, change team and corporate development – are briefly outlined in a steering meeting.

Step 2: "Goal Check"
The objectives of the change processes are individually talked through, and the respective options are set in relation: *What speaks for/against this variant?*

Step 3: "Stakeholder Check"
The next diagnostic task is carried out from the viewpoint of the stakeholders in this change (employees, proprietors, customers, etc.): *What is our appraisal of the options from our current perspective?*

Step 4: "Cost/benefit"
In conclusion, the participants position the three alternatives in a "Cost/benefit" portfolio.

Step 5: Further procedure – particularly communication – is agreed on.

What you need:
- Flipchart or laptop and projector

Our comment:
Not all changes need as a matter of course to be managed by a change team! Line management could be a good alternative.

TEAM STAFFING BASED ON MICROCOSM ANALYSIS

When to use it:
The enterprise decides to rely on teams for the implementation of change, which means that staffing choices are vital to its success. The teams should reflect the enterprise's characteristics (microcosm approach, integration of all relevant differences).

What it achieves:
The selection is made under the aspects of "getting the best people onto the team" and "finding the optimal combination".

How to proceed:
Step 1: Those responsible for the staffing first work individually on the central questions: *"What are the different logical systems that distinguish our enterprise?" "What are the trends in terms of hard cuts/new growth in our enterprise?" "What hard cuts & new growth are foreseen in the change process?"*
"What requirements result from this for the selection of key players?"

Step 2: The results are consolidated and summarized in criteria for team staffing.

Example:

Criteria / People	Time with the company (< 1, < 2, > 2 years)	Department – Manufacturing/Administration/Sales	Attitude – conservative/ progressive	Experience with hard cuts	Experience with new growth

Step 3: Proposals for team staffing are entered into this model. (Goal: Get the best people.)

Step 4: The individual columns are analyzed. Objective: The best combination. The selection is gradually narrowed down. Experience has shown that this involves some backtracking and crisscrossing.

Step 5: The responsible parties make the staffing decisions.

What you need:
Flipchart/laptop and projector

Our comment:
When in doubt, decide in favor of an "explosive" combination that clearly illustrates the differences in your organization.

THE "RED RIBBON"

When to use it:
The organization is on the verge of a transformation. The new is still unfamiliar, and the transition is a matter of concern to many managers and employees.

What it achieves:
In a simulation, the participants become aware of the dynamics the transition entails.

How to proceed:
Step 1: The room is separated into halves with a red tape. These fields are signposted "old" and "new". The participants are all in the "old" field.

Step 2: Groups discuss the following central questions:
- "What are we proud of/where are we unique?"
- "What do we want to take with us/transfer/preserve?"
- "What will be left behind, what will we depart from?"

The various points of view are exchanged in brief statements in the plenum.

Step 3: The ribbon is "officially" cut: One at a time, everyone steps from "old" to "new", and comments from their perspective: *"What does this transition mean to me?"*

Step 4: A summary is worked out in groups, then consolidated in the plenum.

What you need:
- Large room without chairs
- Red ribbon
- Scissors

Our comment:
A bit theatrical – but it works!

TRAVELING TO FOREIGN WORLDS (EXAMPLE: SEMINAR HOTEL)

When to use it:
Key individuals are dealing intensively with change management issues. They wish to complement their preparations with ideas from outside sources.

What it achieves:
The sensibility for one's own actions increases through the observation of examples for success from other sectors or systems. The discussion of differences and points in common leads to new solution ideas. The perception for one's own success factors increases.

How to proceed:
The following example describes a prototypical procedure in a seminar hotel, where the management team is staying. This hotel has received numerous awards for excellence in the past.

Step 1: The group is divided into several sub-teams, which define their "observer focus". In this example:

The teams determine their analytical approach:
- Interviews
- Document analysis
- "Undercover" observation
- etc.

They have a fixed "time budget" for the accumulation of information (e.g., two hours).

Step 2: The groups fan out and collect information.

Step 3: In seminar rooms, each group sifts through their results and forms hypotheses on what constitutes this company's special success factors, then prepares a presentation.

Step 4: The presentations are exchanged in the plenum.

Step 5: The results are now consecutively consolidated – openly, for all participants. The groups are mixed.

Step 6: Summary and operationalizing (*Who does what?*) of results.

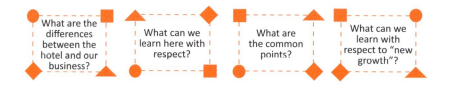

What you need:
- A "system" that can be observed (in this case, the seminar hotel)
- Facilitation material for the groups
- Possibly a camera; dictaphone

Our comment:
You will be amazed how complex a "seminar hotel system" can be!

PHASE 3 INTERVENTIONS: QUICK WIN PORTFOLIO

When to use it:
The change project is in progress; initial implementation results are foreseeable. But there is no coordination or strategy for quick wins.

What it achieves:
A "dramaturgy" of quick wins that has an impact on all important stakeholder groups and generates implementation energy.

How to proceed:
Step 1: The steering group (management team or project team) collects all project results that have proved viable up to this point. Each sub-segment manager goes through his or her planning and writes it down on separate Post-it notes.

Step 2: The individual results are entered in the following quick win portfolio.

Step 3: The overall image is collectively evaluated. The objective is a well-balanced portfolio that distributes the quick wins across all phases and includes all important stakeholders.

Optimization questions:
- Have the quick wins gotten off to a good start, or should some of them be brought forward, or postponed?
- What is the effect on our enterprise; how relevant are the quick wins for our everyday routine?

Step 4: The responsible managers summarize the results and determine implementation steps.

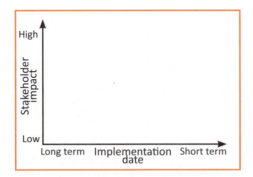

What you need:
- A large wall for the portfolio
- Post-it notes (large format)

Our comment:
Have you ever experienced a genuine quick win?

STAKEHOLDER IMPACT ANALYSIS

When to use it:
It is unclear how the individual stakeholders are specifically affected by the change project, to what extent they have been informed, and how clear the next steps are to them.

What it achieves:
The change management team obtains an overview of the status from the stakeholder outlook. The quality of control measures is improved.

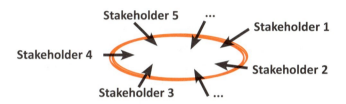

How to proceed:
Step 1: In a brainstorming session, the change management team lists major stakeholders and arranges them in a diagram (if the team has already prepared a diagram, it can be used as a starting point).

Step 3: For every group of stakeholders, the group now answers two questions and assigns a value to the answer:
- *How well is the respective group informed about the change?* (0% to 100%)
- *Are the stakeholders clear on their next steps, tasks and contributions?* (0% to 100%)

Step 3: The assessments are transcribed onto the graph. They serve as a starting point for overall evaluation of the current situation and action options.

What you need:
- 2 pinboards
- Flipcharts

Our comment:
Check if you really have "something" for all stakeholders!

THE MANAGEMENT TEAM SPEECH

When to use it:
Numerous parties are demanding a clear positioning of management. The stakeholder interests are complex and contradictory. There are different positions in the management team itself.

What it achieves:
The management team deals more clearly with the diverse interests. There are clear communication messages.

How to proceed:
Step 1: The various stakeholders are presented in a brief analysis. A three-person team is commissioned to draft a speech on the "state of the nation" (the designated, actual speaker should not be a member). The remaining participants form pairs and decide on a stakeholder perspective. If there are not enough participants for all stakeholder groups, the pairs take several perspectives.

Step 2: Parallel group work:
Three-person team: drafts the speech, prepares the address and allocates roles.
Stakeholder pairs: answer the questions:
What distinguishes our position?
What do we expect of the management team?

Step 3: The speech is held, questions are clarified.

Step 4: The stakeholder pairs provide feedback:
- What were our emotions during the speech?
- What appealed to us positively?
- What do we see critically?

Step 5: Improvements are worked out in the plenum. In conclusion, the person who held the speech summarizes his/her findings.

What you need:
- Writing material

Our comment:
Controversial discussion enhances the quality of the speech!

CHANGING THE GENERAL FRAMEWORK; STRENGTHENING OPTIONS FOR NEW GROWTH

When to use it:
The change is becoming increasingly dynamic. Now it is a matter of strengthening the growth options.

What it achieves:
New conditions break up the routine and as a result, new options for action arise. Employees become aware of the demand for innovation.

How to proceed:
Option 1: Bring in a creativity and innovation consultant, who makes improvements to the workspace – including furnishing, color and sound design, lighting and plants.

Option 2: Support your employees in the design of creative working environments, also in the case of virtual workstations.

Option 3: Organize creative sessions in unique settings, such as cafes, amusement parks or wellness hotels. Your imagination sets the limits here.

Option 4: Introduce a system for implementing innovations and measuring their effectiveness. The system should include objectives for innovation frequency as well as their profit contribution.

What you need:
Imagination – and the courage to translate it into reality.

Our comment:
Surprises beget surprises. Small changes often have a big effect.

INNOVATION MARKET

When to use it:
There is a great variety of initiatives and plans for innovation in the enterprise, but people don't see the big picture yet. Incentive systems are lacking.

What it achieves:
The company's innovative capacity is strengthened, innovative key players are given market-oriented incentives; constructive competition is promoted. The big picture is experienced by everyone.

How to proceed:
Step 1: Preparation: Review and summarize current innovative plans and projects in an overview.

Announce the innovation market in an internal advertisement. Employees currently involved in innovations are invited to a kickoff event; additional submissions are actively solicited.

Step 2: Kickoff: present the submissions to all participants (preferably in a market setting). Senior management communicates the objectives and procedure for the innovation market. The submitted innovation projects compete for people and resources. They receive feedback and ideas for their further work from the other market participants (possibly from the different stakeholder perspectives).

Whoever wants to invest in innovative ventures offers resources; whoever wants to contribute competencies and experience negotiates collaboration with innovation teams.

Senior management sets the framework (e.g., time capacity per employee, overall budget) and ground rules. Frameworks and ground rules that promote autonomy, self-initiative, intense communication through self-management and reciprocal challenge have proven successful in the past.

Step 3: The innovation teams continue their work independently, or build networks and synergetic relationships with other teams.

Step 4: The teams prepare an innovation market, which is broadly advertised in the company. They compile the previous results of their work and specify what they additionally want to offer, and how.

Step 5: A great deal of information is exchanged during the innovation market. A jury – or all participants – vote for the "most effective" innovations.

Step 6: The prizewinners give a "press conference" for an audience relevant to them.

What you need:
Facilitator, consultant and project team for planning and managing the innovation market as a process tailored to individual needs.

Our comment:
The innovation market is most effective if understood as a process (with preparation & follow-up). It consolidates the orientation towards innovation and exploits innovative potential.

LATERAL THINKING: RAISING TEAMS' INNOVATIVE POTENTIAL

When to use it:
An innovation team is in the kickoff phase. All key players assemble for a retreat session with the objective of promoting initial innovation potentials.

What it achieves:
Every participant is positively encouraged to think about the company's future; the spectrum of possible solutions widens.

How to proceed:
Step 1: Put yourself in the position of someone who you have always wanted to be. Concentrate on the following: *What is my everyday life like in this situation? What am I proud of? What are my dreams?*

Step 2: Form small teams (3 to 4 people).
Go for a walk. Imagine that you meet each other by coincidence, get to know each other, and hear about your partner's firm and the issues people there are dealing with.

Now go together to a place where you feel comfortable – where you would otherwise never go – to deal with the following question:
From our perspective, what would be totally different/surprising and innovative for this company?

Step 3: Exchange of views among groups in the plenum.

Step 4: Each group takes over other groups' ideas and works on them (What is productive about this → What is its potential?).

Step 5: Exchange

What you need:
Flipcharts/laptop for documentation

Our comment:
Innovation should also be fun – the "dream question" renders dream results!

"FUTURE CABARET": SCENES FROM THE FUTURE

When to use it:
An initial vision is documented or discussed; it is still abstract and lacks action-orientation.

What it achieves:
By playing through concrete scenes, it becomes possible to experience the future – each participant translates their abstract vision into action. Processing this provides ideas for further developing the vision.

How to proceed:
Step 1: The participants form groups of three to five. Each group is given the task of preparing a scene:
- The scene should be typical for the future ("business-relevant").
- It should integrate elements of hard cuts and new growth.
- Everyone in the group plays a part, everything is allowed.
- The group should give the scene a title.

Step 2: The groups prepare their scenes.

Step 3: The sequence of the scenes is determined; the moderator writes down the names on a flipchart. Piece for piece, the scenes are played out; action is interrupted in the event of spontaneous applause, and every scene is applauded.

Step 4: (possibly the next morning): The scenes are discussed in mixed groups (every scene should be represented by a member). Central questions:
- What has become particularly clear for our vision?
- What were the key scenes?
- What have the scenes emphasized?
- How has our vision now been supplemented?
- What has not been addressed, and why not?
- What have we learned for hard cuts and new growth?

Step 5: Exchange in the plenum; an editing team works on the formulation of the new vision.

What you need:
- Stage/platform on which the groups play out the scenes
- Flipchart
- Video camera

Our comment:
Highly suitable for the evening session of a retreat!

DEALING WITH CONTRADICTIONS: COST/BENEFIT

When to use it:
Perceptions of the current situation and views on necessary steps for further development diverge widely. Discussions are characterized by polarization; a resolution of conflicts is nowhere in sight.

What it achieves:
Participants are given the opportunity to experience confrontation with "opposition" as a vital necessity for the further development of the change process. This enables them to recognize that every intervention has its price. Pros and cons become clear, and polarizations lose their force.

How to proceed:
In a working group – in which all important representatives of the "problem" are included – the individual aspects are worked out according to the following basic structure:
- *What is the issue/problem?*
- *What is its opposite?*
- *What is the positive aspect of the opposite?*
- *What is the negative aspect of the opposite?*

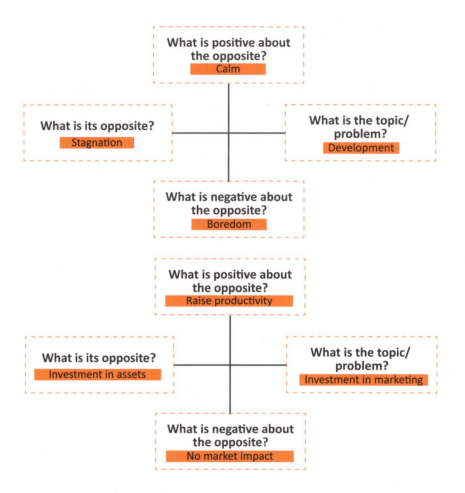

In conclusion, the group determines options and scrutinizes their possible implementation.

What you need:
The people who are fundamentally concerned by the problem all in one room – and impartial facilitation.

Our comment:
This technique can also be applied in individual coaching.

"STAND UP OR REMAIN SEATED"

When to use it:
The organization is in the midst of a change process. There are diverse trends and perceptions in the enterprise. Their distribution in the company is not clear. Clarity on this is, however, very important for the further procedure.

What it achieves:
In a large-scale event – in which a majority of the workforce or a representative cross-section is present – these differences become quickly and pointedly visible for everyone.

Those responsible use this information to give shape to the further change process.

How to proceed:
Step 1: Preparation: Identify the relevant differences of opinion/perception regarding the success of the change.

Example: To what extent will the effects of the change be felt on the following levels? my person/my team/the whole organization

Step 2: Present these differences to the participants (5–10 min.).

Step 3: Working individually, each participant assesses what the perception/answer is on each of the different levels, e.g., my person, my team and the whole organization:
- very much?
- average?
- not at all? (5 min.)

Step 4: Analogously, each of the levels (e.g., teams, the whole organization) are requested to give their answers:
- not at all: remain seated
- average: stand up
- very much: stand up and raise one hand (3–5 min.)

Step 5: For each of the levels, ask flash questions about all three positions: *What made you decide this way, what impression do you have of the overall process?* (40 min.)

Step 6: Continue work in the plenum:
1. Minimal variant: Those responsible for change management and implementation take a position and draw conclusions (15 min.)
2. More extensive variant: delegates discuss the positions in the plenum, in working groups, etc., and draw conclusions for the further management of the change process

What you need:
- A room in which everyone can see everyone else (or video transmission)
- Presentation equipment
- Sound system (depending on the size of the room)
- Group size: 25 to 1,000 (or more)

Our comment:
The initial selection of differences is crucial! These must be of relevance for implementation and emotionally appealing. Really make use of the information received as a motor for shaping the change process further.

MINI EVALUATION – CHANGE STATUS

When to use:
The company is undergoing change in numerous areas; a wide array of subprojects is being taken on. The managerial staffs' appraisal of the progress is divergent.

What it achieves:
Clarity on which change phase the subprojects are located in. Development of suitable control measures for the change as a whole and for subprojects.

How to proceed:
Step 1: The representatives of the individual projects form groups and assess subproject status using the phase model: In which change phase are we currently?

Step 2: Afterwards, they position themselves in the room according to their assessment. Together (and possibly with representatives of other subprojects that have positioned themselves in the same phase) they discuss the reasons for their position. (*Why are we standing here? What is the special characteristic of our position?*)

What you need:
- A room with floor markings indicating the 5 change phases described earlier (without chairs in the beginning)
- Chairs that can be quickly set up
- Flipcharts

PHASE 4 INTERVENTIONS: EVALUATING PILOT PROJECTS – CHECK-UP FOR FURTHER IMPLEMENTATION

When to use it:
The initial pilot projects are underway. Reactions vary. Numerous rumors are coursing through the company about experiences made in their implementation. It remains unclear which implemental steps promise the most success.

What it achieves:
A common understanding is achieved of the status of pilot projects and their implementation. The quality of implementation is enhanced.

How to proceed:
The following participants are invited to work in the response team:
- Pilot project developers
- Management (decision-makers)
- Project manager and clients
- Stakeholders: experts/users in daily business
- Working groups are formed under the aspect: *"With whom do (I think) I share a similar view of the current situation?"*

Step 1: Central questions for discussion in the groups:
1. Rumors: What have we heard about the pilots?
2. *What do we most urgently want to know about the pilots or their evaluation in their implementation concepts?*

Step 2: Plenary: Three highlights per group are briefly presented.

Step 3: As far as possible, "live" presentations of the pilot projects:
- Successes/failures/ups and downs
- Lessons learned on hard cuts and new growth
- An overview of the implementation concept
- What should we preserve/change/attain?
- How can we measure success?

Step 4: Questions from the groups regarding clarification of these points.

Step 5: In-depth discussion in the working groups:
1. *Why will the concept fail?* (devil's advocate role)
2. *Why will it succeed?* (promoter role)
3. *Which questions still need to be discussed?* The group selects a "questioner".

Step 6: The facilitator collects the questions ("hot potatoes") and documents these on a flipchart.

Step 7: Listening and dialogue
- **Inner circle:** The questioner and whoever would like to respond move into the inner circle.
  a) The questioner is interviewed by the facilitator:
     – What is the question?
     – Why is it important?
     – What are the criteria for a good answer?
     – Whoever wants to answer moves into the inner circle.
  b) The "answerers" repeat the question in their own understanding. Only after agreement is reached on the question can they answer, pose questions in return and develop variants or ideas.

  Objective: Answer the question or clarify further action.
- **Outer circle:** listens (follows the exchange, analyzes it, notes resonances).

Step 8: Overall view: The facilitator draws a line through the room representing a scale from 0% to 100%.
- Everyone answers the central question: *"How high do I assess the project's current chances for implementation?"* From an *overall corporate viewpoint*, i.e., abstracting from one's own perspective.
- Everyone positions himself or herself on the scale; the facilitator interviews the participants on their respective positioning and their assessment of the overall image.
- Optional: Statement from the client and project manager.

What you need:
- Facilitation cards
- Presentation documents
- Masking tape

Our comment:
Broad participation and a controversial discussion are essential success factors! Important: clear and "strict" facilitation.

SYMBOLIC ACTION: "WASTEPAPER BASKET – MUSEUM – SHOWCASE"

When to use it:
Most of those concerned have now realized that as the change moves forward, the organization has to depart from fundamental routines/behavioral patterns – some dear, some detested. A concrete new outline of the future is already emerging.

What it achieves:
In a symbolic action, leaving things behind but also embracing the new become topics of discussion. The departure from good but outdated behavior patterns takes place in an appreciate way, opening the door onto new ways of doing things.

How to proceed:
Preparation: The participants (key players for the change) are asked to prepare themselves to answer the following questions:

- Question 1: *What must we leave behind, even if it was functional and important?*
- Question 2: *What must we leave behind because it has always been dysfunctional and unimportant?*
- Question 3: *What must we strengthen in order to be successful in the future?*

Step 1: Workshop/large-scale event
The participants discuss (in groups of three) various approaches to the three questions. They write down core messages for each question on cards. Each participant represents/answers one of the questions in turn.

Step 2: The "museum"
The representatives for question 1 assemble in front of the "museum pinboard". The facilitator asks for different perspectives and arranges the subject areas in groups. The overall image is discussed and decided in the group. The two other groups listen.

Step 3: The "wastepaper basket" (same procedure as Step 2 with representatives for question 2)

Step 4: The "showcase" (same procedure as Step 2 with representatives for question 3)

Step 5: Preparation of an implementation plan
Still focusing on their respective perspectives, the groups work on the following central questions:
- What can we do to successfully translate the wastepaper basket, museum and showcase into practice?
- What do we need for this?
- What could be the next step?

Step 6: The groups present their results/proposals. Those concerned are asked for their views (approval/refusal). Clear responsibilities are defined for the next steps (to-do list).

Step 7: The participants return to their original groups of three, and discuss:
- How consistent is the overall image?
- What is most important to us in terms of content, emotion and structure?
- What are our recommendations for further action?

What you need:
- A "wastepaper basket" pinboard
- A "museum" pinboard
- A "showcase" pinboard
- Facilitation material

Our comment:
The "museum" gives a good visual representation of appreciation for the "outdated".

SYMBOLIC IMPLEMENTATION OF THE MAIN CHALLENGE

When to use it:
The objectives have been clearly communicated and accepted; they are highly challenging, and can be concentrated in core messages.

What it achieves:
The most important stakeholders become aware of exactly what is happening. The status of the project's development becomes understandable, focus is strengthened.

How to proceed:
Step 1: The core team (e.g., project team, managing director) analyzes the change process in relation to its core messages. Depending on the group size, discussions are held with the whole group or in subgroups. The central questions are:

- What are the process's most important objectives (regarding substance, timing, social considerations, etc.)?
- Which stakeholders are most important for their achievement?

The results are documented on a flipchart.

Step 2: Brainstorming in subgroups

- What symbols could stand for these objectives? (e.g., final date: clock; cost objective: moneybag, etc.)
- At which locations and through which media are the target groups most accessible (e.g., employees: reception area, elevator, canteen; proprietors: conference room, billboard in front of the private house, etc.)?

Step 3: Presentation of ideas in the plenum, joint brainstorming on the central question:

What are possible symbolic actions that could provide the relevant target groups with a clear picture of how far the change process has progressed so far towards its goal?

Step 4: Afterwards, ideas are short-listed, compiled and scaled in a portfolio.

The team decides on the best alternative and allocates responsibility for its implementation.

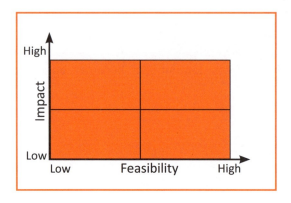

What you need:

- A workshop room
- Flipchart or computer

Our comment:

Digital countdown displays in reception areas, billboards on the company grounds or continually updated info boxes in elevators (to name a few examples) have proven successful in practice.

PHASE ARCHITECTURE WITH CLEAR HANDOVERS
EXAMPLE: PROJECT → LINE

When to use it:
The change process is taking place over a longer time period, during which the tasks and social dynamics change. A particularly abrupt transition in the process is the handover of implemental responsibility from projects into the line, e.g., to managing directors or the management team.

What it achieves:
The employees and managerial personnel have a clear idea of the change milestones. The handover of responsibilities is clear; the results of the last phase are acknowledged, and the requirements and responsibilities for the new phase are defined and agreed upon.

How to proceed:
Step 1: Together with the client, the project team clarifies the phase structure, the handover time and how previous work will be evaluated.

Step 2: Project team workshop

The project team evaluates results so far on the basis of the project mandate, stakeholder feedback and benchmarks with other projects.

Results up to now	% finished	Finish by	Next tasks	Responsible

Based on these results, the project team prepares a "phase conclusion report" that encompasses the results, timetable, costs and the relationships with the most important stakeholders.

The handover to the new responsible personnel is organized in similar fashion. Individual project team members prepare a handover work package. This (real) package contains information on the already compiled results, but also future work packages for managerial personnel and possible performance indexes for these areas.

Step 3: The handover retreat

The business management invites all members of the project team as well as managerial personnel and key individuals to this session.

The project team organizes the first half of the retreat; afterwards, line management has its turn.

At the start, the participants individually compile their most significant experiences with the project so far – from their own personal perspective. The emotional impact of the described incidents is rated on a scale of –100 to +100. A "timeline" is collectively drawn on the pinboard. The project team has already prepared files for the handover and placed these in postal packages, which are personally handed over to each involved manager.

Those "taking over" spontaneously and publicly portray how they intend to meet the requirements and expectations. In the end, the project team is "praised" and "unburdened" by the client (overall director of the change process).

What you need:
- Project presentations
- Laptop, projector
- Facilitation material
- A large room

"CUSTOMER PARLIAMENT" 2

When to use it:
A "Customer Parliament" has already been held in the preceeding year. The results of the same could be useful for further development.

What it achieves:
- Continuation and expansion of the previous year's event
- Direct, personal appeal to all relevant customers
- In the foreground: customer retention; new business as secondary objective
- Not a re-run: again, an event with innovative character
- Follow-up on the previous year: Where has implementation been accomplished? How can we further develop our partnership?

How to proceed:
Step 1: Preparation
- Select customers (current/long-standing/prospective)
- Send out invitations, announce the selection
- Make internal preparations: What items from the previous year have been implemented?
- Present invitees with a reminder and/or a questionnaire to help them tune in to the coming event

Step 2: (Day 1) "Customer Parliament"
- Basic idea: Last year, the "Parliament" passed a basic law, which could be considered the "constitution". Now, it is time to make constitutional amendments or pass laws that will increase its effectiveness.
- The government (business management) starts with a speech on the "state of the nation".
- The parliament debates, withdraws for fraction group meetings, and – after a general debate – passes amendments or laws.
- Employees are "only" observers (journalists and/or photographers) and do not actively participate in the discussion; the event is possibly broadcasted "live" in another room.

Step 3: (Day 2) Employee retreat
- Reflection on the results of the Customer Parliament
- Executive management: How do the results affect our general strategy?
- Groups: How do the results affect our specific project strategies?
- Decision on how to proceed after the end of the retreat: each customer should be contacted personally.

Step 4: Follow-up phase
- Every participant should be contacted personally (with general info and an individualized response)
- Film on CD
- Customer newspaper

What you need:
- General requirement: Plenary assembly hall to accommodate all participants (a room not too large in relation to the number of participants, to create a relatively intimate atmosphere)
- Side rooms for "fraction group meetings"
- A room for broadcasting the proceedings to employees

Our comment:
A pleasant side effect: New possibilities for collaboration and new business often emerge as a result of intense discussions!

COMPREHENSIVE PROJECT WORK

When to use it:
Implementation projects are running in all areas of the enterprise. These have originated partly in top-down decisions, partly in proposals coming from sub-divisions, but also in the personal intiative of individuals.

What it achieves:
This project landscape is "scanned" to determine the extent to which it actually comprehensively covers the organization's crucial issues. The deployment of projects becomes more focused and efficient.

How to proceed:
Step 1: Analysis

The representatives of the management team or change team compile an overview of the projects currently underway, including their objectives, activities, costs and the involved employees (please note: This step can often take months!).

Step 2: Management team event

In a workshop, the projects are first presented in their entirety (key data). Afterwards, they are evaluated in working groups according to various criteria/levels. The facilitators (internal and/or external) have prepared a small index card for each project.

Group 1: divides up the projects according to what process they chiefly pertain to, e.g.:
- Innovation process
- Production process
- Marketing process
- Service process
- Support processes

Group 2: allocates the projects to current strategic directions of impact, e.g., TOP FIVE OBJECTIVES of the year.

Group 3: allocates the projects to the individual corporate sectors.

Group 4: arranges the projects according to temporal maturity.

The results are presented in the plenum; afterwards, the groups are mixed in "cross-sections" and discuss:
- How do we see the overall image? (e.g., bundles vs. "white spots on the map")
- Are the projects really hitting the nerve issues of the organization?
- What conclusions can we draw (termination, postponement, redefinition of ongoing projects)?

Step 3: Start a comprehensive project portfolio:

Someone is appointed or volunteers to take on responsibility for this.

What you need:
- Post-it notes with the project names
- 4 pinboards or a flipchart

Our comment:
If for some reason you are not able to address the organization's "crucial issues", it's better not to do this exercise!

PHASE 5 INTERVENTIONS: MEETING CHECK-UP

When to use it:
Everyday routine has already "settled into place". There are established meeting structures, and things have begun to proceed in certain patterns. However, doubt is arising among management whether the prevailing behavior patterns and the topics chosen for discussion are appropriate and/or helpful for anchoring the achieved change in the company.

What it achieves:
The company routine is seen "through new lenses", in light of reflection on one major meeting (e.g., a meeting of the management team) that serves as an example. In an initial reflection, the quality of the meeting – especially the selection and treatment of topics – becomes manifest. It becomes clearer, to what extent and in what direction the meeting has been adapted to the change. It becomes possible to identify essential levers for anchoring the new.

How to proceed:
Meeting preparation and procedure "as usual". A "Meeting Check-Up" is carried out as the last item on the agenda.

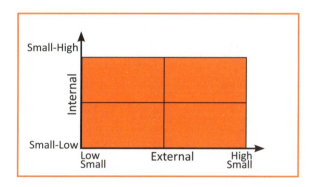

Step 1: Contents and procedure are analyzed in subgroups.

Group 1: *What contribution do the present-day meeting topics make in the following dimensions?*
- Increase of internal efficiency
- Improvement of market/customer position

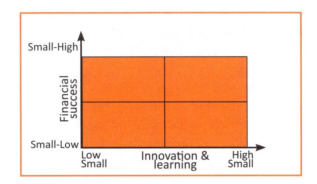

Group 2: *What contribution do the present-day meeting topics make in the following dimensions?*
- Financial success of the enterprise
- Innovation and learning

Group 3: *How do we rate the meeting's procedure?* The participants rate the individual topics in terms of ...
- **Information quality**

  low   high
- **Quality of discussion**

  low   high
- **Degree of decision-orientation**

  low   high

Step 2: To conclude the rating, the groups develop images and associations for the way the meeting runs: *Our meeting is like ...*

Step 3: The groups then present their results. A plenary discussion on the following central question is held:
- *Are we dealing with the right topics?*
- *Are there any "white spots" on the map?*
- *Are we working efficiently?*
- *What is our overall impression? How great is the need to make changes to our meetings, on a scale of 0 to 100%?*
- *What are the next steps?*
- *Where are the benefits and added value of our meetings?*

What you need:
- 3 pinboards
- Prepared facilitation cards with the agenda topics
- 1 participant or external specialist for facilitation

Our comment:
Be on the lookout for "unproductive" behavior patterns that may have crept in.

REGULAR REVIEW GROUPS

When to use it:
Improving the qualification of employees is an essential feature of change processes. Appropriate courses have been offered, events have been held, and a series of (pilot) projects have offered new experiences. Now the new knowledge and skills gained need to be reinforced and consolidated.

What it achieves:
The new experiences are shared and reflected upon in small groups. The quality of implementation increases and the employees taking part have more assurance in dealing with new aspects of their work. Cross-divisional thinking is promoted, implementation issues are discussed, and immediate solutions are developed.

How to proceed:
Step 1: Selection of participants (managerial personnel, project managers and key individuals).

Step 2: Kickoff event with the participation of all concerned employees and the entire management. Information is provided on overall architecture and review trios are established, as well as a team for overall control; a typical review trio meeting is simulated.

Step 3: Regular review trio meetings; work on the following levels:
- Personal insights
- Points in common/differences
- Reflections on the company's overall situation
- Drawing of consequences for both individuals and the trio
- Formulate a core message for the control team

Step 4: The steering team evaluates the ideas and provides feedback on the overall situation.

Step 5: There is a semi-annual "Sounding Board" for evaluation of processes and contents.

What you need:
- Infrastructure for the events
- Intranet platform for the exchange of information

Our comment:
The composition of the review trio should be as "mixed" as possible.

KEY ACCOUNT EVENTS

When to use it:
The new processes are clearly established internally and first experiences have been gathered. The enterprise has a wide array of relations to important key customers. The relationship with these customers is one of trust and candid openness.

What it achieves:
The change makes itself manifest in the relationship with the key customers. New processes, beneficial for both sides, become transparent. New possibilities for improvement arise as the result of a mutual learning process. The relationship is emotionally strengthened.

How to proceed:

Preparation:
Step 1: External consultants individually interview account managers or the account team members from Company A and the relevant customer contacts from Company B on the topic: *"What changes have there been in collaboration in the past year? Which topics are we particularly concerned with?"*

Step 2: Interviewer documents the results

Step 3: Preparation for a "mini-diagnosis" in a half-day event

Event:
Step 1: Welcoming, presentation of objectives, introduction of participants

Step 2: Reflection of the diagnostic results 1: "Customer" viewpoint (Company A)

Step 3: Reflection of the diagnostic results 2: "Supplier" viewpoint (Company B)

Step 4: Processing in groups
- *How consistent is the diagnosis concerning our company? What confirms my current view of the other company? What is new?*
- *Where do we perceive points in common, differences?*
- *Which topics should we work on?*

Step 5: Exchange in the plenum

Step 6: Work on future-oriented detail topics in mixed groups; each working group additionally develops a motto for collaboration in the next year.

Step 7: Exchange

Step 8: Concluding constellation: All participants position themselves in the room.

Follow-up:
Letter to the participants with minutes and agreed actions, possibly video documentation

What you need:
- A room
- Circle of chairs
- 2 flipcharts, pinboards, projector

Our comment:
The number of participants depends on the business constellation (from 8 to 100). The courage to be candid pays off!

PEER-TO-PEER CONSULTING/COLLEAGUE SUPPORT

When to use it:
The change is being broadly implemented. New experiences are being gathered in many different parts of the organization. The number of those involved has increased sharply. Now it is a matter of learning from successes and consolidating them.

What it achieves:
Recipes for success are multiplied in the organization through mutual "collegial consultation". The employees recognize new possibilities for dealing with their respective challenges. The motivation to venture out onto new ground increases. By means of this role-change approach, a balance of give and take is achieved.

How to proceed:
The following gives an example from a meeting with nine participants:

Step 1: Parallel groups of 3 (A, B and C); discussion of the question: *"Which topics do we want consultation on from the colleagues?"* Topics are decided upon and the group makes notes on them.

Step 2: Interviews (A ↔ B ↔ C): Group B interviews Group A on the topic that Group A would like consultation on (then: C → B; and finally: A → C). The interviews are held publicly, audible for everyone in the room.

Step 3: Formation of hypotheses and recommendations for a lasting implementation; the groups work on the central questions:
- What are our hypotheses on this topic? Why are things the way they are? What can be read between the lines?

After that:
- Based on our consultant role, which recommendations do we make?

The results are documented on a flipchart.

Step 4: Presentation and discussion: The groups present their results in turn; the respective topic providers ask questions.

Step 5: Implementation check and feedback

The groups go back to separate work on the central questions, taking into account the presentations by their "consultants".
- Which hypotheses impressed us most?
- How implementation-relevant are the recommendations for us?
- What do we implement, and how?

Step 6: Reactions and results are exchanged in the plenum.

Step 7: Final round: *What has been achieved today? What can we learn for the next session (what can we "intensify"; where can we "do things differently")?*

What you need:
- A room with a circle of chairs
- Possibility to work in separate rooms
- 3 flipcharts

Our comment:
The group size is absolutely variable; we recommend a facilitator for larger groups.

"RESARCH TEAM", QUALITATIVE EVALUATION

When to use it:
In various parts of the organization, the new is flourishing. In others, things have not changed much. The reasons for this are the subject of highly divergent conjectures and attributions.

What it achieves:
Dealing with diverse perceptions creates a new surge of energy. The individual divisions redefine their change strategy.

How to proceed:
Step 1: The management team asks a group of key individuals to form a "company culture research team" with the task of fathoming the different existing approaches. Selection criteria are: representation of the various corporate trends/commitment to dealing with the change (pro or contra). Qualitative, open interviews are the recommended method.

Step 2: Self-diagnosis (Workshop 1): An expert (internal or external) explains the method of open, qualitative interviews. The group members conduct reciprocal "test interviews" for self-diagnosis. The basic assignment is: Conduct an interview in which you determine the status of change in your interview partner's division.

Parallel interviews, each with two interviewers and two interviewees.

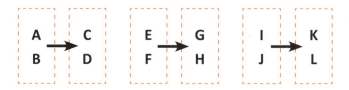

Switch roles in a second round:

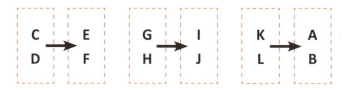

The interviews are evaluated by the interviewers: *What are the determining behavior patterns in this area? What images and perceptions are prevalent? What is the emotional state of the interviewees?* In a process of reflection, this experience is collectively analyzed, and deductions are made for the next steps.

Step 3: Interview planning (Workshop 2):
The group draws up an environmental analysis: *Who/what are the essential stakeholders in this process?* This serves as the basis for the selection of interview partners in the various areas of the company. The group agrees upon the basic interview sequence, and who will contact whom.

Step 4: Interviews and evaluation:
The interviews are conducted in pairs and recorded. These recorded interviews are evaluated by a different pair (cross evaluation).

Step 5: Integration of results (Workshop 3):
The results are presented by the respective evaluators; the interviewers provide feedback:
- What corresponds with the image we had?
- Where was our impression different?
- Which topics should we evaluate in more detail?

Results are integrated into an overall picture, and major hypotheses are formed. In addition, cross-sections of interviewers, evaluators and uninvolved persons are grouped to work on the central questions:
- What are our main hypotheses?
- Which quotes particularly substantiate this?
- Control question: *Does anything speak against this hypothesis?*

After the exchange in the plenum, the participants determine further actions (options: further evaluation/further interviews/communication).

Step 6: Reflection of the results to the interview subjects and management. Overall subject: *How do we see the status of the different corporate divisions in relation to our overall change process?*

In a workshop, the group conveys the results to those concerned. Response is visualized by asking participants to position themselves in the room on a scale from 1 to 10.

Based on their positions, working groups are formed. They continue discussing the response by considering the questions: *What confirms our viewpoint? What's surprising? Where do I disagree? What are the consequences?* Afterwards, delegates from each group discuss the results and draw consequences in an inner circle. In conclusion, the management team decides how things will continue.

Step 7: Broad communication throughout the company

What you need:
- Recording devices for the interviews
- Presentation infrastructure
- Workshop rooms

Our comment:
Openness sets an example! Don't forget communication!

IMPACT DIAGNOSIS OF "CORPORATE CONTROL SYSTEMS"

When to use it:
Change is being implemented gradually. The question is now: Which control systems have an intense multiplier effect on the implementation of the change goals, and which further developments need to be prioritized?

What it achieves:
Management (line, project team) prepares a clear image of the necessary developmental priorities for the control systems. The change process is "systematically" supported, increasing the overall coverage.

How to proceed:
Step 1: In a management retreat, the status of the current system is analyzed. The responsible members briefly present this from their respective point of view (example: MBO; MIS; IT, personnel development; strategy process, etc.)
- Current objectives
- Concerned corporate sectors, processes, individuals
- Planned further developments

Step 2: In small groups, the participants form hypotheses regarding the systems:
- Which systems are supporting which change objectives at the moment?
- Which systems or partial aspects are basically sabotaging consistent implementation?
- Where do we see need for development?

In conclusion, the hypotheses are summarized in the entire group.

Step 3: The people responsible for a system each choose sparring partners, with whom they prepare implementation consequences with timelines for the respective system.

Step 4: The individual proposals are presented and brought into relation with each other in an overview presentation (pinboard/projector).

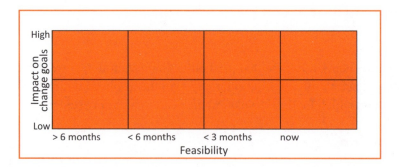

Implementation decisions are made based on this overview. Depending on resources, an implementation plan is made – either immediately or commissioned for the next meeting.

What you need:
- Pinboard or laptop with projector
- Meeting room

Our comment:
Attention: The question *"Which systems could sabotage our change objectives?"* has explosive potential.

WHAT DO WE GET RID OF?

When to use it:
New systems have already been introduced, now comes the integration into an overall system. It is still unclear which standard systems are valid, and which will be replaced – and if so, by what.

What it achieves:
Managers and employees become aware that the "new" has not been simply added to the "old", but that it also has a relieving effect. Letting go of certain things makes it possible to concentrate on the essentials.

How to proceed:
Step 1: The members of the management team (managers from all units) prepare the following central questions at the meeting:
- Which control/management instruments can we safely eliminate now that they have been replaced by new ones (example: key account lists that are now available online)?
- Which systems should we integrate in order to create synergies (example: integration of market, production and financial data)?

Step 2: Warm-up: To start with, the participants "fantazise" about what proposals for "chucking things" the respective managers will put forward.

Step 3: Presentation of proposals, including reactions to the fantasies – we know from experience that quite a few additional ideas can result from this. These are documented on cards/Post-it notes.

Step 4: Evaluation of ideas in a portfolio.

Step 5: Decision and further procedure: Activities and responsibilities – including the communication strategy – are agreed on in a "to-do list".

Step 6: Broad communication of highlights throughout the company.

What you need:
- Pinboard
- Cards/Post-it notes

Our comment:
If well applied, these interventions can significantly relieve the burden of employees.

TRANSFORMATION CLOSING EVENT

When to use it:
The transformation has been successfully anchored in the organization, but it still feels "new".

What it achieves:
The individually concerned parties – but also the organization itself – become aware of the lessons learned from the transformation experience. In terms of emotions as well as in accounting terms, this phase is brought to a conclusion. An opportunity is provided to discuss open questions or relational issues. The event has a positive effect on relations to the stakeholders and intensifies focus on the future.

How to proceed:
Step 1: Preparation
- The responsible persons determine who will participate on the basis of a stakeholder analysis. The more comprehensive and varied, the better: there is no maximum limit (3 to 10,000 participants – the budget should be clarified beforehand).
- In the invitation the participants are asked to bring along a symbol (small object) that stands for the overall transformation process. If the transformation process had been begun with a presentation of symbols, these starting-symbols should also be brought along.

Step 2: Conclusion event with the external stakeholders
- This part can be held on the first afternoon of a 1.5 day workshop.
- The participants are positioned in the room according to their "origin", i.e., homogeneous stakeholder groups sit together in a circle of chairs.
- After a brief introduction explaining the objectives and the manner of proceeding – but not the contents – of the workshop, the stakeholder groups set to work, beginning with a discussion of their symbols.
- Central questions:
  - *How did I experience the transformation process (positively/negatively in relation to business/innovation/organization, etc.)?*
  - *What does my symbol express in particular?*

- *How substantial is the transformation's success from our point of view (on a scale from 0 to 100)?*
- *Are there any open questions or unaccomplished tasks?*
- *What is our message to the other stakeholder groups?*

- In the plenum, each stakeholder group takes a position and describes its symbols. Before the presentations, the facilitator asks the other groups: *"What do you think group x's message will be?"* Symbols are placed in the middle of the room (or presentation boards on the walls). The core messages are documented, the success scale values are assigned, and open issues are put in a topic bank. The overall image is commented in a plenary discussion. Those responsible for implementation address the open issues, and agreement is reached on who will take them on.

Official report of the project manager, steering committee or responsible managers:

- The groups are now mixed, and the focus is on "learning". Central questions are discussed: *What have I learned in the course of the process? What have we learned as an organization regarding*
    - my role,
    - dealing with hard cuts,
    - dealing with new growth,
    - the overall steering of the transformation?
- Form: A-B-C-interviews (A interviews B; C listens and then provides feedback; the interviews proceed in turn). From this, the groups formulate a maximum of three findings and three recommendations. These are exchanged in the plenum.
- Personal feedback: Everyone has the opportunity for a brief feedback discussion with three participants (5 to 10 min.). The facilitator sets the time everyone chooses a partner and has a feedback talk. Partner change after 10 minutes.
- Back to the future: The participants return to their stakeholder groups and discuss priorities for the future. Central questions: *What are our main priorities for future action? Where have we reached consensus in the group? Where do differences remain?*
- The priorities are clearly transported in brief statements in the plenum.

- As a conclusion, there is a collective farewell. The event finale takes place in the form of a party, a ceremony or a concluding evening.

What you need:
- A large room
- Pinboards/flipchart/laptop and projector
- Markers for the circles of chairs
- Name-tags (for large events)
- Facilitation material

Our comment:
Ensure variety in the group. Anyone who has something to contribute should be able to participate.

ALL INTERVENTIONS AT A GLANCE

Overview table
Architectures/designs/interventions

Phase 1
- The change begins with me
- Starting a vision process with key players
- "Customer Parliament" 1
- Past – Present – Future
- "Learning Organization" questionnaire
- Creativity blockers
- Illustrating the necessity of hard cuts: eliminate luxury
- "Take a stand": Constellations on essential change dimensions
- Environment analysis
- Analysis of forms of capital

Phase 2
- Quick wins and "go to market" workshop 1
- Quick wins and "go to market" workshop 2
- External sparring-partner systems (SPS) for hard cuts
- Strategy retreat with key players
- Structure decision – who should drive the change: management team, change team or corporate development department?
- Team staffing based on microcosm analysis
- The "red ribbon"
- Traveling to foreign worlds (example: seminar hotel)

Phase 3
- Quick win portfolio
- Stakeholder impact analysis
- The management team speech
- Changing the general framework; strengthening options for new growth
- Innovation market
- Lateral thinking: Raising teams' innovative potential
- "Future cabaret": Scenes from the future
- Dealing with contradictions: Cost/benefit
- "Stand up or remain seated"
- Mini-evaluation – change status

Overview table
Architectures/designs/interventions (cont.)

Phase 4
- Evaluating pilot projects – check-up for further implementation
- Symbolic action: "Wastepaper basket – Museum – Showcase"
- Symbolic implementation of the main challenge
- Phase architecture with clear handovers
  Example: project -> line
- "Customer Parliament" 2
- Comprehensive project work

Phase 5
- Meeting check-up
- Regular review groups
- Key account events
- Peer-to-peer consulting/colleague support
- "Research Team", qualitative evaluation
- Impact diagnosis of "corporate control systems"
- What do we get rid of?
- Transformation closing event

APPENDIX

APPENDIX

How this second edition came about – acknowledgements

This book is for managers, consultants and all those who are promoting transformation in organizations.

"Managing Cuts & New Growth" is a new approach to change management that integrates our 20 years of consulting and management experience, as well as our research initiatives in this field.

It is a result of our long-term co-operation as consultants and managers – together with our clients and organizations.

We started our research in the 1990´s and published "Harte Schnitte/Neues Wachstum" in 2002 for the German speaking countries. As our consulting work has become much more international since then, we decided to renew the book and publish it in English. We are very proud to be releasing the second edition now.

We are addressing managers and consultants as well as all those who want to create inspiring change processes and achieve sustainable results in execution. Moreover, as passionate consultants we would like to contribute to our community of practice on how to establish customized transformation processes based on systemic thinking.

Our book is the result of work in progress; we received a great deal of support and valuable insights. During our work as managing partners at Neuwaldegg Consulting Group we learned and profited a great deal from the work and animated discussions with our colleagues. This intensive work went on with our new teams, who are challenging us – thus pushing our approaches to change management and corporate development even further.

We thank Annika Serfass for her outstanding contribution to the innovation article and treasure hunt case study as well as to resilience as an essential ingredient of organizations and leaders to promote sustainable change. She also did research on change management studies and did the project management for this second edition. Nicole Rimser was again great in doing elegant and clear charts and graphical work. We also want to thank Pia Ottacher for the project management. The meticulous proofreading was carried out by Sigrid Buhl and Stephanie Delgado Martin.

Above all, we also want to thank our families, partners and friends for their patience and encouraging support while we were writing this book – anything but daily business for us!

With this book, we would like to contribute to the further development and innovation of systemic approaches, and give impulses for theoretical and practical discussions.

We are looking forward to your feedback and dialogue. You can reach us via e-mail at:

heitger@heitgerconsulting.com alexander.doujak@doujak.eu

Vienna, January 2013 *Dr. Barbara Heitger, Dr. Alexander Doujak*

Brief glossary

Architecture[70]

The term "architect" stems from the Greek and means "master builder". Just as architects plan rooms and thus create settings in which different things can happen, consultants plan social, temporal, spatial and substantive design elements for the pre-structuring of processes. By "architecture" we mean the structure and the setting of the consulting process. Fluidity in the boundaries between architecture and design is a familiar phenomenon. Architecture determines that something takes place and influences *what* actually takes place. Architecture constructs areas that leave room for development and provides structures for processes.

Examples:

- Clear contracts, clear project roles, defined project length
- Diagnosis
- Reflection Workshop
- Steering Group
- Dialogue Group
- Sounding Board
- Large group events
- Work with internal project management
- Work with business management
- Multiplier forums or meetings
- Coaching sessions (professional, process-oriented, personal)
- "Train the Trainer" modules
- Evaluation, i.e., performance control/reviews
- Facilitated departmental and team discussions on the quality of internal co-operation
- Staff work in the consulting system

---

[70] C.f. Königswieser/Exner, 2001, pp. 45 ff.

Autopoiesis[71]

Autopoiesis means "self-creation" – a term coined by Maturana and Varela. Originally restricted to biological systems theory, the term has also been adopted by other system-theoretical schools of thought, above all social systems theory (Willke and Luhmann). Maturana was concerned with finding a criterion by which "life" could be defined. Based on the standpoint of systems theory, he developed the "Living Systems" theory. What makes a system into a living system is self-generation – autopoiesis. This self-creation refers to the system's development of new structures, its processes of self-preservation and its fundamental self-control and self-organization. The system is not controlled from the outside, but is "informationally self-contained". Relationships and roles are elements of social systems, generated by the developing systems themselves.[72]

Design[73]

By design, we mean the planning of a communication session (workshop, large group, coaching session, etc.). Not only the simple order of events, but also the working mode (group or individual work), the type of discussion (e.g., following a lecture) and the anticipated effect of the individual steps are specifically planned. The design determines how substantive, social, temporal and spatial dimensions of the communication are organized in a given setting.

This can be compared with the interior design of a building. A design should include the following four dimensions:

- Time
- Space
- Content
- Social interaction

Diagnosis[74]

We use the term "diagnosis" to describe the phase, step or project that serves to obtain relevant information about a system. The diagnosis can be extensive

---

[71] C.f. http://www.dietrichlensch.de/texte/oti/autopoie.html
[72] C.f. Willke, 1993; Maturana/Varela, 1987; http://www.dietrichlensch.de/texte/oti/autopoie.html
[73] C.f. Königswieser/Exner, 2001, pp. 147 ff.
[74] C.f. Königswieser/Exner, 2001, pp. 52 ff.

(a project of its own) or brief (mini-diagnosis during a project). It surveys a system's information, assumptions and images with respect to boundaries, objectives, interpersonal interaction patterns, resources and problems, etc. The diagnosis of the system provides orientation to the consultants. It provides the basis for hypotheses and interventions. The diagnosis is an intervention in itself, and is conducive to building personal relationships of trust between consultant and client systems via discussions, individual and group interviews, observations, etc.

Intervention[75]

Intervention means targeted communication (i.e., with a calculated effect on the partner) between psychological and/or social systems that respects the autonomy of the system in which the intervention is being undertaken. Interventions have the function of:
- Relieving the burden on individuals
- Opening up contradictions
- Collecting information
- Proximity-distance regulation
- Stimulation of system formation
- Conveying alternative perceptions
- Emphasizing emotional aspects

Systemic intervention[76]

Systemic intervention can be described as targeted communication in awareness of the precariousness of attempting to effectively influence an autonomous social system. Accordingly, what sets system-theoretical intervention strategies apart is that they identify and limit the risks of interventions in autonomous systems, thus making them easier to tolerate.

Systemic intervention technique[77]

Some typical systemic intervention techniques are:
- Circular questioning
- Paradoxical intervention

---

[75] C.f. Königswieser/Exner, 2001, pp. 41 ff.
[76] C.f. Königswieser/Exner, 2001, p. 17.
[77] C.f. Königswieser/Exner, 2001, pp. 35 ff.

- Symptom prescription
- Reinterpretation or reframing
- Splitting
- Positive connotation, positive symptom evaluation

Social systems[78]

The social systems that constitute the consulting context can be differentiated into three types: The Client System, the Consultant System and the Consultation System. The following list shows the main features of the systems involved in the consulting process. They are:

- Systems, not environments
- Autonomous or autopoietic
- Self-referential
- Not trivial or heteronomous
- Social, not mechanical, organic or psychological
- Organizations, not systems of interaction, groups, networks, functional subsystems or societies

Systemic consulting[79]

In our understanding of systemic consulting, interventions are ideas or suggestions which the client system is free to use as it sees fit. The scope of possible influence is very limited. Consultants can only facilitate awareness of the contradictions between change and preservation; it is the client system that decides how this will be dealt with. Everything has a function in relation to its meaning; how functionality is defined lies with the client system.

---

[78] C.f. Königswieser/Exner, 2001, pp. 20 ff.
[79] C.f. Königswieser/Exner, 2001, pp. 24 ff.

Bibliography

Amidon, Debra M.
   Innovation Strategy for the Knowledge Economy, Ken Awakening, Butterworth – Heinemann, Frankfurt am Main, 1997.

Beer, Michael/Nohria, Nitin
   Breaking the Code of Change, Harvard Business School Press, Boston, 2000.

Beer, Michael/Nohria, Nitin
   Cracking the Code of Change, Harvard Business Review, 3/2000, pp. 133–141.

Bennis, Warren/Mische, Michael
   The 21st Century Organization, Jossey Bass Publishers, San Francisco, 1995.

Berkun, Scott
   The Myths of Innovation, O'Reilly, Sebastopol, 2007.

Bommer, M./Jalajas, D.
   The threat of Organizational Downsizing on the Innovative Prospensity of R&D Professionals, in: R&D Management Vol. 29, 1999, pp. 69–82.

Bower, Joseph L./Christensen, Clayton M.
   Disruptive Technologies: Catching the Wave, in: Harvard Business Review, January, 1995.

Boyett, Joseph H.
   Beyond Workplace 2000, Plume Pinguine, New York, 1996.

Bridges, William
   Transitions – Making Sense of Life Changes, Perseus Books, 1980.

Burke, W. Warner
   The New Agenda for Organization Development, Organizational Dynamics, Summer 1997.

Cascio, W. F./Young, C. E./Morris, J. R.
   Financial Consequences of Employment Chance Decisions in Major U.S. Corporations, in: Academy of Management Journal, Vol. 40, pp. 1175–1189.

Charan, Ram/Tichy, Noel M.
   Every Business is a Growth-Business, Random House, Chichester, 1998.

Chase/Dasu
   Want to Perfect Your Company's Service? Use Behavioural Science, in: Harvard Business Review 6/2001, pp. 79–84

Christensen, Clayton M./Raynor Michael E.
   The Innovator's Solution – Creating and Sustaining Successful Growth, Mcgraw-Hill Professional, 2003.

Cummings, Thomas G./Worley, Christopher G.
   Organization Development and Change, South Western, Div of Thomson Learning, 2004.

Dannemiller, Tyson
   Associates Whole-Scale Change, Berrett-Koehler Publishers Inc., San Francisco, 2000.

Dougherty, D./Bowman, E.H.
   The Effects of Organizational Downsizing on Product Innovation, in: California Management Review Vol. 37, 1995, pp. 28–44.

Downs, Alan
   Corporate Executions: The Ugly Thruth About Layoffs – How Corporate Greed Is Shattering Lives, Companies and Communities, Amacom, New York, 1996.

Duarte, Deborah/Tennant-Snyder, Nancy
   Strategic Innovation – Embedding Innovation as a Core Competence in Your Organization, John Wiley & Sons, 2003.

Dyer, Jeff/Gregersen, Hal/Christensen, Clayton M.
   The Innovator's DNA – Mastering the Five Skills of Disruptive Innovation, McGraw Hill, 2011.

Edvinsson, Malon
   Intellectual Capital, Harper Business, New York, 1997.

Edvinsson, Leif/Malone, Michael
   Intellectual Capital – Realizing your Company's True Value by Finding its Hidden Brainpower, Harper Business, New York, 1997.

Ernst & Young
   The Drivers of Financial Reputation, EYGM Limited, 2007.

Foster, Richard/Kaplan, Sarah
   Creative Destruction – Why Companies that Are Built to Last Underperform the Market – and How to Successfully Transform Them, Currency/Doubleday, New York, 2001.

Fritz, Robert/Senge, Peter M.
   The Path of Least Resistance for Managers – Designing Organizations to Succeed, Mcgraw-Hill Professional, 1999.

Gandolfi, Franco
   Learning from the Past – Downsizing Lessons for Managers, 2008.

Galbraith, Jay
   Designing Dynamic Organizations – A Hands-On Guide for Leaders at All Levels, Mcgraw-Hill Professional, 2001.

Gertz, Dwight/Baptista, Joao
   Grow to Be Great, Moderne Industrie Publishers, Landsberg am Lech, 1996.

Gryskiewiecz, Stanley
   Positive Turbulence – Developing Climates for Creativity, Innovation and Renewal, Jossey-Bass Publishers, San Francisco, 1999.

Hambrick, Donald (ed.)/Nadler/Tushman
Navigating Change – How CEOs, Top Teams and Boards Stem Transformation, Harvard Business School Press, Boston, 1998.

Hamel, Gary
Leading the Revolution, Harvard Business School Press, Boston, 2000.

Hamel, Gary
The Future of Management, Harvard Business School Press, Boston, 2007.

Hamel, Gary/Prahalad, C.K.
Competing for the Future, Harvard Business School Press, Boston, 1994.

Hammer, Michael/Champy, James
Business Reengineering – Die Radikalkur für das Unternehmen, Campus Publishers, Frankfurt am Main, 1994.

Hargadon, Andrew/Sutton, Robert
Building an Innovation Factory, Harvard Business Review May-June 2000, pp. 157 ff.

Hirschhorn, Larry
The Workplace Within, MIT Press, Cambridge, 1999.

Huber/Glick
Organizational Change and Redesign, Oxford University Press, Oxford, 1994.

Hunter, Scott
The Negative Effects of Downsizing, www.associatedcontent.com , 2007.

Hurst, David K.
Crisis & Rewenal – Meeting The Challenge of Organizational Change, Harvard Business School Press, Boston, 1995.

Huseman, Richard/Goodmann, John
Leading with Knowledge – The Nature of Competition in the 21st Century, Sage Publications, London, 1999.

Huselid, Mark/Becker, Brian/Ulrich, Dave
The HR-Scorecard, Harvard Business School Press, Boston, 2001.

Jacobs, Peter K.
Minding the Muse – The Impact of Downsizing on Corporate Creativity, Harvard Business School Press, Boston, 23 May 2000. http://hbswk.hbs.edu/item/1518.html

Janes, Alfred/Prammer, K./Schulte-Derne, Michael
Transformationsmanagement – Organisationen von innen verändern, Springer Publishers, Vienna, 2001.

Johansen, Bob
Leaders Make the Future – Ten New Leadership Skills for an Uncertain World, Berrett-Koehler, 2009.

Joyce, Teresa/Kilman, Ralph
Profiling Large-Scale Change Effects, OD Journal 2/1999.

Kantner, Rosabeth Moss
 When Giants Learn to Dance, Unwin Paperbacks, London, 1990.

Kaplan, Robert S./Norton, David P.
 Balanced Scorecard – Translating Strategy into Action, Schäffer-Poeschel, Stuttgart, 1996.

Kates, Amy/Galbraith, Jay R.
 Designing Your Organization, Wiley & Sons, 2007.

Kieser, Alfred
 Downsizing – eine vernünftige Strategie? Harvard Business Manager, 2/2002.

Kim, Chan/Mauborgne, Renée
 Blue Ocean Strategy – How to Create Uncontested Market Space and Make the Competition Irrelevant, Harvard Business Review Press, 2005.

Kirckpatrick, Donald
 Evaluating Training Programs – The Four Levels, Berrett-Koehler Publishers Inc., San Francisco, 1994.

Königswieser, Roswita
 Die Auswirkung schockierender Nachrichten – Psychische Bewältigungsmechanismen und Methoden der Überbringung, in: Betriebswirtschaft Vol. 5, Poeschel Verlag, Stuttgart, 1985.

Königswieser, Roswita/Exner, Alexander
 Systemische Intervention – Architekturen und Designs für Berater und Veränderungsmanager, Klett-Cotta-Verlag, Stuttgart, 1999.

Kotter, John P.
 Leading Change, Harvard Business School Press, Boston, 1996.

Kotter, John P./Cohen, Dan S.
 The Heart of Change – Real-Life Stories of How People Change Their Organizations, Mcgraw-Hill Professional, 2002.

Krizanits, Joana
 Selbstmanagement in Transition. In: Hernsteiner 1/2002.

Krogh, Georg von/Ichijo, Kazu/Nonaka, Ikujro
 Enabling Knowledge Creation, Oxford University Press, New York, 2000.

Lagadec, Patrick
 Preventing Chaos in a Crisis – Strategies for Prevention, Control and Damage Limitation, McGraw-Hill, New York, 1991.

Lawler, Edward E./Worley, Christopher G.
 Built to Change – How to Achieve Sustained Organizational Effectiveness, Wiley & Sons, 2006.

Leifer, Richard/McDermott, Christopher
 Radical Innovations, HBS Press, 2000.

Leonard, Dorothy
  Spark Innovation Through Empathic Design, in: Harvard Business Review 6, November/December, 1997.

Loehr, Jim/Schwartz, Tony
  The Making of a Corporate Athlete, in: Harvard Business Review 1/2001, pp. 120–128.

Low, Jonathan/Siesfield, Tony
  Measures That Matter, Boston, Ernst & Young, 1998.

MacCoby, Eleanor E. et al (ed.)
  Readings in Social Psychology, Holt, Rinehart and Winston, New York, 1958.

Maes, Jeanne/Rushing, Daniel/King, Deborah
  Corporate Strategies – Reassessing the Outcomes of Downsizing, in: OD Journal 4/1997, pp. 9 ff.

Management Center Europe
  Implementing your Strategy through your People Innovation, in: The Executive Issue Vol. 33, July 2008.

Markides, Constantinos C./Geroski, Paul A.
  Fast Second – How Smart Companies Bypass Radical Innovation to Enter and Dom- inate New Markets, Wiley & Sons, 2004.

Maturana, Humberto/Varela, Francisco J.
  Der Baum der Erkenntnis – Die biologischen Wurzeln menschlichen Erkennens, Goldmann, Bern, München 1987.

Mishra, Aneil K./Mishra, Karen E./Spreitzer, Gretchen
  Preserving Employee Morale During Downsizing, in: Sloan Management Review, Cambridge, Winter, 1998.

Morris, James R./Cascio, Wayne F.
  Downsizing After All These Years, in: Organizational Dynamics, Winter 1999, pp. 78 ff.

Nadler, David A./Nadler, Mark B./Tushman, Michael L.
  Competing by Design – The Power of Organizational Architecture, Oxford University Press, 1998.

Noer, David M.
  Healing the Wounds – Overcoming the Trauma of Layoffs and Revitalizing Downsized Organizations, Jossey Bass, San Francisco, 1993.

Nonaka, Ikujiro/Takeuchi, Hirotaka
  The Knowledge-Creating Company – How Japanese Companies Create the Dynamics of Innovation, Oxford University Press, New York, 1995.

Ornstein, Robert
  Multimind, Junfermann, 2nd ed., Paderborn, 1989.

Patton, Michael Quinn
  Utilization Focused Evaluation, SAGE Publications, Thousand Oaks, Calif., 1997.

Pettigrew, Andrew (ed.)
　The Innovating Organization, Sage Publications, London, 2000.

Plender, John
　A Stake in the Future – Making the Stakeholder Society Work, Nicholas Brealey Publishing Ltd., 1997.

Prahalad, C.K.
　Managing Discontinuities – The Emerging Challenges, Industrial Research Institute Inc., 1998.

Schrage, Michael
　Serious Play – How the World's Best Companies Simulate to Innovate, Harvard Business School Press, Boston, 2000.

Senge, Peter M.
　The Fifth Disciplin – The Art and Practice of the Learning Organization, Doubleday/Currency, New York, 1990.

Sheffi, Yossi
　The Resilient Enterprise, MIT Press, 2005.

Simon, Walter
　Levers of Control – How Managers Are Innovative Control Systems to Drive Strategic Renewal, Harvard Business School Press, 1995.

Simons, Robert
　Levers of Organizational Design – How Managers Use Accountability Systems for Greater Performance and Commitment, Mcgraw-Hill Professional, 2005.

Sparrer, Insa; Varga von Kibéd, Matthias
　Ganz im Gegenteil. Tetralemmaarbeit und andere Grundformen systemischer Strukturaufstellungen, Carl-Auer-Verlag, Heidelberg, 2000.

Strebel, Paul
　Breakpoints – How Managers Exploit Radical Business Change, Harvard Business School Press, Boston, 1992.

Sutton, Robert
　Weird Ideas That Work. 11 ½ Practices for Promoting, Managing and Sustaining Innovation, Penguin Books Ltd, London, 2001.

Taffinder, Paul
　Big Change, John Wiley & Sons, Chichester, 1998.

Tennant Snyder, Nancy; Duarte, Deborah L.
　Strategic Innovation. Embedding Innovation as a Core Competency in Your Organization, Jossey-Bass, San Francisco, 2003.

Tharp, Twyla
　The Creative Habit. Learn It and Use It for Life, Simon & Schuster, New York, 2003.

Tomasko, Robert M.
　Rethinking the Corporation, Amacom, New York, 1993.

Tomasko, Robert M.
Downsizing – Reshaping the Corporation for the Future, Amacom, New York, 1990.

Tuckman, Bruce
Developmental Sequence in Small Groups, in: Psychological Bulletin 63 (6): 384–399, 1965.

Turner, Freda
Downsizing: Who is the Real Loser?, WebPronews, 8 February 2008. In: http://www.webpronews.com/downsizing-who-is-the-real-loser-2003-02

Tushman, Michael/O'Reilly III, Charles
Winning through Innovation, Harvard Business School Press, Boston, 1997.

Ulrich, Dave
Human Resource Champions, Harvard Business School Press, Boston, 1997.

von Krogh, Georg/Ichijo, Kazuo/Nonaka, Ikujiro
Enabling Knowledge Creation, Oxford University Press, Oxford, 2000.

Weick, Karl E.
Drop your Tools – An Allegory for Organizational Studies, in: Administrative Science, Quarterly 41, 1996, pp. 301 ff.

Weick, Karl E.
Sensemaking in Organizations, Sage Publ., Thousand Oaks, Calif., 1995.

Weick, Karl E./Sutcliffe, Kathleen M./Quinn, Robert E.
Managing the Unexpected: Assuring High Performance in an Age of Complexity, Wiley & Sons, 2001.

Willke, Helmut
Systemtheorie ll, Gustav Fischer-Verlag, UTB für Wissenschaft, Stuttgart, Jena 1994.

Wimmer, Rudolf
Organisationsberatung: neue Wege und Konzepte, Gabler, Wiesbaden, 1992.

Internet sources

American Management Association: www.amanet.org

http://www.businessweek.com/archives/1996/b3457016.arc.htm

http://ceco.polytechnique.fr/CHERCHEURS/LAGADEC/PLENGLISCH.html

http://www.iq.uni-hannover.de/vorlesung/qs1/KAP01/k01.htm

http://www.infed.org/thinkers/senge.htm

http://www.dietrichlensch.de/texte/oti/autopoie.html

http://www.mckinseyquarterly.com/Organizing_for_successful_change_management_A_McKinsey_Global_Survey_1809

http://www.ch.capgemini.com/m/ch/tl/Change_Management_2005.pdf

THE AUTHORS

Dr. Barbara Heitger

Born 1958 in Münster/Westphalia (Germany)

Founder of Heitger Consulting GmbH, Managing Partner.
Group dynamics trainer & academic advisor to the Austrian Society for Group Dynamics and Organizational Consulting (OEGGO),
lecturer for MBA courses and universities, academic advisor to Carl Auer Publishers.
Author and speaker on topics of strategy, change and leadership.

Education and Experience:
University studies in law, sociology and political science.
Systemic consultant trainings, supervisor, founding member of the Austrian Coaching Council, depth psychology therapy training, consultant, project manager in a bank and an international IT corporation; study trips to the U.S. Managing partner of consultants group Neuwaldegg for 17 years.

Consultant for 25 years for family businesses as well as corporations.
Main emphases:
- Corporate development and change management
- Integrated consulting of strategy work, change and leadership efficiency
- International leadership development programs
- Large scale change initiatives
- Strengthen management teams
- Strategic innovation and agile organizations

Publications on strategy development, project management, strategic repositioning of internal service providers and human resources, change management, systemic consulting and management development in several books and numerous articles.

Dr. Mag. Alexander Doujak

Born 1965 in Klagenfurt (Austria)

Founder and managing partner of Doujak Corporate Development
Head of the supervisory board of Palfinger AG
Member of Extended Board Constantia Industries AG

Education and Experience:
Ph.D. degree in Commerce at the Vienna University of Economics and Business Administration, study visits in Boston (MIT, Harvard University).
Training in international project management and systemic consulting, long-standing board member at the International Project Management Association, executive management positions in the media industry. Broad management expertise in corporate development, global strategy and management of change.

Main emphases:
- Corporate Development of global market leaders (management positions as well as consulting)
- Top-Executive Coaching (individual coaching of executive board members/CEOs and coaching of executive teams)
- Integral strategy and corporate development projects, combining aspects of innovation and rationalization (hard cuts and new growth)
- Strategy development and implementation, Change Management
- Strategic Innovation
- Professional development of internal and external consultants

Publications on change management, strategic innovation, project management, project portfolios, re-engineering as a development process, IT and change management.